Language in school and community

Edited by Neil Mercer

Edward Arnold

© Copyright Edward Arnold 1981

First published 1981 by
Edward Arnold (Publishers) Ltd
41 Bedford Square, London WC1B 3DQ

British Library Cataloguing in Publication Data

Language in school and community.
1. English language – Spoken English
2. English language – Usage
I. Mercer, Neil
428′.3   PE1068

ISBN 0-7131-6347-X

Filmset by Northumberland Press Ltd,
Gateshead, Tyne and Wear
Printed in Great Britain by Richard Clay
(The Chaucer Press) Ltd, Bungay, Suffolk

Contents

Preface

Although research into language development and language use has grown dramatically in recent years, the implications of this research for educational policy and practice have not been at all adequately explored. It is often difficult to relate the interests and findings of researchers to the practical needs of teachers, but this is nevertheless essential for systematic innovation and evaluation in education to take place. This book attempts to make these kinds of connections. Its basic theme is: what is known about the relation between children's language experience in and out of school, and what implications does this have for educational policy and classroom practice? It consists of a collection of chapters by authors who are all, in various ways, involved in research into language and education, and most of whom have been directly involved in teaching and/or the development of courses and materials on language for teachers. The integration of chapters in the book arises from their authors' shared belief that a better understanding of language and education will only emerge from a critical examination of school language use in its broader social context and not from a continued narrow emphasis on the disabilities or deprivations of particular children, as individuals or as members of social groups.

Language in school and community has been put together in Britain during a time of severe educational cutbacks, in which many people responsible for the development and implementation of ideas like those presented in this book – teachers, advisers, researchers and others – are finding the scope, or even the very existence, of their jobs under threat. Talk about educational 'economies' is, of course, euphemism; what is at issue is the political priority given to improving the education of most British children. There is no doubt that if the present circumstances continue, the changes in educational policy proposed and implied in this volume will not take place at the rate they should.

There is another, more explicitly ideological opposition to the introduction of new ideas in educational policy and practice which has become apparent in recent educational debates. This mainly takes the form of proposals for the reassertion of 'traditional' educational values, the recreation of an age in which 'the basics' of education were supposedly better taught and learnt. What the traditionalists are really advocating, however, is a nostalgic return to the times when educational 'success' and 'failure' were simply considered less problematic. Language development often figures in these 'back to the basics' arguments, but the true basis for the development of children's skills and confidence in communicating is not to be found in traditional language shibboleths and outmoded pedagogies. It lies instead in a meaningful and systematic relationship between school language work and children's broader language experience.

The book is divided into three parts. The two chapters in Part I serve to some extent as a preparation for the latter parts, by examining the language demands of school learning from different, complementary perspectives. In Part II specific, contemporary issues in the relation between the cultures of school and community are considered, and in Part III authors critically and constructively discuss aspects of school language work.

Acknowledgements

Many of the ideas in this book originally came together in the preparation of Open University course *PE232 Language Development*. I would like to acknowledge here the support and stimulation of OU colleagues during that time and in the preparation of this book. I also wish to express my appreciation to those external contributors to that course, school teachers and academics, whose comments and advice helped initial ideas develop, and intentions become practical realities.

Neil Mercer
Milton Keynes, December 1980

Part I

Language and school learning

Part I consists of two chapters, each of which considers the demands that school makes on children's ability to use language. While some issues are discussed in both chapters – in particular misunderstandings between teachers and children about words and concepts used in school – the authors provide different, complementary perspectives on this theme, based on the applied disciplines of linguistics and social psychology.

Katharine Perera's aim is to show how school places special, and often problematic, kinds of language demands on children, even those who are already fluent speakers of their native language. She demonstrates how difficulties of comprehension can arise for both spoken and written language, at the different linguistic levels of vocabulary, sentence structure and discourse. Of particular interest in her treatment of reading comprehension is her comparison of the demands of children's fiction and non-fiction. In common with the later chapters by Pam Czerniewska and Sally Twite, Katharine Perera's chapter very clearly demonstrates the practical benefits a teacher will gain from an understanding of language structure.

In Chapter 2, Mercer and Edwards's concern is with the 'ground-rules' of teaching and learning – the underlying principles or rules of interpretation which define the ways in which problems are to be approached, and explanations framed, in school. Their argument is that the nature of classroom communications can best be understood in relation to these ground-rules, and that problems for both teachers and children often arise because of their implicit, taken-for-granted nature. A strong implication of this approach is that educational success or failure is not comprehensible purely in terms of the abilities or problems of individual children (or teachers) but in terms of the degree of shared understanding upon which the teacher–learner relationship is based. This point of view is echoed elsewhere in the book, most explicitly in the chapters by Wiles and Kochman.

Part I
Language and school learning

1

Some language problems in school learning*

Katharine Perera

Introduction

When children first go to school, the majority of them have already acquired a great deal of language. They can talk happily, and often at great length, about things that are happening or that have happened. However, this predominantly narrative and descriptive type of language, important though it is, is not the only kind of language that they will meet or need in school. The world of the school is generally more formal than the world of the home, and the learning of academic subjects requires rather different kinds of language from the everyday language we find in conversation or in children's news stories. I think there are three areas in which this more formal, more academic language can cause difficulties: the first is that the child might have difficulty in understanding what the teacher says; the second is that he might have difficulty in understanding textbooks and work-cards in subjects such as maths, social studies and science; and the third is that he might have difficulty in writing appropriately about academic topics.

Understanding the teacher's spoken language

Unfamiliar vocabulary

There are plenty of examples, from all age groups, of pupils not understanding what the teacher has said. One of my favourites comes from a student of education who wrote in a final exam paper about the child development theories of P.R.J. But I think that misunderstanding of oral language is more widespread at primary level. We can identify three different sources of this misunderstanding. The first is where the teacher uses unfamiliar vocabulary. This may be a word which has two meanings, one concrete and one abstract. The teacher may intend the

* This chapter is a revised and extended version of an article that was first published by the Open University in 1979 under the title *The language demands of school learning*, as a supplementary reading to Block 6 of course P232, *Language Development*.

abstract meaning but the young child is much more likely to assign the concrete interpretation to the word. There is an example of this in Laurie Lee's autobiography, *Cider with Rosie*. Describing his first day at school, he remembers that the teacher told him to 'Wait there for the present' – and he went home at the end of the day bitterly disillusioned because he was not given one. On the other hand, the unfamiliar vocabulary may be archaic or unusual words that the child has not met at all before. Here there is a tendency for him to associate them with words he already knows. There are many examples to be found in children's misinterpretations of the language of school assemblies, as in, 'Our Father, which art in heaven, Harold be thy name.'

Ambiguous reference

The second type of oral misunderstanding is where the adult gives a verbal explanation accompanied by a pointing gesture and the child misunderstands the reference of the verbal explanation. A friend of mine, when she was a young child, was in a car with her parents and, as they drove past an airfield, she pointed at something and asked, 'What's that, Mummy?' Her mother replied, 'It's a hangar.' 'What's it for?' 'It's where they keep the aeroplanes at night.' The point is that my friend was actually pointing to a wind-sock, not to a hangar at all. The name 'hangar' seemed perfectly appropriate for what she was looking at – it was, indeed, hanging – and when she heard the improbable explanation that it housed aeroplanes at night, she decided sagely that it was another example of the adult whimsy that she kept meeting in story-books. It was several years before she associated the definition with the appropriate object.

Unfamiliar use of sentence patterns

The third type of oral misunderstanding is where the teacher uses a grammatical construction that the child does not interpret correctly. This is particularly common with commands and rebukes. To very young children adults tend to use direct commands such as, 'Don't do that' or, 'Put your toys away now'. On the whole, adults do not use this kind of language to one another. We soften our commands in various ways. When the child first goes to school, he starts meeting adult-type commands and rebukes and does not necessarily recognize them for what they are. Joan Tough (1973) has a recording of an infant classroom where the teacher says things such as, 'Jimmy, would you like to put your toys away' and 'I wonder who hasn't put his toys away yet' and it is very clear to the observer that Jimmy simply does not understand that this means, 'Put your toys away'. He is not being perverse or disobedient; he just does not recognize these adult forms yet.

Implications for the classroom

I am not suggesting that teachers should not use such forms – if they did not, children might not learn them – but I think it is important for them to be alert for the children for whom they are totally unfamiliar. This is harder than it sounds, because children are very good at following what others are doing, at picking up cues from their environment, so they often behave appropriately without necessarily understanding the language at all. It is possible, by using a blend of structures, to lead the child gradually from the direct to the polite form of a command, e.g.

Put your toys away, would you, Jimmy, please.
Would you put your toys away please, Jimmy.
Would you like to put your toys away, Jimmy.

Understanding the language of textbooks

The difficulties that pupils can meet in trying to understand the language of textbooks and work-cards are more prevalent and more serious than any problems that the teacher's spoken language may cause. This is because written language is generally more formal than oral language; it is not accompanied by gestures and facial expressions; and it cannot, of course, respond to any obvious misunderstanding on the part of the child in the way that the teacher can. In addition, reading is essentially a private activity, whereas listening is a public one, so the child who is reading is not able to take a lead from the behaviour of other children in the class. But modern teaching styles put a great deal of weight on books and work-cards: mixed-ability and mixed-age teaching mean that class lessons are difficult and group work preferable. The report on primary education in England (DES, 1978) shows that 61 per cent of seven-year-olds and 49 per cent of nine-year-olds are taught in mixed-age classes. Presumably, this means that a great deal of their work is done on an individual or group basis, rather than as a class. But, of course, group work requires the pupils to work from books and work-cards because the teacher cannot be with all the groups at once. Lest we should think that this problem can be overcome by the good and energetic teacher who makes her own work-cards, tailor-made for the needs of each group, it is worth noticing how very difficult this task is. Writing clear, simple, explanatory prose is not easy. Indeed, when the Effective Use of Reading Project team in Nottingham assessed the level of difficulty of teacher-produced worksheets, they found, for example, that one set produced for a first-year, mixed-ability secondary group was comparable in difficulty with the standard 'O' level textbook in the same subject.

Sources of difficulty in reading can be pin-pointed at the level of the word, the sentence and the discourse. In order to illustrate different types of reading difficulty, I have chosen examples from textbooks in use in English schools. I have selected some books that are in use in primary schools and others that are in use in secondary schools. All the secondary books are said to be suitable for the first two years of secondary education. The books have all been published for the first time during the past 15 years. Apart from these restrictions, the selection of the books was a random one. There is no intention here to criticize these books in particular or textbooks in general. The linguistic features of a book constitute only one of the aspects by which it may be judged; subject-matter, presentation, interest level and so on are also very important. Neither do I intend to suggest that all textbooks for children should be written in the simplest possible language; if they were, pupils would lose one very valuable means of extending their reading and language abilities. Rather, I believe it may be helpful to draw attention in as precise a way as possible to areas of difficulty so that teachers are able to offer detailed help and guidance to their pupils as they tackle the demanding kind of formal language that is found in subject text-books. It is perhaps worth commenting that individual examples may not seem particularly difficult; indeed, they may seem no harder than the language found in children's fiction. However, a characteristic feature of academic writing is that difficult constructions tend to occur frequently, sometimes with several in one sentence, and this concentration of difficulty can be a stumbling block for the struggling reader.

Each of the examples from a textbook is identified by a letter; the key to these letters is given on page 27.

Reading difficulties at word level

Familiar words with special meanings

There are three main sources of difficulty at word level; the first is when words which are familiar to the children are used in unfamiliar ways. For example,

> The camel *caravans* trudged the old silk *roads* between the ancient cities of Constantinople and Peking. (B)
> Priests generally *arose* at a later period in time when there were special holy buildings called temples. (K)

Children will understand the words 'caravan', 'road' and 'arose' but it is likely that the meanings they assign to them will not enable them to interpret these particular passages appropriately. The first extract may suggest a holiday highway rather than a rough track; the second example may give rise to the belief that priests got up late. In a sense, the very familiarity of these words is a disadvantage because the child thinks he understands them when really he does not. An additional problem with such familiar words is that the writer may take them for granted and not explain or highlight them in the text. In *The Developing World: Geography Two* (G), the following seemingly familiar words occur in one nine-page unit of work:

estate, roots, grub, nap, battery, stock, cake, mean, litter, relief.

It seems likely that a twelve-year-old pupil will be able to assign a meaning to each of these words but it may not be the technical sense that the writer intends. For, although these words are not capitalized in the text (unlike the obviously specialist vocabulary), they all have technical rather than everyday meanings, i.e.

estate:	farmland
roots:	root-crops (e.g. carrots)
grub:	to uproot a hedge
nap:	pile on cloth
battery:	shed for hens
stock:	cattle
cake:	cattle-food
mean:	average
litter:	bedding for hens
relief:	height of land

A study that illustrates the difficulty that apparently familiar words can cause was carried out by Hull (1979), who showed that only half of the fourth year secondary pupils he tested understood the meaning of the term 'Western leaders' in a passage of modern history: responses included 'footballers' and 'fashion designers'. There were problems too with this extract from a geography book:

It is also the chief fishing port of Holland; herring and white fish are caught in the North Sea. Flushing (22,000) and the Hook of Holland (3,000) situated as far out to sea as possible, are packet stations.

Asked what the 22,000 referred to, only 16 per cent of the pupils mentioned population; nine 'O' level geography students thought that it referred to fish.

It is worth noting here that some writers are particularly sensitive to the problems of the multiple meaning of some familiar words, e.g.

The scientist is a curious person – not of course soft in the head – but curious about things, wanting to know why they do this or that. (I)
Another fact we often want to know about a body (this is what a scientist calls a 'thing' – a book, a pencil, ... a coin – all these are 'bodies') is the space it takes up. (I)

Technical vocabulary

The second source of difficulty at word level is technical vocabulary. This is something that teachers and writers are very aware of; technical words are often capitalized, italicized or underlined in the text; they are generally explained or illustrated and there may be a glossary. Additionally, they may be the focus of comprehension questions. However, there is no doubt that too great a concentration of technical vocabulary can make reading very daunting for all but the best reader. These are some examples of the more unusual vocabulary young readers meet:

muezzin, pommel, mantlets, trebuchet, effigy, Doge, Bezant. (A)
After *retting*, the fibres are removed at the mill by *scutching*. This ... is followed by *hackling* ... (B)
garrison, motte, bailey, culverin, saker, minion, machicolations, impressment, martello, garderobe, trebuchet, mangonel. (C)
stratum, scarp, humus, isolines, isohyets, tsunamis, caldera, sawah, carboniferous, levees. (G)

I think that technical vocabulary can be fairly roughly divided into two types. The first consists of words that are necessary and helpful. Such vocabulary encapsulates some of the key concepts of a subject discipline. Its use is essential because non-technical words will be either too imprecise or too circuitous to do the job efficiently. The second type is jargon, that is vocabulary which is not essential to clear or concise thinking in the subject but which simply replaces one word with another, usually longer and harder, one. I believe that it is important for teachers to consider carefully how much of their 'subject vocabulary' is essential and how much unnecessary. To illustrate this from the technical vocabulary of linguistics, I think that the word 'phoneme' belongs to the first type; it is essential for clear and accurate thinking in the subject and cannot be validly replaced by the more general term 'speech-sound'. On the other hand, the terms 'exophasia' and 'endophasia' to label audible speech and sub-vocal speech seem to me to be examples of the second type, jargon; they have no advantages over the simpler everyday terms.

Several studies have shown that technical vocabulary may cause comprehension difficulties. Otterburn and Nicholson (1976) tested 300 secondary children's understanding of 36 common terms used in mathematics at CSE level. Only 14 of these words were understood by more than half the subjects. These are some of the words that were not understood:

factor, gradient, intersection, multiple, parallelogram, product, ratio, symmetry.

Between 1975 and 1977 Johnstone (1978) conducted an experiment with over 6,000 English and Scottish children who were about to sit for 'O' level examinations. The subjects were given chemistry examination questions in either their original form or in a simplified form; even where only one word in the question was altered, scores for the simplified questions were considerably higher. For example, 80 per cent of the subjects got the following question right:

Which one of the following is *not* a pungent gas?
A Sulphur dioxide
B Hydrogen chloride
C Chlorine
D Oxygen

The percentage of correct responses rose to 95 when the word 'pungent' was replaced by 'choking'. Johnstone comments, 'It was clear that if pupils failed to answer a question correctly we could not assume that only their chemistry was faulty.'

Whatever the specialist area, technical vocabulary can cause problems. It probably has to be learnt slowly, with plenty of opportunity to try it out in 'safe' situations until it becomes familiar. Prestt (1976), writing of science by work-cards, points out that it is not possible for a child to enter into a dialogue with a work-card, so he does not have any way of making new terms and concepts his own; there is always a danger that technical terms remain merely a set of impressive verbal labels.

Formal vocabulary
Thirdly, the necessary use of technical terms by textbook writers frequently leads them to use general vocabulary that is noticeably formal. It is as if there is a feeling that specialist terminology does not collocate happily with everyday expressions and must be embedded in prose that is appropriately elevated in style. This means that, even where every technical word is essential and carefully chosen by the author, the overall level of vocabulary difficulty may be higher than it need be. For example,

Locate your pulse in your wrist. (I)
These lochs *afford* deep water berthage capable of taking the giant tankers of the future. (J)
Nowhere *in excess of* 850 metres, the faulted hill masses have been dissected by ice. (J)

Locate, *afford* and *in excess of* are not technical terms; their replacement by the less formal expressions *find*, *provide* and *higher than* would not do violence to the subject discipline being taught but would help to make the style less formal and more accessible to the young reader.

Reading difficulties at sentence level
At sentence level there are several grammatical constructions that can

cause difficulty for the weak reader. There are three different underlying reasons why such constructions can present problems. One reason is that some sentence patterns occur infrequently in speech and so the struggling reader is not able to predict what might come next, as the language structure is not part of his oral linguistic repertoire. The second reason is that it can be difficult to identify quickly the grammatical constituents of a sentence when the cues to structure which are provided in speech by intonation contours are not present. The third reason is that some constructions, which are relatively easy for the listener or the normally skilful reader to interpret, are difficult for the slow reader because his slowness prevents him perceiving the whole grammatical constituent as one unit.

Sentence patterns less frequent in speech than writing
Several studies (e.g. Pearson, 1976; Ruddell, 1965; Tatham, 1970) have shown that young children read more easily and more accurately when the text consists of sentence patterns that occur in their speech than when it contains constructions more frequent in written than oral language. Other studies (e.g. Clay, 1969; Goodman, 1967; Weber, 1970) have examined children's oral reading errors and found that children tend to say what they *expect* the text to say; if the text does not match their expectation then they make an error. Clearly, a young reader's grammatical expectations will derive chiefly from his own oral language. This strongly suggests that some of the more literary sentence constructions will be a source of difficulty for the inexperienced or struggling reader. Some sentence patterns that are rarely found in children's speech are subject nominal clauses, concealed negatives, some types of ellipsis, word order altered for stylistic purposes, and various kinds of coordination and subordination.

Subject nominal clauses
Young children use nominal clauses as object of a sentence,

e.g.:
John thought *that he would win*

but rarely as subject. Examples of nominal clauses functioning as subject of the sentence are:

> *That the level of the sea rises and falls twice in every 24 hours* is obvious to anyone at the seaside. (F)
> *Whether the difference is great or small and whether True North lies east or west of Magnetic North* depends on the position of the observer on the earth's surface. (F)

Sometimes subject nominal clauses are introduced by a question word. This can lead the inexperienced reader, who is not skilful enough to check ahead for the presence of a question-mark, to expect a question rather than a statement, e.g.:

Why this was so is very puzzling. (B)
What proved to be of particular interest were the isobars. (F)

Concealed negatives
Some sentences have a negative meaning without an obvious negative marker such as 'not', 'no', or 'never', e.g.:

We *rarely* have a completely cloudless sky in Britain. (B)
Most people stayed in their home region and *hardly* went further than the nearest town or city. (K)

Reid (1972) has shown that young readers tend to interpret such sentences with positive meanings, e.g.:

We have a completely cloudless sky in Britain.

Clearly, if this interpretation conflicts with other evidence in the text, or with the reader's knowledge of the world, it is likely to cause confusion.

Ellipsis
Because conciseness is favoured in writing, authors may omit words which are unlikely to be omitted in speech. For example, subordinate adverbial clauses may occur without subject and lexical or auxiliary verb, e.g.:

When in battle, the knights wore red tunics over their armour. (A)
The holy man learnt certain actions which he hoped, *when performed*, would result in winning the favour of the gods. (K)

Ellipsis commonly occurs in relative (or adjectival) clauses. In their oral language acquisition, children first learn to use full relative clauses, e.g.:

John saw the man *who was wanted by the police*

and only later acquire the more literary version,

John saw the man *wanted by the police*.

Relative clauses with ellipsis can cause problems for the reader, e.g.:

Enzymes *present in the cells of the body* begin the breakdown of glucose. (I)

Here, since the child expects the subject 'Enzymes' to be followed by a verb, he may read 'present' as a verb (pre'sent); so, ignoring 'in', he begins the sentence:

Enzymes present the cells of the body ...

He expects this to be followed by 'with' and is confused when he meets the verb 'begin'. It is generally felt that shorter sentences are easier for young readers than long ones. This is very often the case but where there is a choice between a short unfamiliar construction and a longer familiar one it is likely that the longer one will cause fewer difficulties, e.g.:

> Enzymes *which are present in the cells of the body* begin the breakdown of glucose.

Altered word order

Writers depart from normal word order for various reasons. They may wish to link a sentence smoothly with the preceding discourse, e.g.:

> They wanted to keep their gods happy. *This* they did by offering them gifts. (H)

An author may use a cleft construction to emphasize an important word or phrase, e.g.

> *It was the priest* who decided whether or not a person's sacrifice was acceptable. (K)

Some writers are clearly not happy to use the type of prepositional construction that occurs in speech, preferring a more formal word order:

> And climate, as shown in the Introduction, to a great extent controls the activities *in which* it is possible for us to engage. (F)

And word order may be altered simply for variety, e.g.:

> Above the mountain passes and caravan routes, along military and pilgrim roads, towered these castles. (A)

Whenever the word order does not match the order that the reader would use in speech, he is slowed down in his reading (until he becomes familiar with these literary patterns) because the text does not match his linguistic expectations.

Some types of coordination and subordination

Generally young children are able to join phrases or clauses using the coordinating conjunctions 'and', 'but' and 'or'. It is noticeable, however, that authors of textbooks often use 'or' in a way that is very rare in speech, e.g.:

> It revolved *or* moved round in a circle. (D)
> And so the electric current, *or* the rate at which the electrons are flowing, must be the same all round the circuit. (I)

In these sentences, instead of contrasting two *different* things (e.g. hot or cold; black or white), the authors are using 'or' to link two phrases which refer to the *same* thing; the second phrase is a gloss on the first and 'or' could be replaced by 'that is'. But in the same books 'or' is also used with its more common contrastive meaning, e.g.:

He could play the viol *or* flute. (D)

It is obviously difficult for the reader to work out which meaning of 'or' he is faced with unless he knows the meanings of the two phrases that have been joined. And of course he only needs the second, explanatory phrase if he does *not* know the meaning of the first one. Sometimes complex conjunctions, such as 'either ... or', 'not only ... but also', can cause reading difficulties. Reid (1972) suggests that 'not only' is often interpreted with a negative meaning, so children may misunderstand sentences such as this:

The earth *not only* travels on its orbit round the sun, it *also* rotates on its axis, taking 24 hours to make one complete revolution. (F)

Then there are subordinating conjunctions which may be used differently in writing and in speech. To young children, 'once', is probably most familiar as an adverb, meaning 'at one time', e.g.:

Once he had a lot of money.

In the following example, however, 'once' is used as a subordinating conjunction, meaning 'as soon as':

Once the Holy Men organized themselves properly they soon realized that they possessed power over life and death. (K)

'If' can also be used in a rather unusual way, e.g.:

If there was not much daylight, neither were there many ways of providing artificial light. (C)

Normally we expect a condition to be followed by the consequence of that condition, e.g.:

If there was not much daylight, people went to bed early.

But here, one condition is followed by another. The sentence could be paraphrased:

If it is true that there was not much daylight (and it is true) then it is also true that there were not many ways of providing artificial light.

Problems caused by the absence of intonation cues

The second major source of grammatical difficulty at sentence level is the absence of intonation cues to constituent structure. In speech, one of the very important roles of intonation is the division of utterances into grammatically relevant word groups. In writing, of course, this source of information is lost; and punctuation serves to demarcate only some of the larger grammatical units. This means that the reader may be confronted with a string of words without necessarily being aware of the grammatical relationships between them. Such a difficulty arises in object nominal clauses and in relative clauses if the writer does not include a clause-marker to draw attention to the structure of the sentence.

An object nominal clause can occur with or without the clause-marker 'that', e.g.:

John believed (*that*) *the story was true.*

Hakes (1972) has shown that such sentences are easier to interpret when the clause-marker is present. When the clause-marker is not included, it is easy for the reader to 'chunk' the sentence inappropriately, treating 'the story' as the object of the verb 'believe', e.g.:

John believed the story.

This tendency is increased if the remainder of the sentence comes at the start of the next line. When 'that' is included in the sentence, the structure is as clear to the eye of the reader as it is to the ear of the listener.

A relative clause may be introduced by a relative pronoun. The pronoun has to be present if it functions as the subject of the relative clause, e.g.:

I met the man *who won the prize.*

But the relative pronoun can be omitted if it is the object of the relative clause, e.g.:

I met the man (*whom*) *your friends admire.*

Fodor and Garrett (1967) have shown that such sentences are understood more readily when a relative pronoun is included. If there is no relative pronoun, two noun phrases occur together and it can be difficult to sort out the grammatical constituents, e.g.:

A Professor James knows breeds dogs.

Here it looks at first as if 'Professor James' is the subject of the sentence and 'knows' the verb. If 'that' or 'whom' were included, it would be clear that 'professor' is part of one constituent and 'James' part of another, e.g.:

A Professor *that James knows* breeds dogs.

Examples from school textbooks of these two constructions are:

Object nominal clause without clause-marker

He feared *the Saracens might conquer his country too.* (A)

The weak reader may think the sentence reads:

He feared the Saracens

and then be confused by 'might conquer'.

Relative clause without relative pronoun

Prince Alexius offered to give the Crusaders the money they needed. (A)

In this sentence also it is easy for the reader to stop too soon, thinking that the sentence ends at 'money'. Particularly if the line division is unhelpful or if the reader is not sensitive to the function of full-stops and capital letters, he may think that 'they needed' is the beginning of a new sentence. These are further examples where longer sentences, with clause-markers included, are easier to read than their shortened versions.

Problems caused by inadequate reading speed

Inadequate reading speed causes problems when the text contains long grammatical constituents or when one grammatical constituent is interrupted by another. In order for sentence meanings to be interpreted, the reader has to hold in Short Term Memory all the words that form a grammatical constituent. Only when the grammatical subject, for example, is present as a complete unit in Short Term Memory can it be processed and then left safely on one side to await the rest of the sentence. If any grammatical constituent exceeds the capacity of the reader's Short Term Memory, therefore, he will not be able to process all the words in the constituent together and will have difficulty in perceiving the grammatical relationships within the sentence and, hence, in arriving at its meaning.

It is difficult to find precise measurements of the capacity of Short Term Memory. However, there is wide agreement that its capacity is strictly limited both in terms of the number of items it can store and in terms of the length of time it can hold them. It seems to be able to hold five to nine items at a time (Miller, 1956) for a period of a few seconds, perhaps three or four. ('Items' are not precisely defined; they may be words or phrases, so the storage capacity is for more than nine words so long as they are grammatically related.) Exactly how long these items can be retained depends partly on how much attention is being paid to the task and also on how much effort is needed to process the information that is being received. Once a meaning has been synthesized from the items in Short Term Memory, the processed 'chunk' can be shunted into a less vulnerable memory store. This store, where material can be held for several minutes, is sometimes called Long Term Memory (e.g. Hellige, 1975) but this is rather a confusing designation as the label is more often applied to the permanent memory or knowledge that a person has; Gough (1972) has coined a more explicit, if cumbersome, name: the Place Where Sentences Go When They Are Understood (PWSGWTAU).

Using figures from the eye-movement studies of Taylor *et al.* (quoted in Massaro, 1975, p. 294), we can suggest an approximate average reading speed for six-year-olds of 80 words per minute, for nine-year-olds of 160 w.p.m. and for twelve-year-olds of 200 w.p.m. From this, allowing a Short Term Memory of 3.5 seconds' duration, we can very roughly assess that, at these reading speeds,

(a) six-year-old readers will be able to hold four to five words in Short Term Memory (i.e. 80 w.p.m. $\div$ 60 = 1.3 words read per second, $\times$ 3.5 = 4.6 words held in STM);
(b) nine-year-olds will be able to retain eight to ten words (i.e. 160 w.p.m. $\div$ 60 = 2.6 words read per second, $\times$ 3.5 = 9.3 words held in STM);
(c) twelve-year-olds will manage ten to thirteen words (i.e. 200 w.p.m. $\div$ 60 = 3.3 words read per second, $\times$ 3.5 = 11.6 words held in STM).

Of course, if the reader is reading at a slower speed than the average for his age, either because he is a weak reader, or because difficult vocabulary and unfamiliar concepts are slowing him down, then he will be able to store proportionately fewer words. All this means that, if a grammatical constituent is longer than the reader's Short Term Memory capacity, or if it is interrupted by another construction that exhausts the storage space in Short Term Memory, the reader will have to struggle to make sense of the passage. Reid (1972) shows that, given a sentence like this:

The girl standing beside the lady had a blue dress

many seven-year-old children think that 'the lady' was wearing a blue dress. Obviously, the six-word constituent 'the girl standing beside the lady' has overloaded their Short Term Memory and so 'the girl' has been lost.

Long grammatical subjects are a particularly severe source of reading difficulty because they may leave the reader in doubt about the word that actually 'does the action' of the verb. The following are some examples from textbooks of sentences with long grammatical subjects. I have used capital letters for the 'head' word of the subject and for the verb to draw attention to the distance between these two vital parts of the sentence.

A LINE of these charging knights with lowered lances WAS a frightening sight to the enemy. (A)
A SYSTEM in which nobles are given estates of land in exchange for the use of their soldiers IS CALLED feudal rule. (H)
The only WAY to rid themselves of this feeling of guilt or to avoid any likely punishment by the gods WAS to offer them gifts. (K)

These subject phrases range from nine to twenty words, requiring reading speeds of approximately 150–350 words per minute. In each case the 'head' word is singular and is followed by a singular verb, but several other nouns in each subject phrase, including the one immediately preceding the verb, are plural. (An examination of about 17,000 noun phrases (Quirk *et al.*, 1972) showed that not only are complex noun phrases more common in serious and scientific writing than they are in fiction and informal speech, but also that a higher proportion of these complex constructions occur as subjects of clauses in the academic modes than in the more informal types of language.)

Like long grammatical subjects, interrupted constructions also place a heavy burden on the reader's memory, e.g.:

They in turn were followed *after over a century of domination by lesser states* by the Persians. (H)

The most common type (*there is probably one of this kind hanging on the wall of your classroom*) consists of a small glass tube filled with mercury. (F)

Concentration of difficulty

All these examples of sources of reading difficulty at sentence level can be found in most kinds of written language. The special difficulty of academic, or textbook, written language is that it frequently contains a higher concentration of difficult features than fiction does. It is particularly common for textbooks to contain sentences that consist of several clauses, e.g.:

They heavily outnumbered the invaders, yet in the end the Spaniards won because they were brave, because they had better weapons, because many Indians took their side and because many Aztecs suffered from a terrible disease called smallpox which came from Europe with the Spaniards. (E)

There are seven clauses in this sentence, which is conceptually as well as linguistically difficult. The reader needs to sort out that 'they' were the Aztecs and 'the invaders' were the Spaniards; that there were more Aztecs so you would expect them to win (this expectation is implied but not stated) but they did not, for a variety of reasons. The reasons are particularly difficult because the first three are strengths of the Spaniards but the fourth is a weakness of the Aztecs.

The following sentence has only three clauses but, nevertheless, it contains many difficult features:

The use of machinery on this scale and the fact that until recently the Prairie farmer concentrated on the growth of only one kind of crop enables him to run his farm with far fewer labourers than the English farmer whose activities include the cultivation of a variety of crops and the keeping of animals. (F)

Here, the subject of the main verb 'enables' is the coordinated pair 'the use ... and the fact ...'; the complete subject phrase is 26 words long. The clause 'that the Prairie farmer concentrated ...' is interrupted by the phrase 'until recently'. After a comparative construction, the sentence concludes with a relative clause which has an object that is 12 words long.

The first of the two examples I have given here is a sentence that is 45 words long; the second example contains 55 words. An American computer analysis (Kucera and Francis, 1967, p. 376) has shown that the average sentence length for 'general fiction' is 14 words and for 'learned and scientific writings', 24 words. So, on average, sentences in textbooks can be expected to be roughly twice as long as sentences in fiction. And these particular examples are three and four times as long as the average sentence in fiction. Long sentences such as these with complex internal relationships place greater burdens on the reader's Short Term Memory and on his syntactic abilities.

Reading difficulties at discourse level

Even if the reader can understand all the technical vocabulary of the passage and has no difficulty at sentence level he may still not be able to make sense of the text as a whole. There are frequent instances of pupils understanding all the constituent sentences of a passage and yet not understanding the relationship between them, i.e. not understanding the point that is being made. Pupils will frequently remember a dramatic or vivid example without having any idea of the generalization it was intended to exemplify.

The structure of factual prose

The movement and structure of factual prose are very different from the chronological narrative of fiction. A paragraph may consist of a generalized statement, followed by detailed examples given as evidence of the truth of the first statement; or there may be several apparently disparate examples strung together to be followed by a concluding statement which draws out the similarity between each of the earlier cases; the writer may put forward one point of view and then turn round and put the opposite point of view; or he may give a series of facts, following each with his own opinion or interpretation; and so on. Unless pupils are able to recognize which type of paragraph construction they are reading and to understand the structure of the author's argument, they are unlikely to understand each sentence properly – it will remain an isolated unit, unrelated to the whole.

Writers usually signal the relationships between their ideas and signpost their readers through the text by means of conjunctions and sentence adverbs. There are the additive words which show that the writer is bringing extra evidence to prove his point, e.g. 'furthermore', 'in addition', 'similarly', 'moreover'; there are the contrastive words which show that the author is changing direction, e.g. 'on the contrary', 'conversely', 'however', 'notwithstanding'; there are the concluding words that show he is making a point, e.g. 'therefore', 'consequently', 'accordingly', 'hence'. It is all too easy for children to slip over these words completely when they read; even if they do read them, it is very likely that they will not interpret correctly the relationship that is being signalled. A project at Monash University in Australia (Gardner, 1977) tested secondary pupils' understanding of about 200 of the connective words that are used in scientific writing and found that 11 of them were understood by only 50 per cent of fifteen-year-olds. (Examples are 'similarly' and 'that is'.) Three words, including 'moreover', were only understood by up to 30 per cent of this age group. This suggests that a passage which a writer has constructed with care becomes, to the unskilled reader, just a collection of more or less random sentences. These connective words occur widely in all types of academic writing, not just in scientific texts as is sometimes suggested, e.g.:

Similarly, the Iroquoian Indians thought that the Master of life sent nothing but 'good' things to the earth. (K)
They had, *moreover*, to make all their own houses. (F)

Sometimes the connective words connect with an idea so far away in the text that the reader has to hold a great deal in his head if he is to understand the link that is being made, e.g.

It was food, however, which was the key to any siege. If the garrison did not bother to lay in stocks of every item they could not hope to withstand an attack for very long. Here is Salisbury castle collecting stores together in 1173. [12-line list of stores]. The handmills were kept for grinding up the corn to make flour and the malt was used for brewing beer. I like the idea of keeping a spare chain for the drawbridge and a spare rope for the well. *Equally* if they began their siege at the wrong time of year when perhaps there were no crops growing, the attackers could find themselves in difficulty. (C)

The first sentence is a general statement which is followed by two statements of detail: 'If the garrison did not bother to lay in stocks . . .' and 'Equally if they began their siege at the wrong time of year . . .' The link between the two is marked by the connector 'equally' but the two sentences are so far apart that it takes a skilled reader to make the connection. The difficulty is exacerbated by the unusual use of the pronouns *they* and *their* to refer to a noun that has not yet been introduced. (Understandably, it is more normal for pronouns to follow the nouns that they refer to.) In, 'Equally if they began their siege . . .' *they* refers not to the garrison who have already been mentioned but to the *attackers* who are not specified until the end of the sentence. This makes it more likely that a reader will erroneously relate *equally* to the immediately preceding sentences rather than perceiving its function of marking a contrast with the second sentence in the paragraph.

Problems of interpretation at discourse level can also arise when an author, striving for an elegant written style, tries to avoid excessive repetition within a paragraph. Consider the following extract:

> Throughout the Middle Ages and up until the establishment of Clydesdale's trade with North America, the east coast was Scotland's premier commercial and manufacturing area. Today, the regions bordering on the Forth are growing rapidly. Closer ties with Europe may hasten this process and the supremacy of the Clyde may one day be seen as a brief interlude in which the historical heartland of Scotland was eclipsed but for a short period. (J)

In this paragraph, the relative industrial strengths of the west and the east of Scotland are being compared. So that the comparisons do not become boringly repetitive, the writer refers to the west as *Clydesdale* and *the Clyde*, and to the east as *the east coast, the regions bordering on the Forth* and *the historical heartland of Scotland*. In order to understand the author's conclusion that the east coast looks set to surpass the west in importance once again, the reader has to have a very clear idea of the geographical positions of the Clyde and the Forth and to be alert to the range of substitute expressions that are used.

Non-fiction compared with fiction

Apart from the structural features that have been mentioned, there are some general differences between fiction and non-fiction which tend to make non-fiction intrinsically harder to read. This is an oversimplification, of course; it is possible to find examples of very difficult novels and easy textbooks. However, the generalization does allow comparisons to be made which throw some light on the problems children face when they read factual prose.

It is worth noticing initially that people who write fiction are first and foremost *writers*. They are drawn to writing and – more importantly – their work is published, because they have a talent for it; they know that writing is a craft and they write and rewrite until their prose is as good as they can make it. On the other hand, writers of textbooks are generally good at their specialist subject; they may not have any particular writing skills at all. As geographers or historians or whatever, they are likely to be very concerned about what their academic colleagues think of their command and presentation of their subject. They may scrutinize their manuscripts for accuracy, balance, fairness and so on but they do not necessarily pay the attention to language that we expect from a novelist.

Secondly, whenever a writer sets out to produce a work of fiction, he has to create a self-contained world which is credible to the reader and which can be entered by him while he reads the book. Whether a novel is set in the past, the present or the future, whether it is a work of fantasy or realism, the author strives to present characters and settings in such a tangible way that the reader feels that he is there too. Strangely enough, non-fiction, which is always written about the real world, often seems more distanced from it. Textbook writers expect their readers to bring their own knowledge of the world to their reading (and this knowledge may well not be as extensive as the author assumes) and they do not, generally, paint vivid word-pictures. The following extract from a historical novel shows how Cynthia Harnett (1959, pp. 17–18) humanizes the historical fact of narrow streets:

> Bendy enjoyed sticking his head out [of the window] and finding himself suspended almost half-way across Paternoster Row, with the attic window of the house opposite so near that he could toss apples backwards and forwards with the boy who lived there.

Following from this is the fact that fiction is always about people – or robots or animals who behave like people and have human emotions. When people appear in non-fiction they do things such as ploughing fields, inventing the steam engine or discovering gravity, but they are rarely presented as rounded human beings who experience joy and sorrow, fear, excitement and disappointment. Then there is much non-fiction which is not about people at all but about objects and processes in the physical world, such as the working of a dynamo or the formation of fold mountains, and some is about abstractions like the nature of kingship or the concept of freedom. In broad terms, a text is usually more remote the fewer references it has to human lives, feelings and opinions. Rudolf Flesch, who designed one of the most widely-used formulae for measuring readability (Flesch, 1948) was very aware of the importance of 'human interest' in a book and, in fact, his formula is in two parts, one to measure linguistic complexity and the other to measure human interest. Because the second part of the formula is rather more complicated to apply, it is rarely used in modern readability studies. Flesch found, however, that it corrected anomalies that occurred when the first part was used on its own. He assessed the readability of two psychology textbooks using the formula and compared the results with students' subjective ratings of the books. On the measure of linguistic complexity alone, the book that the students found hardest to read should have been easy, according to the formula, and the text that they rated as most readable had a score that suggested it was very difficult. When the 'human interest' part of the formula was applied, it showed that the book the students considered readable was high in human interest, the unreadable one very low. This finding lends support to the intuitively obvious notion that writers differ enormously in their ability to write compellingly about abstract topics. Two extracts from science textbooks, selected by Whitcombe (1973), illustrate this vividly. They are both about acceleration due to gravity. The first is intended for CSE pupils:

> One method of measuring the acceleration due to gravity, is to time a free fall by an electric clock capable of measuring one-hundredths of a second. The apparatus consists of an electro-magnet (M) which is energized by a switch incorporated with the electrical supply to the clock. A steel ball with a piece of paper between itself and the iron core is held by M. When the switch is pressed, the current in M is cut off and the ball begins to fall. Simultaneously, the clock is switched on. After falling a height h the ball strikes a hinged plate X. This then breaks contact and the clock automatically stops.... On repeating the experiment with magnetic materials with different mass in place of the ball, practically the same time of fall is obtained. Thus all objects, no matter what their mass may be, fall under gravity with the same acceleration.

This is written in the traditionally impersonal style of scientific prose, where falls are timed, switches pressed and experiments repeated without any mention of the human beings who do these things. The second extract is taken from a book that is designed and marketed for abler students who are following an ONC course:

> Until the seventeenth century it was generally believed that heavy weights fell to the ground more quickly than light ones. Galileo, an Italian scientist (1564–1642), tested this theory. The story says that in the presence of the assembled University of Pisa he dropped two different weights simultaneously from the top of the Leaning Tower. They reached the ground at the same instant. However true the story, he showed that all things falling freely move with the same acceleration. A lead shot and a cannonball take the same time to fall through the same height. A feather takes longer because it does not fall freely; it is buoyed up by the air. If, however, you release a feather from the top of an evacuated bell-jar it will fall like a lump of lead. Experiments show that the acceleration of a freely falling body is about 32.2 ft/sec.² It is called the acceleration due to gravity and is denoted by 'g'.

The anecdote about Galileo not only personalizes the topic but also serves to make the important point that scientific discoveries are made by real people, rather than coming into existence by themselves.

Another difference between fiction and non-fiction is that the narrative of a story has strong chronological ordering, whereas a textbook does not. This becomes obvious when we think that teachers very rarely ask pupils to read a paragraph or a chapter of a story in isolation from the rest of the book and they certainly would never ask them to read chapter ten, then chapter two, followed by chapters seven and nine. With textbooks, however, this is a perfectly legitimate thing to do. It is possible whenever the chapters each form a self-contained section of the book. For example, in a book on the Tudors and Stuarts, the first four chapters are titled: 1. The Tudor Kings and Queens; 2. Tudor Homes; 3. Sailors and Ships in Tudor Days; 4. How the People Lived in Tudor Times. These chapters can perfectly well be read in any order. In addition, the subsections within some chapters are also self-contained and movable. The fourth chapter, for example, includes the following sections: How they dressed; Poor people and beggars; Punishments; Soldiers; Smoking; At the theatre. We know from experience that the hardest part of a novel is usually the beginning. At first we have to struggle to get into the fictional world that the author has created, to get to know the characters, their names, relationships, and so on. But once we have made that effort, the dynamism of the narrative, combined with our desire to learn what happens, carries us on and the reading becomes progressively easier. In contrast, every time a reader starts a new section in a non-fiction book, it is like starting at the beginning of a novel. Because there is no chronological sequence, no necessary growth of one section from another, there is very little dynamism to carry the reader forward. This means that much stronger motivation is needed to keep reading a textbook than a novel.

The last comparison that I shall make between fiction and non-fiction is a consideration of the lay-out of the text on the page. It is revealing to think about the function of headings and subheadings. Although the chapters in fiction often have titles, they do not strictly need them. They could be numbered one to twelve without making the reader's task any harder. This is not true of non-fiction; because there is no chronological sequence, no narrative thread to guide us, we need to be cued in to the subject matter. Chapter headings are therefore much more important in non-fiction than in fiction. Subheadings within a chapter are very rare indeed in novels (Joyce's *Ulysses* is the only example I can think of) but they have an important function in non-fiction, where they reveal the high-level structure of the discourse. If the reader ignores the subheadings, some paragraphs become much more difficult to interpret. Consider the following extract, which comes at the beginning of a new section:

> Edinburgh and other burghs on the shores of the Forth estuary formed the nucleus of Scotland's trade and industry and Glasgow was not a great medieval city with a tradition of artisan craftsmanship like Paris or London. The impetus for the city's growth came with the Treaty of Union in 1707 when trade with the colonies was legally permitted. (J)

The point at issue here is the identity of 'the city' in the last sentence. Skilful readers have no difficulty in recognizing that it is Glasgow but those who are less able are easily led astray by the prominence of Edinburgh at the beginning of the paragraph. In this case, the title of the chapter is 'Glasgow and the Clyde' and the subheading at the start of this extract is 'Beginnings'. Clearly, the likelihood of the young reader correctly identifying 'the city' is greatly increased if he reads both headings before starting this section. The lay-out of non-fiction can also cause problems when the understanding of the text depends on a simultaneous interpretation of a graph or map or diagram, which may even be on another page. It is very difficult for an unskilled reader to move from his point in the text to a chart and back again and, perhaps, to continue doing this for a whole paragraph. Whalley and Fleming (1975) showed that students spent 20 per cent more time studying diagrams when they were printed immediately next to the appropriate part of the text than when they were separated from it. Diagrams on a different page from the related written material were not looked at at all.

Studies of textbook difficulty

Considering all the difficulties of vocabulary, grammar and discourse structure that academic writing presents, it is not surprising that there are numerous studies suggesting that the textbooks used in schools are often too difficult for the pupils they are intended for. For example, Gould (1977) has shown that CSE biology texts are more suitable for 'A' level students. In an American study, Galloway (1973) looked at books of nine different types, ranging from *Macbeth* to maths, and tested sixteen-year-old students' understanding of them. She found that all the books were too difficult for the students to read independently, except the advanced geography book. Not surprisingly, the hardest of all was the poetry book – but at least teachers feel it is a legitimate, indeed fundamental, teaching activity to help pupils prise out the meaning of a poem, whereas problems of language comprehension are seen as peripheral to the 'main' business of teaching maths or science.

Implications for the classroom

Apart from a careful selection of textbooks in the first place, I believe that there are at least three ways in which teachers can help children to overcome difficulties they meet in reading textbooks and work-cards. Firstly, an examination of several books makes it clear that a few types of difficulty tend to recur in any one text; one author may frequently use unusual patterns of word order; another may often use interrupted constructions, and so on. If teachers are aware of a structure which may cause difficulty and which is likely to be recurrent, then they can draw their pupils' attention to it, explaining that it is a feature of that writer's style.

Secondly, since lay-out and the use of headings, subheadings and so on have a much more important role in non-fiction than in fiction, I feel that it is worth teaching these conventions explicitly and encouraging children to read the chapter title and all the section headings before they start reading a chapter so that they have an idea of the contents and organization of what they are about to read. (It is interesting that there is a strong feeling that to do this with fiction is somehow cheating; that we spoil a story by looking at the last page before we start. This just emphasizes how different the techniques of reading fiction and non-fiction are and how important it is that children should be aware of the differences.) Occasionally, the teacher might prepare a worksheet consisting of some paragraphs from a text-book the class is using with the subheadings left out. Pupils can try to provide helpful titles for each section and can then compare their choice with the author's. (Such an exercise proves that writers do not always choose the best headings!) Apart from drawing their attention to the presence and function of titles, this task is an excellent means of discovering whether children have understood the gist of the passage and not been distracted by illustrative details.

Thirdly, I think that it can be worthwhile for teachers occasionally to read good non-fiction aloud to the class. After all, infant teachers read stories daily to their pupils and so children become familiar with the typical language of stories, such as 'Once upon a time' and 'happily ever after' and so on, and with the organization and development of a narrative. By the time children start to read subject textbooks, they are probably halfway through the junior school. It is unusual for them to hear this kind of language read aloud, and they may no longer have systematic timetabled help with reading by this stage. So, generally, children are expected to 'pick up' the formal language of academic subjects with rather little explicit help. But if they hear this kind of language well read, they will learn some of its characteristic vocabulary, sentence patterns and types of discourse organization in a pleasant and natural way.

Writing about school subjects

Children in primary schools do a great deal of writing of stories, news and so on. Anything with a strong chronological sequence, be it an imagined story or an account of the growth of some mustard and cress, is relatively easy to write about because the order of events in time imposes an order on the narrative. Similarly, anything that is written as a personal account is generally easier than something that is distanced, impersonal and formal. At some stage, most children will need to write impersonally, and also to write descriptive, explanatory and argumentative pieces which do not have their own intrinsic ordering. Teachers need to decide when children should make the move from personal, informal writing to a more scholarly presentation and how they should be helped to make it. There are distressing accounts of children's writing being sharply criticized because, although they have clearly understood the subject matter, the academic conventions have not been respected. For example, a college student wrote:

My first notion of the change in emphasis between junior and grammar school came when I had to write an essay on Neolithic man for my first piece of history homework. I started, 'My name is Wanda and I am the son of the headman in our village'. The history master read it out to the rest of the class in a sarcastic voice – everybody laughed and I felt deeply humiliated. I got 3/20 for covering the page with writing. I hated history after that until the third year.

(Martin, 1976, p. 16)

And then there is this example from a fourteen-year-old boy's geography homework:

'An erratic is quite an exciting result of glaciation, as a large rock not geologically the same as its surroundings may be found perched incredibly precariously on smaller stones. This is an erratic.' The teacher has put a red ring round the word 'exciting' and written in the margin, 'No need to get excited about it'.

(Cashdan and Grugeon, 1972, p. 119)

On the other hand not all teachers require their pupils to write always in the academic mode of the subject. In *Understanding Children Writing* (Burgess *et al.*, 1973) there is a marvellous account of the chemical structure of polythene by a seventeen-year-old girl who has obviously been told to write for the layman; her piece is 'dedicated to the dedicated non-scientist' – a short extract cannot do justice to the clarity and humour of the piece:

One of the curious things about carbon atoms and about most other atoms come to that, is that they appear to behave as though they possess arms, each terminating in an eager hand, ready to grab at some stray hand belonging to another atom in order to satisfy their perpetual lust for security. Carbon is not only willing to hold hands with members of its own species, i.e. other carbon atoms, but also associates quite readily with members of different species, e.g. hydrogen atoms (which unfortunately for them have only one hand, restricting them to monogamy).

(Burgess *et al.*, 1973, p. 31)

I would not want it to be thought, however, that I believe pupils should always be allowed to write informally or personally about factual, academic topics. There is currently a tendency to believe that it is good for children to write in the personal style and bad for them to have to write in impersonal language. I think that this is an unfortunate polarization. I believe that it is valuable to learn to handle more formal styles of written language. But I believe that teachers need to be aware of all the difficulties such language entails and to be prepared to share good models of academic writing with their pupils, to discuss its value with them, and then to give them explicit and precise help in mastering that most demanding form of language for themselves.

Key to textbooks used for examples

Books in use in primary schools

A: BAILEY, V. and WISE, E. 1969: *Focus on History: The Crusades.* London: Longman.

B: EVANS, H. 1973: *The Young Geographer, 3.* Exeter: Wheaton & Co.

C: GREGOR, H. 1972: *History Picture Topics: Castles in Britain.* London: Macmillan.

D: LEWIS, B. 1971: *People in Living History.* Edinburgh: Holmes McDougall.

E: LINCOLN, J. D. 1977: *History First Series: Montezuma.* Cambridge: Cambridge University Press.

Books in use in secondary schools

F: CAIN, H. R. and MONKHOUSE, F. J. 1967: *Graded Geographies, Book 1: General Geography.* London: Longman.

G: CRAWFORD, S. 1970: *The Developing World, Geography Two, A New Man.* London: Longman.

H: HA, W. H. and HALLWOOD, C. L. J. 1969: *A Pictorial World History, Book 1.* London: Longman.

I: MEE, A. J., BOYD, P. and RITCHIE, D. 1971: *Science for the 70s, Book 1,* London: Heinemann.

J: REID, R. W. K. 1974: *Scotland.* Aylesbury: Ginn.

K: WIGLEY, B. and PITCHER, R. 1969: *The Developing World, Religion One, From Fear to Faith.* London: Longman.

References

BURGESS, C. *et al.* 1973: *Understanding Children Writing.* Harmondsworth: Penguin.

CASHDAN, A. and GRUGEON, E. (eds.) 1972: *Language in Education.* London: Routledge & Kegan Paul.

CLAY, M. M. 1969: Reading errors and self-correction behaviour. *British Journal of Educational Psychology* **39**, 47–56.

DES 1978: *Primary Education in England.* London: HMSO.

FLESCH, R. F. 1948: A new readability yardstick. *Journal of Applied Psychology* **32**, 221–33.

FODOR, J. and GARRETT, M. 1967: Some syntactic determinants of sentential complexity. *Perception and Psychophysics* **2** (7), 289–96.

GALLOWAY, P. 1973: How secondary students and teachers read textbooks. *Journal of Reading* **17**, (3), 216–9.

GARDNER, P. L. 1977: *Logical Connectives in Science.* Mimeographed report to the Australian Education Research and Development Committee.

GOODMAN, K. S. 1967: Reading: a psycholinguistic guessing game. Reprinted in Singer, H. and Ruddell, R. B. (eds.) 1976, *Theoretical Models and Processes of Reading*. Newark, Delaware: International Reading Association.

GOUGH, P. B. 1972: One second of reading. In Kavanagh, J. F. and Mattingly, I. (eds.), *Language by Ear and by Eye*. Cambridge, Massachusetts: MIT Press.

GOULD, C. 1977: The readability of school biology textbooks. *Journal of Biological Education* 11, 248–52.

HAKES, D. T. 1972: Effects of reducing complement constructions on sentence comprehension. *Journal of Verbal Learning and Verbal Behaviour* 11, 278–86.

HARNETT, C. 1959: *The Load of Unicorn*. Harmondsworth: Puffin.

HELLIGE, J. B. 1975: An analysis of some psychological studies of grammar: the role of generated abstract memory. In Massaro, D. W. (ed.), *Understanding Language*. London: Academic Press.

HULL, R. 1979: Words are not English. *Trends* 3, 37–43.

JOHNSTONE, A. 1978: What's in a word?. *New Scientist*, 18 May.

KUCERA, H. and FRANCIS, W. 1967: *Computational Analysis of Present-Day American English*. Providence, Rhode Island: Brown University Press.

MARTIN, N. *et al.* 1976: *Writing and Learning across the Curriculum, 11–16*. London: Ward Lock.

MASSARO, D. W. (ed.) 1975: *Understanding Language*. London: Academic Press.

MILLER, G. A. 1956: The magical number seven, plus or minus two: some limits on our capacity for processing information. *Psychological Review* 63, 81–97.

OTTERBURN, M. K. and NICHOLSON, A. R. 1976: The language of CSE Mathematics. *Mathematics in School* 5 (5), 18–20.

PEARSON, P. D. 1976: The effects of grammatical complexity on children's comprehension, recall and conception of certain semantic relations. In Singer, H. and Ruddell, R. B. (eds.) *Theoretical Models and Processes of Reading*. Newark, Delaware: International Reading Association.

PRESTT, B. 1976: Science education: a reappraisal. *School Science Review* 57, 628–34.

QUIRK, R., LEECH, G., GREENBAUM, S. and SVARTVIK, J. 1972: *A Grammar of Contemporary English*. London: Longman.

REID, J. 1972: Children's comprehension of syntactic features found in some extension readers. In Reid, J. (ed.), *Reading Problems and Practices*. London: Ward Lock Educational.

RUDDELL, R. B. 1965: The effect of oral and written patterns of language structure on reading comprehension. *Reading Teacher* 18, 270–5.

TATHAM, S. M. 1970: Reading comprehension of materials written with select oral language patterns: a study at grades two and four. *Reading Research Quarterly* **5**, 402–26.

TOUGH, J. 1973: *Focus on Meaning.* London: Allen & Unwin.

WEBER, R. M. 1970: A linguistic analysis of first-grade reading errors. *Reading Research Quarterly* **5** (3), 427–51.

WHALLEY, P. C. and FLEMING, R. W. 1975: An experiment with a simple recorder of reading behaviour. *Programmed Learning and Educational Technology* **12** (2), 120–3.

WHITCOMBE, V. 1973: Every teacher a teacher of English. *English in Education* **7**, 43–56.

2

Ground-rules for mutual understanding: a social psychological approach to classroom knowledge

Neil Mercer and Derek Edwards

Communications in context

For their practical work in science, a class of twelve-year-olds had been set the task of creating a vacuum by boiling off water from a conical flask. The teacher explained the procedure, and the principles involved, before the pupils did the experiment themselves. Afterwards, three pupils wrote down these observations:

Pupil A: ... the air was vacuumed and the water was taking the air's place and the water shot up the tube because of the vacuum.

Pupil B: ... the heat made the air expand till the air passed down the tube and made the water rise into the flask so the flask was vacuumed.

Pupil C: ... the air has come out but the vacuum is left.

(From Twite, et al., 1969, p. 90)

If these responses had been made in an examination, these pupils would no doubt suffer because they do not provide an explicit, 'scientific' description of what they had observed, and do not show, in writing, that they fully understand the scientific concept of a 'vacuum'. What any teacher concerned with these children would wish to know, however, is why they had failed to do these things.

Explanations of the quality of children's performances on such tasks are most usually framed in terms of characteristics of the children themselves. For example, they had not paid sufficient attention (though two at least do seem to have observed the details of the process), they have poor vocabulary development (i.e. are unable to use scientific terms like 'vacuum' appropriately), they are unable to grasp scientific concepts (due to low IQ, or poor cognitive development?) or they are simply inarticulate ('linguistically deprived', perhaps?).

Here is another example. Two third-year remedial boys are discussing, on their own in a quiet room, some of the difficulties they face with maths lessons:

A: I can't do my maths very well because of the hard words ... gremorry, grometry or something like that, I don't know what the words mean, you know, it gets me real muddled.

B: I know what it means it means a three-sided figure, but we had another word and it meant four-sided.

A: It gets me all muddled up, and that, when I sit there and I sit there for nearly a whole lesson, you know, and I think I can't do it, you know it makes me think I can't do it when I don't know the word.[1]

Another case of 'vocabulary problems', or limited cognitive development? Such examples have, on many occasions, been used by researchers and teachers to try to define children's inadequacies, and hence explain their position as low achievers in the classroom. One such researcher whose research has proved particularly influential amongst primary and junior school teachers, is Joan Tough. Her concern is with 'the particular needs of those children who are at a disadvantage within school because of their experience of using language at home' (Tough, 1976a); the underlying philosophy of her research owes much to the work of Bernstein.[2] In one part of her research, she asked seven-year-olds to describe to an adult how something worked; in one case they had to say why a 'squeezy' soap container made a good water-pistol. She claims that 'advantaged' (i.e. middle-class) children were able to show they understood the underlying principles of operation, while disadvantaged children could not.

For example:

Tom (an 'advantaged' child): It's because when you squeeze it, it's not hard, and so all the air is pushed out. Then when you put it in the water and don't squeeze, the sides go back and so the water goes in and takes the place of air. Then you squeeze it and the water is forced out through the little hole up the tube and makes a jet.

Mark (a 'disadvantaged' child): You get it like that. You squeeze it. Go like that. And so like that.

Tough uses such examples to justify her claim that 'those uses (of language) which were thought to reflect complex thinking more frequently appeared in the talk of the children of the advantaged groups' (Tough, 1977 p. 159). In other words, the children's inadequate language is taken to reflect inadequate thinking.

We would argue, however, that there is no reason to believe from this example that Mark did not know how the water-pistol worked. From Tough's description of the experimental setting, and from the nature of his speech, it is clear that he was simultaneously *demonstrating* to the researcher, by physical action, how it worked. The verbal explanation was only part of his total explanation. Tough does not judge Mark and Tom's explanations by any general criteria of communication adequacy,

[1] From a tape-recorded discussion available on PE232 Cassette Side 4 (Open University, 1979).

[2] For a more detailed discussion of Tough's research, and the Schools Council Project for which it forms the basis (Tough, 1976a; 1976b), see Mercer (1979).

such as whether the child is succeeding in conveying information to a listener who is really ignorant of the situation. She is instead judging their performance in terms of their conformity to educational language, whereby children are expected to provide explicit verbal demonstrations of their understanding for teachers (or researchers) who already possess the knowledge in question.

Mark's 'inadequate' performance may, therefore, be seen as the result of an unresolved misunderstanding between the researcher and the child about the nature and purpose of the task being attempted, a misunderstanding for which at least some of the blame must fall on the researcher. We are not, of course, proposing that all children have equal educational potential, or that educational failure is simply the result of misunderstandings about school work. But we will argue in this chapter that any constructive analysis and assessment of children's performance in school must take account of the social context in which that performance is elicited, and that the contributions of all participants in any educational interaction – e.g. a dialogue between a teacher and child, or the whole sequence consisting of a teacher's presentation of some topic or body of knowledge to a class, followed by their classwork on that topic – must be regarded as intrinsic and inseparable parts of one educational process.

Returning to the first example quoted in this chapter; how can we judge the children's ability to understand concepts like 'vacuum' without knowing how their teachers had explained the special, academic meaning of this word? It seems likely from the way the second child used 'vacuumed' as a past participle that his most meaningful experience of this term has been at home – vacuuming the carpet. Perhaps their teacher assumed that the scientific usage was commonsensical, or would become so through usage; likewise with the remedial boy's 'grometry' teacher. Perhaps, to their own educational disadvantage, the pupils had intentionally and successfully 'bluffed' their teacher into thinking that they *did* understand what was going on. One London teacher (Powell, 1978) found to her surprise that her pupils had managed to complete perfectly acceptable assignments for the secondary school science curriculum while continuing to think that 'evaporation' meant thickening milk, and that 'liquids' were something thick and sticky, like *Fairy Liquid*. These pupils had made sense of these words, but only on the basis of their out-of-school experience.

Why do such misunderstandings arise and persist, and what do they reveal about the process of teaching and learning? In order to begin to answer this question, it is necessary to examine the role of mutual understanding in education, rather than simply the cognitive and linguistic abilities of children.

Educational ground rules

When teachers, examiners or testers ask questions or pose problems for children to answer, there are always particular rules of interpretation which define the sort of answer which is appropriate, and these rules of interpretation ('ground rules' as we will call them) are generally implicit rather than overtly stated. Let us examine some contrasting examples:

1. It takes three men six hours to dig a certain sized hole. How long would it take two men working at the same rate?
2. John runs faster than George. Nigel runs slower than George. Who is the fastest?
3. Who was the more successful king of England, George IV or George V?

Superficially, these are straightforward questions, all involving verbal reasoning about the characteristics and activities of certain people. But of course, question 3 is rather different from the others. It concerns real historical persons and demands reference to facts, considerations, events not specified in the question. Questions 1 and 2 are abstract and hypothetical, one essentially a matter of arithmetic and the other a matter of logic. John, George, Nigel and the men digging the hole are in no sense real – they are merely arbitrary but convenient tokens with which to pose abstract problems which would remain essentially the same if rewritten in terms of the comparative lengths of three rivers, or the times taken by several taps to fill a tank with water. However, none of this is explicit in the questions themselves.

'Ground rules' define not correct answers, but appropriate ones. The distinction can be clarified in terms of our three questions. Consider question 1. An inappropriate answer would involve a misinterpretation of the abstract nature of the question. For example, it could be argued that, despite working at the same rate, some people work more efficiently than others, such that a change of personnel will have a complex effect on total time expended, and besides, a reduction or increase in expended time will lead to complications due to fatigue, number of tea breaks, etc. Moreover, if the same hole were re-dug the ground would be easier to work; if it were dug somewhere else, the ground would be different. No matter how ingenious such an answer might become, it is simply *inappropriate*. Similarly with question 2 – one is not supposed to point out such unquestionable truths as that people do not always run their fastest, so that maybe Nigel was having an off day. By contrast, an *incorrect* answer would be one where the question was interpreted appropriately, but wrongly reasoned or calculated. (For example, if it takes three men six hours that makes two hours each, so two men should take four hours. Clearly, according to this calculation, two men work better than three!) The same applies to question 3 also; an incorrect answer would contain historical errors and poor arguments, while an inappropriate one, given the terms of the question, might begin 'I don't believe in monarchies anyway, so there is no way in which any king can be considered successful ...'.

As Margaret Donaldson (1978) has recently stressed, formal education demands of children the ability to deal with abstract logical problems, and hypothetical states of affairs, and increasingly so as they get older. What is at issue here is not the development of such abilities, of what Piaget for instance calls 'formal operational intelligence', but rather the fact that these and other sorts of classroom expertise are communicated, demonstrated and assessed in ways that depend on *shared* rules of interpretation, ground-rules for *mutual* understanding that largely remain implicit. And of course children differ considerably in terms of how far their own modes of language, communication and argument, and particularly the nature and extent of their accumulated knowledge and experience, are at one with those of the school.

The issue here is not one of inherent intelligence or reasoning ability, but one of mutual understanding. The problem is social-psychological, not psychological, not inherent in the child but in the encounter between child and school. Its cultural nature can be illustrated by a quotation from a paper by Ulric Neisser in which he describes and interprets some cross-cultural research by Michael Cole:

> For some years Michael Cole and his associates ... have been studying cognitive processes in a Liberian people called the Kpelle. They are an articulate people, debate and argument play an important role in their society. Many are entirely illiterate never having gone to school. Like members of traditional societies everywhere, unschooled Kpelle get poor scores on tests and problems that seem easy to people with some formal education. The following example gives some idea of the reason why:
>
> *Experimenter*: Flumo and Yakpalo always drink cane juice (rum) together. Flumo is drinking cane juice. Is Yakpalo drinking cane juice?
>
> *Subject*: Flumo and Yakpalo drink cane juice together, but the time Flumo was drinking the first one Yakpalo was not there on that day.
>
> *Experimenter*: But I told you that Flumo and Yakpalo always drink cane juice together. One day Flumo was drinking cane juice. Was Yakpalo drinking cane juice that day?
>
> *Subject*: The day Flumo was drinking cane juice Yakpalo was not there on that day.
>
> *Experimenter*: What is the reason?
>
> *Subject*: The reason is that Yakpalo went to his farm that day and Flumo remained in town on that day....

Such answers are by no means stupid. The difficulty is that they are not answers *to the questions*. The respondents do not accept a ground rule that is virtually automatic with us: 'Base your answer on the terms defined by the questioner'. People who go to school (in Kpelle-land or elsewhere) learn to work within the fixed limitations of this ground rule.... It is clear that (unschooled) subjects take their particular actual situation into account more fully than schooled people do, when they are presented with formal problems. This may seem to be a poor strategy, from the problem setter's point of view. In general, however, it is an extremely sensible course of action. In the affairs of daily life it matters whom we are talking to, what we are measuring and where we are.... Intelligent behaviour in real settings often involves actions that satisfy a variety of motives at once – practical and interpersonal ones, for example.... All this is different in school. We are expected to leave our life situations at the door, as it were, and to solve problems that other people have set.

(Ulric Neisser, 1976, pp. 135–6)

Clearly this example is similar to those we have been discussing. Despite the inclusion of culturally-appropriate activities, such as drinking 'cane-juice', the unschooled Kpelle do not deal with the question in the way the experimenter intends. They treat it as a 'real-world' problem, rather than a purely formal, logical one. Of course, it would have been wrong for the experimenter to assume from the answers that his 'subject' was simply being illogical or stupid. The answers are quite reasonable if one accepts the alternative ground-rule that the questions are to be taken to refer to actual persons, or persons in a fictional story. We are told that the Kpelle are skilled in debate; it is quite possible that they were trying to avoid being tricked into giving the simple logical answer (that Yakpalo was also drinking cane juice) and were demonstrating their ingenuity in thinking up alternative possibilities.

We have tried to illustrate here just one sort of ground-rule, of direct importance to the business of classroom education. Learning in school, as Bruner (1972) and Donaldson (1978) have stressed, is often disembedded from the everyday sorts of occasions in which we reason and use language. What tends to happen is that when faced with logical, disembedded problems (well represented in the Piagetian operational thinking tasks that Donaldson discusses), children unused to the conventions of interpretation, or ground-rules, of such questions will treat them as contextually embedded, real-world ones and answer accordingly. One of us (D.E.) asked his ten-year-old daughter the question about the men digging the hole. She replied, 'It depends how strong they were.' Having been informed that the men are understood to work equally well, she revised her answer to 'Four hours'. Then, appreciating the unlikelihood that two men are more productive than three, asked 'Do they have bulldozers or spades?' The same child had no problem with several three-term series problems (typified by question 2 on p. 33).

It is not that such inappropriate answers are simply wrong or unintelligent. This is immediately obvious if we put the problem into a real-world context. Imagine that three men have actually taken six hours to dig a hole outside one's house, and are about to block access to the house by digging another similar one alongside it. But one of the men had gone home ill. We want to calculate the time we are likely to be inconvenienced; but how? The sorts of questions that were previously inappropriate now become very important. Was the sick man's performance impaired when helping to dig the first hole? What about lunch breaks, work schedules, equipment, etc? What if the sick man, or a replacement, returns when the second hole is half dug? What about simply asking the men how long they are likely to take? Indeed, anyone who did otherwise, such as making arithmetical calculations of the sort required in question 1, would probably be considered rather silly.

The cues that distinguish the abstract, logical problems from 'real-world' ones can be subtle; they depend on prior experience with problems of a similar sort. For example, our problem questions (1, 2 and 3 above) can be specified as particular examplars of more general types of problem according to both context and form. In terms of context, question 1 is likely to appear as part of an exercise in mathematics, along with other arithmetical questions, as part of a maths lesson, in a maths textbook or otherwise, perhaps, presented by the mathematics teacher. In terms of its form, the question is recognizably one of a general type in which certain participants in a process (men digging holes, taps filling water tanks, etc.) are accorded a certain measured characteristic (time taken, temperature achieved, or whatever), and one is required to calculate a value of that characteristic for a different number or nature of participants. Similarly, question 2 is of a sort which occurs in certain IQ tests, having the form of logical syllogism known as a three-term series such that, given two related premises, a particular conclusion can be reached as a logical deduction. Question 3 will normally occur in the context of a history lesson or examination, and refers to actual historical persons who will undoubtedly have been dealt with ('done') in class or in a set text. Put this way, the questions may appear rather more abstruse than before we started to analyse them! But of course, recognizing that the problems are of one sort or another would not normally be a conscious and explicit business. Indeed, the discovery and identification of different sorts of educational problems, of the cues by which they are distinguished and acted on, and of the criteria by which children's responses are assessed, requires empirical research of the sort we are as yet only beginning to undertake.

The cues which distinguish the abstract from the 'real-world' problems can be disguised so as to fool even sophisticated and well educated adults into confusing the one with the other. Even forewarned as you are, try the following puzzle:

Three old ladies have just enough money to club together to purchase a second-hand television set at £45. So, each contributing £15, they take the £45 to the shop and give it to the salesman, who passes it on to the shop manager. The manager informs the salesman that the set has been reduced to £40, and gives him back £5 to return to the old ladies. The less than honest salesman decides to pocket £2 and gives the old ladies £1 each. Thus, the old ladies are delighted to have paid a net amount of only £14 each. But thrice £14 is £42, which, added to the salesman's £2, accounts for only £44. What has happened to the other £1?[3]

We have to stress that we have been considering here just one albeit general and important sort of ground-rule: one concerning the appropriateness of different sorts of answers to questions whose terms of reference are merely arbitrary tokens of the concrete expression of essentially abstract logical or arithmetical puzzles. The point we want to make is that the whole business of education is based on similar sorts of ground-rules, on *implicit* knowledge and rules of interpretation, such that the extent to which these are truly shared by teacher and learner is always crucial. Education is about the establishment and assessment of *shared* understandings; it is social-psychological, not simply a matter of the psychology (knowledge, motivation, intelligence, stage of cognitive development etc.) of individual children, or indeed of their inherent linguistic or sociolinguistic competence.

Let us take a step backwards, away from particular sorts of ground-rules in the classroom, and consider for a moment the role that ground-rules have in terms of our general understanding of education as the transmission of human knowledge. We have here a contentious notion already, that education is 'the transmission of human knowledge'. This implies that knowledge is something like material possessions that are handed down from generation to generation; the learners are more or less passive recipients. The more recently dominant Piagetian model is that of education as the fostering of mental growth, or cognitive development, such that education needs to be tailored to the particular requirements of the child's own stage of development. Clearly there is some value in both of these views, and the issues are not merely philosophical – they have had a direct and fundamental bearing on how teachers teach, especially in our primary schools.

[3] We are, unfortunately, unable to give proper credit to the author of this puzzle. The confusion arises because the puzzle presents a real-world situation, in which prices change as transactions take place in real time, and during which specific people and sums of money appear and reappear, but asks for a mathematical analysis. One way of unravelling this confusion is to point out that the figure £44 actually has no reality whatsoever, since it is formed by adding the salesman's £2 to the sum of £42 of which it is already part.

Our interest in the ground-rules of mutual intelligibility has led us to emphasize a rather different point of view than these. It is that human cognition is itself essentially socio-cultural rather than psychological. It is a product of communication as well as something to be communicated, and the major means of communication is language. We refer to 'human' cognition in order to stress the role of language. It is not merely language itself which is the special hallmark of the human species, but the intimate role it has in the nature of human knowledge and thought. The communications of animals serve the purpose of directing and managing actions, interactions and social-emotional relationships in the here-and-now. Animals take with them to the grave, as Bruner, Vygotsky and others have remarked, whatever skills and knowledge they have acquired in life which cannot be overtly demonstrated in action. Human cognition, its principles of operation as well as its contents, transcends personal experience and is a function of generations of human culture, established and changed through acts of communication, and acquired by children through acts of communication. This process is, in the broadest sense, what we call 'education'.

We believe that this inherently social nature of human cognition has been underestimated in the traditions of developmental and cognitive psychology which underline our practices of formal education. The dominant paradigms, both traditional and 'progressive', have separated the roles of teacher and learner, and placed the onus on the learner. So learners are seen as the passive recipients of what is taught, or else their learning is a function of their inherent cleverness (as measured by IQ tests and the like), or else they are active processors of knowledge, in the Piagetian sense, such that what is learned is essentially a function of their own developing cognitive structures. Our view, if we may state it provocatively, is that knowledge does not meaningfully exist until it is shared. Human cognition is inherently 'intersubjective', designed to be communicable and acquired through acts of communication, represented in communicable symbolic forms (language, pictures, diagrams, etc.). Knowing and learning are not psychological but social-psychological processes. Knowledge and reasoning, cognitive skills such as reading, writing and remembering, can only be demonstrated, recognized, taught, assessed, as all of these terms imply, through acts of communication. And the essence of these communications is that meanings are shared. The single goal of education, one that links teaching, learning and assessment, is the establishment of intersubjectivity – that is, the establishment not merely of cognitive skills in the learner, but of skills recognized and validated by the teacher and examiner – a mutuality of cognitions.

All communications, and by implication the nature of knowledge itself, rely on implicit rules of interpretation. No act of communication is totally explicit (Rommetveit, 1974; see also D. Edwards, 1979) – it is meaningful in terms of who says it to whom, in what context, in reference to some domain of things or ideas, and most especially on the basis of some assumptions about the listener's prior knowledge and processes of interpretation. Overt messages, things actually 'said', are only a small part of the total communication. They are like the tips of icebergs in which the great hidden mass beneath is essential to the nature of what is openly visible above the waterline. The process of education, in the broadest sense in which we have defined it, is essentially like all acts of communication. It occurs most tangibly in the exchange of overt messages where mutual intelligibility is heavily dependent on the nature and extent of implicit knowledge and processes of interpretation. It is these implicit bases of mutual interpretation that we are calling ground rules.

One of the points at which education fails is when incorrect assumptions are made concerning shared knowledge, meanings and processes of interpretation. Moreover, these ground-rules generally remain in the realm of implicit assumption. They define not the correct answer but what sort of answer is appropriate, what sort of written composition is required, what sorts of experience, behaviours, speech etc. are appropriate, what levels of explicitness, and much more. For example, when teachers ask for information, what do they want? Do they not know the answer? Do they want to discover whether or not the child knows the answer? Do they know this already, but want the child to demonstrate how explicitly he can convey the answer in formal language? When children answer inappropriately or not at all, to what is this attributed? To the teacher's own lack of explicitness, to a failed mutuality of meaning, or to some deficiency inherent in the child?

To the extent that the success of classroom communications (which includes most of teaching, learning and assessment) depends on implicit bases of interpretation, it is no use taking a purely behavioural view of any more than a view that stresses the individual psychology and competence of the child. Much of what is happening does not directly meet the eye or ear. The sorts of problems we are discussing here are not to be found, at least directly, in any mere record of what was said and done. We have to make inferences, on the basis of what is said and done, about the rules of interpretation that appear to be operating.

The ground-rules approach leads us to make different sorts of inferences from those suggested by other approaches. It leads us to distinguish between incorrect or deficient performances by children, indicative of characteristics of the children themselves, and cases where there is a lack of mutual understanding. And this is just the sort of distinction which needs to be made when we are dealing with children whose cultural, family and linguistic backgrounds do not mesh ideally with those of the teacher or researcher.

Understanding misunderstandings

At this point we can re-address the quesion of why basic misunderstandings about school work between teachers and pupils arise and persist. On the basis of our discussion, at least two reasons can be offered. First, teachers may assume that the ground-rules of classroom work are self-evident, requiring no special explanation. It is recognized that children will need to be taught how to perform certain specific skills, but not that some children, at least, will need to have the underlying principles of schooling itself explained to them. Difficulties for both teachers and learners often stem from the teacher's limited appreciation of the special nature of language in school, of the relation between school language and children's out-of-school experience, and of the justification for promoting certain kinds of language activities (e.g. exactly what children are meant to be learning by engaging in classroom discussions, in writing up practical reports, in summarizing texts, etc.).

Secondly, children themselves may be uncertain or mistaken about what they are expected to do and why, but not reveal this to the teacher. On entering school, motivated pupils quickly realize that teachers' approval is not gained by revealing that they don't already know things that their teachers expect them to. They learn that, in school, the thing to do is to offer what seems to be required by the game, modifying their actions against such feedback as the teacher provides. David Crystal gives this brief real-life example:

> One six-year-old was recorded reading aloud to his toys at home in a flat, stilted, word-for-word manner, though his mother had often heard him read fluently to her. When asked why he was doing it, he replied that in school that was the correct way to read, for whenever he completed a sentence read thus, the teacher's comment was 'Very good!'
>
> (1976, p. 89)

A simple willingness to play the teacher's game, therefore, may contribute to a situation whereby the process of teaching and learning is being undertaken on the basis of erroneous assumptions of common understanding by both teachers and children.

Teacher-talk

One implication of our view of the educational process is that misunderstandings, or failures by children to comprehend concepts and principles inherent in educational activities, cannot be understood merely in terms of individual or social group characteristics of the children themselves. There is some fairly convincing evidence that patterns of communication between parents and children vary both between and within social classes, in such ways as seem likely to affect children's initial appreciation of the nature of classroom communications (e.g. Wootton, 1974; Wells, 1978a, 1978b; see also Stubbs, 1976 Chapter 7; and Mercer, 1979). We are persuaded that some children's language and other experience out of school does prepare them less well for educational achievement than is the case for others; but to try to explain this relative underachievement purely in terms of the children's own intellectual and linguistic abilities and backgrounds is, quite simply, to ignore the interactional nature of the phenomenon. An equally relevant object of our concern must be the communicative behaviour, perceptions and assumptions of the person who controls and largely defines the curriculum in action – the teacher.

If the ground rules of educational activities are such that pupils must work towards a certain set of task definitions and criteria for success, then a prerequisite of their successful performance must be that the teacher makes explicit these conditions, and ensures that pupils' understanding of them is adequate. There are good reasons for believing that such preparation on the part of teachers is often lacking. Barry Cooper (1976), for example, has attempted to stand Bernstein's theory of codes on its head by claiming that school is often difficult for working-class pupils to understand because *teachers* habitually use the kind of inexplicit language (known as 'restricted speech variants') normally attributed to the *children*. He gives the following examples to illustrate his argument:

... a lack of emphasis on understanding in terms of giving reasons is shown in the following example. Mr C., during physics with 1A, was pouring what he called 'distilled' water into a beaker. The following exchange occurred: Anne: that can't be distilled water – it's got germs in it. Mr C. (condescendingly): It's not biologically sterile, it's distilled. That's not the same.
The teacher used his greater knowledge to cut the child down to size – reminding her of her status as an 'ignorant learner'. He did not go on to explain what he meant and why, therefore, Anne's point was 'incorrect'.

(p. 37)

The next example is from a chemistry lesson in which 1 BQ were being taught about elements, mixtures and compounds by Mr G. The teacher performed various experiments and demonstrations. The pupils were gathered around the front bench watching and filling in the results of the teacher's experiments in a table they had drawn up on his instructions. Several pupils, realizing that they need not pay much attention, just copied from his table on the board – in which he put the results. Jill and Sheila, for example, were discussing haircuts. The teacher eventually arrived at the making of the compound hydrogen chloride (a gas). He then, as part of his demonstration, put a lighted splint into it. It should have quietly 'extinguished', but in fact it 'popped'. The latter occurred because of the presence of uncombined hydrogen – left over from the compounding process. The teacher proceeded to tell the pupils that the splint should have extinguished and that they should write this fact down – not what actually occurred. He did not explain the reason for the 'wrong' result to them, but only to me afterwards. The pupils accepted his command to write down what they had not seen without question.

(p. 36)

Cooper argues that the teachers he observed too often failed to take account of the psychological and social circumstances of the children in their class when presenting information; they often failed to make explicit underlying principles in the curriculum material, and they tacitly encouraged the passive acceptance of 'god-given' knowledge by their pupils. In accord with the present writers, Cooper believes that 'explanations of failure need to take account of classroom communication patterns and not merely individual pupil characteristics.' (p. 37).

Pupil-talk

A further implication of our discussion is that any evaluation of a pupil's performance in school has to take particular account of the circumstances in which that performance is elicited. If someone is being evaluated against a certain set of criteria, then their performance is only useful for that purpose if they understand what those criteria are, in the sense that they know what they are being expected to do. Judgements about the quality of children's language are often made without proper consideration of the peculiar language demands of school, and sometimes by people of whom one might least expect it. Douglas Barnes is a researcher who has done much useful and adventurous work, largely aimed at helping teachers identify and encourage the kinds of language use which assist learning in school. In *Communication and Learning in Small Groups*, Barnes and Todd (1977) analyse a set of classroom discussions in secondary schools, and try to distinguish discussion which serves useful educational purposes from that which does not. The discussions are made up of groups of children who are classmates, talking about contemporary issues like 'gang violence'. One of the criteria, used by Barnes and Todd to evaluate discussion is the extent to which the discussants *make their meanings explicit*. Thus, under the heading *Unsuccessful Cognitive Strategies* (pp. 74, 75), they criticize the behaviour of a group (Group 9) who drew extensively on their out-of-school experience to discuss why they thought boys fought in gangs. Barnes and Todd state that 'failure to make meanings explicit ... limits the success of a discussion' (p. 75), and so consider that the children in Group 9 have failed to use the discussion to advance their understanding.

What Barnes and Todd's analysis does not admit is that failure to make some meanings explicit may not limit a discussion's success at all *from the point of view of its members* – they may all have enough out-of-school experience in common to know what each individual member means. It does, however, limit the discussion's success *from the point of view of the observer* – whether a researcher or teacher – who really wants a *demonstration* of learning from the participants. Barnes and Todd expected the children in Group 9 to recognize the discussion as a school task, and follow the appropriate ground-rules. The children, however, whether through ignorance, lack of interest, or misunderstanding, treated it more as an 'ordinary' discussion.

Ground-rules and classroom practice

One of the aims of our recent and continuing research is to describe, in much more detail than is presently possible, the nature and signifi-cance of the ground-rules which are implicitly invoked in teaching and learning. We are using a variety of methods to do this – including the conventional techniques of observing classroom interactions recorded on videotape, and interviewing pupils and teachers about the work they are mutually engaged in. Some of our most interesting results to date, however, have come out of the use of 'activities'[4]. By this term we mean specially constructed procedures which are intended to engage children and teachers in a mutual examination of the assumptions underlying the work they do in school. We ask a teacher to follow a set procedure for examining one aspect of teaching and learning, from which we gather data in different forms; children's work produced in response to the activity, recordings of discussions of the topic by teachers and children and by children themselves, and the teacher's own account of doing the activity and their insights gained by doing it. Activities can be refined when necessary, and new ones developed. The teachers (and to some extent the children) involved are thus acting for us as participant observers and experimenters for our project. They are not, however, simply 'subjects' who are being experimentally manipulated; they are simultaneously engaged in an examination of their own teaching rationale and practice which has direct implications for what goes on in their classroom.

In one activity, for example, teachers and children use unmarked, anonymous pieces of writing (e.g. essays from other years or classes) to examine critically the criteria by which school work is judged. As part of this, children are asked to mark these essays as if they were the teacher. The teachers collaborating with our team found that some junior school children were able to provide evaluations of other children's work which closely matched their own – even though these

---

[4] Some activities of this kind were included, in slightly modified form, as 'Classroom Activities' in PE232 *Language Development*.

children did not always meet these standards themselves. So comments were made about the spelling, punctuation, cohesion and effectiveness of the pieces. Other children, by making uncritical assessments of work teachers considered poor, or by 'failing' pieces of writing simply because they were 'boring', revealed that they had rather different standards of excellence from those of their teachers. Bringing marking criteria into the open in this way in class discussion also means that teachers have to explain and justify the standards they uphold – a task some have found none too easy!

In another activity intended for middle and secondary schools, teachers and pupils consider the language of special subjects, and words which have different meanings in different subject areas (e.g. 'precipitation' in geography and chemistry) or in and out of school (e.g. 'mass'). By encouraging children to identify words they have found difficult, and to create illustrative examples of how such words might be used, teachers can become more aware of problems in this area and how best to plan ways of overcoming them. The teacher of a rather advanced class of nine-year-olds, as familiar with tape-recorders and slide-shows as a previous generation were with blotters and inkwells, was astonished when they all listed 'audio' and 'visual' among the words they didn't understand. The secondary children, quoted earlier in the article, who wrote that in a science experiment 'the air/flask was vacuumed' not only revealed their confusion about the use of the word 'vacuum' in and out of school, but indirectly suggested a way that their teacher might use their existing knowledge of vacuum cleaners to develop their understanding of the scientific concept.

Other activities deal with topics like what makes a good classroom discussion, and why and when explicit language is really required in speech and writing. As we expected, such activities often reveal discrepancies between what a teacher assumes learners know (and so takes for granted) and what their true understanding is.[5] On the other hand, some activities have surprised both us and the teachers involved by demonstrating the extent to which young children are interested and able to take part in meta-discussions about the work they are required to do in schools, its relation and relevance to out-of-school living, and so on. (It might not have been expected, for instance, that an average group of ten-year-olds would be able to contrast the ways they expressed themselves in formal classes and in small groups, or to discuss how

[5] We would include ourselves amongst those teachers who have gained such insights through employing these enquiry methods with the learners for whom we have most recently been responsible (undergraduate university students). One of us (NM) found, for example, that his conception of the purpose, value and criteria for success of tutorial or seminar discussions was sometimes significantly different from that of the students he taught – so much so that a major revision of an established second year social psychology course was proposed.

and why one child tended to take over the role of 'teacher' in group work.) In terms of our interests as researchers, we learn much about the ways participants in teaching and learning construe what they are doing – the expectations and assumptions, shared or otherwise, which guide their actions. From the point of view of the teachers involved, it does seem that using these kinds of activities helps develop a greater awareness of the social, linguistic and cognitive conventions of the classroom. This in turn allows them to make a more critical evaluation of their teaching goals and methods, based on a better understanding of the task facing every child who is trying to make sense of what he or she is asked to do in school.

References

BARNES, D. and TODD, F. 1977: *Communication and Learning in Small Groups*. London: Routledge & Kegan Paul.

BRUNER, J. S. 1972: *The Relevance of Education*. London: George Allen & Unwin.

COOPER, B. 1976: Bernstein's codes: a classroom study. *University of Sussex Education Area Occasional Paper 6*.

CRYSTAL, D. 1976: *Child Language, Learning and Linguistics*. London: Edward Arnold.

DONALDSON, M. 1978: *Children's Minds*. London: Fontana.

EDWARDS, D. 1979: Communication Skills. In N. Mercer and D. Edwards, *Communication and Context* (Block 4, PE232 Language Development). Milton Keynes: Open University Press.

MERCER, N. 1979: Language and social experience. In N. Mercer and D. Edwards, *Communication and Context* (Block 4, PE232 Language Development). Milton Keynes: Open University Press.

NEISSER, U. 1976: General, academic and artificial intelligence. In L. B. Resnick, *The Nature of Intelligence*. New York: Erlbaum.

POWELL, H. 1976: Unpublished B.Ed. dissertation, North East London Polytechnic.

ROMMETVEIT, R. 1974: *On Message Structure*. Chichester: John Wiley & Sons.

STUBBS, M. 1976: *Language, Schools and Classrooms*. London: Methuen.

TOUGH, J. 1976a: *Listening to Children Talking: a guide to the appraisal of children's use of language*. London: Ward Lock Educational.

TOUGH, J. 1976b: *Talking and Learning: a guide to fostering communication skills in nursery and infant schools*. London: Ward Lock Educational.

TOUGH, J. 1977: *The Development of Meaning*. London: George Allen & Unwin.

TWITE, S., CZERNIEWSKA, P., HOEY, M. and MERCER, N. 1979: Appraising the language of the individual pupil. In M. Stubbs, B. Robinson and S. Twite, *Observing Classroom Language* (Block 5, PE232 Language Development). Milton Keynes: Open University Press.

WELLS, G. 1978a: Language use and educational success; an empirical response to Joan Tough's *The Development of Meaning* (1977). *Research in Education* **18**, 9–34.

WELLS, G. 1978b: *Language Development in Pre-school Children* (Part 2). SSRC End of Grant Report HR2024.

WOOTTON, A. 1974: Talk in the homes of young children. *Sociology* **8** (2), 289–95.

Part II
Language and the cultures of community and school

In this part of the book, each chapter examines one issue of current educational significance concerned with the relationship between children's language experience in their community and at school. Much of what has been written in the past on such matters has been cast in terms of the 'deficit', 'disadvantage' or 'handicap' that children's social and linguistic backgrounds entail. If one common message can be drawn from the very different contributions in this section, it must be that the experience and skills in language that children acquire at home and elsewhere out of school are very much an under-valued and under-used educational resource, rather than a handicap.

In Chapter 3, Silvaine Wiles provides a very clear, well illustrated analysis of the often complex language scene in culturally plural class-rooms. She exemplifies ways of responding to language diversity in the classroom, and gives particular attention to ways in which a teacher, working in a normal class setting, can support the development of second-language learners. Dialect variation is also considered, and the extent to which teachers can acknowledge and use the wider repertoire of language skills possessed by bidialectal and bilingual speakers is discussed. In discussing these matters, the author emphasizes the important role of the teacher in organizing learning situations which will enable children to use and extend their language skills. Most of the examples given are from primary schools, but many of the issues and approaches discussed are equally relevant at the secondary level.

The next chapter, by Mercer and Maybin, is also concerned with general educational implications of language variation. Here, however, the main focus is on accent and dialect variation amongst native-speakers of English, and the attitudes which exist in society to 'non-standard' language varieties. One of the authors' basic contentions is that many of the notions which underlie educational policy and practice on language variation are ill-founded; they argue that some kind of bidialectal language policy is a practical possibility, and illustrate ways that teachers can make more positive use of their children's out-of-school language experience. Readers may be interested to relate the discussion here of dialect-related 'errors' in children's writing to the treatment of the same topic by Wiles (Chapter 3) and Sutcliffe (Chapter 6).

Thomas Kochman's earlier writings (e.g. 1972; 1977) may already be familiar to some readers. He has done much to reveal the ways that the communicative styles of black (working-class) and white (middle-class) Americans differ, and how these differences affect interactions between members of these two groups. In Chapter 5 he considers how different expectations on the part of black and white students influence their participation in classroom discussions and debates. Although his examples are drawn entirely from interactions involving black and white Americans, he makes a number of important general points about the value judgements inherent in 'educational' modes of communication (e.g. that discussion and debate must be emotionally neutral), and the positive aspects of communicative styles which are not normally considered appropriate in school (e.g. the willingness of his black American students to be personally accountable for the truth value of a case being argued). His discussion illustrates well the need for teachers (and learners) to be aware of the ways different cultural traditions embody different ways of communicating – a point also made very strongly by David Sutcliffe in the next chapter. There are also interesting comparisons to be made with the experiences of teachers in multi-ethnic classrooms in Britain (e.g. Jeffcoate, 1979) and elsewhere (Darnell, 1979), as well as with the content of other chapters in this volume (in particular, Chapter 2).

The next two chapters are concerned with the languages and cultures of particular ethnic groups in Britain. As Ivan Henry (1980) has pointed out,

> The word 'education' has an everyday meaning of 'formal education at school'. This often leads people to underestimate the importance of the profound education children receive outside school. The distinction between formal education at school and informal education is crucial in any analysis of the education of black children in the larger cities of modern Britain. (p. 134)

In Chapter 6, David Sutcliffe provides a highly informative discussion of the vernacular speech of British children of West Indian descent. He is concerned not only to explain the linguistic structure of the English creoles upon which this speech is based, but also to argue for the educational relevance of the language skills which are part of this speech style. Here his discussion relates very closely to that of Thomas Kochman in Chapter 5; in particular, both authors show that certain skilled ways of communicating, which are valued and encouraged within children's ethnic communities, are at present ignored, undervalued or even discouraged in school. Sutcliffe illustrates how this rigid segregation of language skills need not be maintained, so that, for example, a teacher might use children's existing expertise in oral improvization as a basis for developing effective writing.

Many ethnic communities in Britain now support their own voluntary 'supplementary schools', attended by children after their normal school day is over. These often differ in their scope and style; West Indian 'Saturday schools' are often entirely concerned with the provision of a more disciplined, traditional tuition in basic subjects which parents feel their children lack, while those of the Polish community are more usually concerned with the development of ethnic pride. Asian supplementary schools are amongst the most flourishing of such institutions; they exist in all areas with substantial Asian communities, and hence take a significant, if small, number of children from local state schools as their after-hours pupils. Their aims, organization and curriculum content are not, however, at all familiar to most people concerned with 'mainstream' education. On the basis of her research into such schools in Leicester, Liz Mercer considers in Chapter 7 the role played by these schools in keeping Asian languages and cultures alive in Britain, and in countering the ethnocentricity of state school curricula.

References

DARNELL, R. 1979: Reflections on Cree interactional etiquette: educational implications. *Sociolinguistic Working Paper* **57**. Austin: South West Educational Development Laboratory.

HENRY, I. 1980: White schools: black children. *The Social Science Teacher* **8**(4), 134–5.

JEFFCOATE, R. 1979: *Positive Image*. London: Writers and Readers Publishing Cooperative.

KOCHMAN, T. 1972: Black American speech events and a language programme for the classroom. In C. Cazden, V. John and D. Hymes, *Functions of Language in the Classroom*. New York: Teachers College.

KOCHMAN, T. 1977: *Rappin' and Stylin' Out: Communication in Urban Black America*. Chicago: University of Illinois Press.

3

Language issues in the multi-cultural classroom

Silvaine Wiles

Responding to linguistic diversity

How Ackee and Saltfish became friends

Cecil Saltfish:	Please Mr Paw Paw, would you please untie me?	1
Paw Paw:	How you get yourself in such trouble, stranger?	2
Cecil Saltfish:	It's me, Cecil Saltfish, the trader and I'm tied up	3
	to this tree ... er ... Bully Bullfrog did this when I	4
	sold more beads than he did.	5
Paw Paw:	Well, I not going to untie you, Mr Saltfish, 'cos I	6
	afraid of Bullfrog bite.	7
Reader:	And he hurried away.	8
Cecil Saltfish & Reader:	'Help, Help', shouted Cecil again.	9
Cecil Saltfish:	It's me, Cecil Saltfish, the trader, and I'm tied	10
	up to this tree. Bully Bullfrog did this when he	11
	was jealous when I sold more beads than he did.	12
	Please untie me.	13
Yam:	Me never untie you, Cecil Saltfish. As much as me	14
	like you, me afraid of Bullfrog bite.	15
Reader:	And she hurried away leaving little Yam to keep up	16
	with her as best he could. Before Cecil could recover	17
	from his disappointment, Plantain come past, bent and	18
	straining under the weight of a heavy basket.	19
Plantain:	Why you tie up like that, Mister?	20
Cecil Saltfish:	Because of Bullfrog. He tied me up to this tree when	21
	he ... I ... I sold more beads than he did. You see we	22
	both trade in beads. Please untie me.	23
Plantain:	Well, I'm sorry, but me can't help you. You see, I	24
	afraid of Bullfrog bite.	25

The multilingual and multicultural nature of schools in inner-city areas today is a fact of life. Teachers are commonly exhorted to respond positively to this linguistic and cultural diversity, and while many are keen to do so it is not clear what this might mean in practice. The extract from a puppet play by second-year junior children with which this article starts is, I think, an excellent example of how a teacher[1] was able to draw on the range of linguistic knowledge that her children possessed.

The children had enjoyed listening to and reading the story of 'How Ackee and Saltfish became Friends',[2] a folk story from the Caribbean, and decided that they wanted to present it as a puppet play. With the help of stick puppets, which they made, a small group acted out the story to the rest of the class. They based their retelling on the text of the book where although the narrative is in standard English the dialogue makes some use of dialect features. Interestingly, the children introduced more dialect features as they presented their version of the story. For example in line 7 Paw Paw says, ''cos I afraid of Bullfrog bite' whereas the text had 'because I afraid of Bullfrog's bite'. The children (see also Yam and Plantain) had rightly identified the omission of the noun possessive marker as a feature of Jamaican dialect[3] and corrected the text in the interest of authenticity. Lines 14 and 15 represent further examples of the same process. The book reads 'I can't untie you, Cecil Saltfish, much as I like you. I afraid of Bullfrog's bite.' The child taking the part of Yam has altered this piece of text in five places, and each change is a step closer to the dialect forms that would almost certainly have been used in the original telling of this story. As well as capturing many of the grammatical features of Jamaican dialect the children make a reasonable stab at the appropriate accent too. Most London teachers who have listened to the recording of the play identify several of the children as Jamaican in origin. Interestingly enough this was not the reaction of a group of teachers from the Caribbean in London on an exchange visit. 'That's not dialect' they said. 'That sounds like foreigners trying to speak dialect'. And they were quite right.

Of the five children participating in this section of the play only one had any direct link with the Caribbean. 'Paw Paw's' parents are from Guyana, but 'Cecil Saltfish' is of Greek Cypriot origin, 'Yam' and 'Plantain' of Turkish Cypriot origin and the 'Reader' an indigenous Londoner (you probably noticed the London dialect feature she intro-

---

[1] I would like to thank Donna Anaman of Princess May Junior School for allowing me to use this extract from work initiated and recorded by her with her class.

[2] One of the stories in the 'Reading Through Understanding' Share-a-Story Series, Sapara *et al.*, 1978.

[3] For a discussion of 'Creole features' see Chapter 6 of this volume; also Edwards (1979), Chapter 4.

duced in line 18). It must be stressed that it was the children's choice to use dialect in the presentation of this play. It is equally important to point out that all of them are competent users of 'standard' English. The activity they were engaged in gave them a chance to display something of their range of language competence. They demonstrate a sophisticated knowledge of language variety and appropriate usage, an ability to move closer to the speech forms of others and an excitement and involvement in verbal expression that the teacher will be able to use to advantage as she seeks to provide opportunities for them to develop their linguistic expertise.

It is crucial that we as teachers attempt to build on the positive achievements of our children, their knowledge of, and ability to use, a range of accents, dialects and in some cases languages. It is not always easy however, to see how this might be done. Three of the children who took part in the puppet play spoke other languages at home, but not all children for whom English is a second language are as advanced in their command of two languages as these children. So how do we help children who are in the early stages of learning English? And, equally importantly, is it possible to support their development in the first language while we help them to learn English effectively? I will return to the issue of support for mother tongues other than English later in the article.

Overlapping needs

For a long time now it has been common to see different groups of children as having different or special needs. Elaborate structures for the teaching of English as a second language and the training of specialist teachers to undertake such work have been created in most of the major urban areas. Whilst this has produced a core of teachers with a fund of knowledge about second-language learning and appropriate teaching techniques it has served to make the 'ordinary' class teacher very unsure of her role in the teaching/learning process of these children. If teaching English as a second language requires specialist training, the class teacher will tread warily in this area and look to specialists to provide the necessary help. On the other hand, specialist teachers often feel very isolated, finding it difficult to get an adequate picture of the learning going on in their ESL students' mainstream classrooms. Without this information, which is vital if they are to support the children effectively, they may find themselves in the unsatisfactory situation of teaching language in a vacuum. It is crucial that the two groups of teachers are brought together to share their knowledge and experience, and organizational structures must be found that allow this to happen. Even where children are given special language help outside the general classroom it is almost invariably the case that a large part of their day is spent with their peers in the normal classroom setting.

At a purely practical level it is hardly ever the case that second-language learners form a distinct group in terms of language need in the classroom. It is far more likely that there will be considerable variation ranging from very early stage second-language learners needing a lot of support to advanced bilinguals whose language development needs in English overlap with those of their English mother-tongue peers.

Another group of children who are often singled out as having special language needs are those referred to as 'dialect speakers'. This is a vague and unhelpful term because at one level we are all dialect speakers, it just so happens that for historical reasons some people's dialects are more prestigious than others. It should be borne in mind however that the word dialect as commonly used has negative connotations. How else can we explain the hostile reaction to the use of dialect in school by many teachers and parents? Implicit in the use of this term is a contrast with 'standard' varieties of the language which are seen as having status in society at large. Many children in school have a home dialect that is potentially different in varying degrees from the dialects of their teachers. However, discussion of 'dialect speakers' in school is very often taken to refer to children of Caribbean origin. Once again, global categories of this kind are misleading. Many children of Caribbean origin (probably the majority) are virtually bidialectal[4] and a close look at their oral and written language shows the extent to which they have successfully responded to the language demands of school. As with children for whom English is a second language there is variation and overlap in terms of language development needs. It is tempting but quite inappropriate to categorize children's language abilities and needs in such an oversimplified way. It can lead to expectations and interpretations which are misguided and can prevent us from looking at the language competence of the individual child. This will certainly turn out to be a more complex process but it will be worth it, for a more analytical approach will, in the long run, enable us to respond more appropriately to the language and learning needs of all the children.

---

[4] Some researchers have questioned the notion of bidialectalism where it is used to mean 'having total control of two different dialect systems'. (see Edwards 1979, p. 36). They have argued that in the case of West Indian Creole we are dealing with a continuum rather than a number of discrete varieties. There is constant interplay or interference between different parts of the continuum. It would perhaps be more helpful to see dialect speakers as having a wider repertoire of language ability from which to draw. Evidence of linguistic choice, rather than inability or confusion, would seem a more appropriate way of describing a dialect speaker's language.

The early stage second-language learner

The 'ordinary' class teacher probably feels least happy about her/his ability to cope with a child who has very little English in the general classroom setting. How can s/he ease the child into the wide range of normal class activities and feel sure that the child is benefiting from the experience, and learning English in the process? In this context it is worth considering the results of some research carried out by Ann Fathman (1976) in the USA into the 'Variables affecting the successful learning of English as a second language'. She looked at 500 elementary and high-school students in public schools in Washington who were also receiving extra help with their English in second-language classes. The type of help, in terms of length of time and size of class, varied across the schools. Pre- and post- tests of spoken English were given to all the students to assess the amount of progress made during the school year. The results were quite startling and deserve careful consideration. For example, she found that those students who spent most time in special English classes (two or more hours a day) did not improve as much as those who spent less time in such classes. In her conclusion she points out that because her study only examined a few of the many possible influences on second-language learning the results cannot be used as an argument for or against 'specific ESL programs'. She nevertheless suggests that teachers who wish to create learning environments conducive to improving the English speaking proficiency of their students should (amongst other things):

> minimize the time spent by the student in special ESL classes
> integrate the student in regular school activities from the very start
> teach the student English within the context of other school subjects where possible
> create awareness among the faculty concerning the cultural and linguistic differences of non-native speakers.

She further suggests that although exposure to English is enough to ensure measurable gains in speaking skills over time, it is vital to create environments in which children need to use English and are motivated to do so. In such settings progress is much more rapid. Ann Fathman's findings are extremely heartening for class teachers. They suggest that the general class setting is a conducive environment for second-language learners particularly where the teacher values talk as an important part of the learning process and organizes the learning activities so that the children are motivated to communicate with each other in English. Where class teachers and ESL teachers can work together to achieve conditions which are most favourable to the learning of English as a second language, the children will certainly benefit. Ann Fathman's fourth suggestion (see above) is obviously one area where specialist teachers' insights can be used to the best advantage throughout a whole school.

Supporting children's language development in the general classroom — an example

Let us now consider a class activity which seems to contain many of the variables mentioned above. A group of five-year-old children and their teacher[5] are playing 'Picture Lotto',[6] an activity which will involve them in vocabulary extension, making requests, practice in matching, and all the social learning which is part of small group turn-taking activities; waiting one's turn, abiding by the rules, learning to win and to lose, taking different roles etc. There are four children in the group, Akhtar from Bangladesh, an early stage second-language learner, and three mother-tongue English children, Madelaine, Richard and Christopher. Richard and Christopher are of Caribbean origin. By popular request the group played the game four times. Only Akhtar mutters rather wistfully after the third game 'dinner time, dinner time'. Whilst not wishing to suggest that activities of this kind should always be played several times over, it was useful to be able to record the way in which the children's language use changed over a reasonable stretch of time. A recording of just one session would not have captured this shift. Extracts from each of the games will be considered in an attempt to analyse the verbal interaction and learning taking place.

In the first game the teacher was the caller. The children each had a base card with some of the lotto items on it. The teacher held up individual lotto cards drawn from a pile and expected the children to ask for the ones that were represented on their boards. The first extract is typical of what ensued:

A:	Mine ... Television	1
C:	Cake. Thank you	2
A:	Mines horse	3
R:	Teapot	4
M:	Baby girl. S'mine	5
A:	Bed my.	6

At one point Christopher says, 'I need one more'. This is immediately taken up by Richard who adds 'I need one more'. Akhtar follows this with 'Am! .. Am! . Am! Two, one more'. It is interesting to note that a relevant comment instantly provokes a reaction from some of the other children. Akhtar seems to understand the sense of the remark (did gesture make this clear?) but is unable to express his position clearly.

[5] I would like to thank Rose Taylor of Haselrigge Infants School for allowing me to quote in detail from a recorded activity that she carried out with a small group of children from her class.

[6] Produced by Abbot Toys, although there are other versions of the game.

It is obvious from the extract above that interaction in this game was minimal, just enough to lay claim to the card. Indeed many activities of this nature can be carried out with a minimum of verbal communication. Some messages can be conveyed quite effectively by such paralinguistic features as the raising of an eyebrow, pointing of a finger etc. However the teacher working with these four children had a range of objectives for this activity some of which were linguistic and she decided to change her tactics.

She suggests that they play the game again but this time with a different caller. Christopher immediately offers to take over that role:

T:	All right, shall we play again? Who wants to be the ...	7
	holding the cards up? Right this time ... you've got to ask	8
	for it. When he holds it up ... you've got to say ... ask	9
	Christopher for it.	10
C:	Who got this? Akhtar you got this? What is it?	11
A:	Bed	12
C:	Good boy	13
	....	
C:	Who got that?	14
A:	Um ... apple an orange an a banana	15
C:	Good boy. Put it on the card	16
A:	Good boy	17
C:	Who got this?	18
A:	Mine car	19
C:	Good boy, Who got it?	20
T:	Oh, that's my dad. Can I have it please? Thank you.	21
C:	Who got pram?	22
M:	Oh, I have. Can I have my pram please? Thank you.	23
C:	Got this? Got teapot?	24
A:	This my ... tea. Good boy (laughs).	25
R:	I haven't never got none in.	26
C:	Who got flowers?	27
A:	This mine flowers.	28
C:	Good boy.	29
	....	
A:	My ...	30
C:	My shoes.	31
A:	Shoes.	32
R:	Ar (complaining noises).	33
C:	You'll get some in a minute.	34
	....	
A:	Oh, mine finish.	35
C:	Who got television?	36
R:	Me.	37
A:	This mine finish, mine finish, mine finish, mine finish,	38
	mine finish, mine mine finish.	39
	....	

R:	Please can I have ...?	40
M:	Can I have my house please?	41
R:	Can I have my ... cooker?	42
	Please can I have my bird please?	43
	Can I have my butterfly please?	44

(Richard and Madelaine use this pattern 7 more times before the end of the game.)

....

T:	Can I please have the teapot?	45
C:	Kekkle.	46
T:	Oh sorry. Kettle. That's it.	47

....

The teacher's role

Clearly a lot of things have started to happen during the second playing of the game. Let's start by considering the teacher's participation. She tells the children that this time round they should ask for their cards (not just label them presumably, as in Game 1). Christopher is clearly confused by this instruction and thinks that he is the one who has to ask the questions. He launches in with 'Who got this? Akhtar, you got this? What is it?' (line 11).

In fact the teacher's instruction is not very clear. To her credit she realizes what has happened and decides to bide her time until she can provide an appropriate model which will make clear what she expects from them. Giving clear instructions is a very difficult exercise. In particular the ask/tell/say confusion is well documented for children of this age.[7] But it is worth remembering that opaque written instructions are also a relatively common phenomenon even (or perhaps especially) at the level of public examinations.[8]

It is quite clear from the transcript that providing a model is a much more effective teaching device than giving an explanation. For shortly after the teacher asks for her card 'Oh, that's my dad. Can I have it please? Thank you' (line 21), Madelaine picks up the pattern and says 'Oh, I have. Can I have my pram please? Thank you' (line 23). By the end of the game both Richard and Madelaine have used this pattern many times. They are not learning any new language of course but they are learning what language the teacher thinks appropriate for this class activity. It is interesting to note that it was not necessary for the teacher to say 'Copy the way I speak'. It was sufficient for her to provide the model, and the children, ever sensitive to the linguistic demands of the environment, shifted their language closer to hers.

[7] For further examples see Chomsky (1969) and Wiles (1979, p. 44).
[8] In 1971 I undertook a linguistic survey of certain CSE and GCE examination papers and found that the rubrics often contained structures more complex than anything in the texts (the questions) themselves.

Peer group support

Turning to Christopher, the most marked quality of his contribution to the game is surely the way he instantly assumes a managing role, a role normally associated with the teacher. Consider his first intervention (lines 11 and 13). He asks the questions, he focuses attention ('Akhtar, you got this?'), he insists on the label ('What is it?'), and finally he praises ('Good boy'). But he does more than this. He issues instructions ('Put it on the card', line 16), he provides words for Akhtar when he doesn't know them (*A:* My. *C:* My shoes. *A:* Shoes, lines 30–32), he corrects a wrong label ('kekkle' for 'teapot', line 46) and he deals tactfully with Richard ('You'll get some in a minute', line 34) who is complaining about not having any of his items called. Indeed he handles the game with skill showing how even at five a child has a very clear perception of the role of an organizer or facilitator and an ability to take it on when given a chance to do so.

What about the form of Christopher's language as opposed to the functions he puts it to? A less important aspect, I would argue, but nevertheless worth considering. The most striking feature is the omission of certain parts of the verb in questions such as 'Who got this?' (line 11), 'Akhtar, you got this?' (line 11), 'Who got pram?' (line 22) etc. This could possibly be seen as a Caribbean dialect interference feature. Dennis Craig (1969, p. 66) would probably include it in his category 'Avoidance of standard forms of negatives and questions'. However I feel it could well be a feature of London dialect also as Madelaine uses the same form 'Who got this?' (line 62) when she is caller in Game 4 (see below). (Although we can't rule out the possibility that she was influenced by Christopher's model in the same way that they were all influenced by the teacher's.) It's also probably linked to a general tendency to delete redundant language items when the situation is informal and speed is seen as an essential aspect of an activity. We all question by means of intonation for example, when it seems appropriate (e.g. Tea? Yes, please!)

Richard gets off to a slow start in this game and expresses his frustration very forcibly when he comments 'I haven't never got none in' (line 26). Viv Edwards (1979, p. 68) points to the doubling of negatives as a feature of Caribbean dialects but as she also points out this is a well known feature of many British dialects (see also Hughes and Trudgill, 1979). As with so many of our children's language features it would be a brave person who was prepared to swear hand on heart that this or that language item was due to interference from a particular source. One thing is beyond dispute – the force of Richard's triple negation.

Akhtar, a chance to participate and learn

But the child of greatest concern in this activity is Akhtar. He has not been in England long and it is clear from his participation in the games that his English is at a very early stage of development. He is confused about the use of my/mine (cf. 'mines horse' (line 3), 'mine car' (line 19), 'this my ... tea' (line 25), 'this mine flowers' (line 28), and eventually after prompting 'my ... shoes' (line 31) and finally 'mine finish, mine finish ...' (lines 38 and 39). But he does seem to open up a little in the second game, both linguistically (e.g. 'apple an orange an a banana', line 15) and as a participator. Note how he laughingly congratulates himself, 'Good boy' (lines 17 and 25), surely a way of teasing Christopher for his teacher-like behaviour. The important aspects of Akhtar's behaviour in this activity are his involvement (notice his excitement at completing his board first), his enjoyment and his attempts to hold his own with the very limited amount of English at his command.

In Game 3 Akhtar becomes the caller and the players change boards:

C:	I'm having this one.	48
R:	I'm having this one.	49
M:	I'm having this one.	50

Two short extracts from the game follow:

A:	This?	51
M:	Me. I got it.	52
A:	What's that?	53
M:	Kekkle.	54
A:	Good a girl.	55
	....	
A:	What's that?	56
M:	Can I have my man please?	57
A:	What's that?	58
C:	Can I have my telephone please?	59
A:	This?	60
M:	Can I have my cooker please?	61

As the caller, Akhtar has a problem. He knows very few of the names of the items on the cards. He compromises, simply using 'This?' (e.g. line 51) with rising intonation or 'What's that?' (e.g. line 53). But despite his lack of English he doesn't let the others get away with inadequate replies. Notice that he insists on Madelaine naming the card (Kekkle, line 54). In fact he takes on the teacher's role, in so far as his English allows, with as much enthusiasm as Christopher (cf. Good a girl, line 55). Notice also how the other children stick with the pattern established in Game 2, 'Can I have my ... please?' (e.g. line 57) and Christopher joins them in this. As caller he hadn't had a chance to do this before, but it had clearly not escaped his notice. This form persists throughout the game.

In Game 4 Madelaine is the caller. Two short extracts will suffice to indicate what happens in this final round:

M:	Who got this?	62
A:	My one.	63
	Mine telephone.	64
R:	'Can I have my telephone?' you mean.	65
	....	
A:	Please can I have my fork? And spoon?	66
	Can I have my ... my brush?	67
M:	And what else?	68
A:	Dustbin and brush, please ...	69
	Can I have my ...	70
	Can I have my dog?	71

Akhtar has finally got it together. The constant repetition of the pattern 'Can I have my ...' has enabled Akhtar to take it into his repertoire. It is interesting to note that Richard also (and quite spontaneously) models the structure for him.

Turn-taking activities

I have looked in considerable detail at this one activity because it seems to offer clues about how children learn from the teacher and each other and has implications for how we organize work in the classroom. The nature of certain turn-taking activities leads to the repetition of language patterns. This repetition serves a similar function to the old language drills that were a familiar feature of second-language learning. However the context is transformed. The focus is no longer on decontextualized language but on learning. Akhtar wants to join in the game. He needs to use English to participate and this need motivates him to extend his communication skills.

Another vital aspect of this activity is the extent to which Akhtar's peers support his learning. We have found this to be a widespread phenomenon, particularly noticeable where teachers encourage children to work collaboratively, show that they value cooperative effort and take care to establish groups that work well and harmoniously together. This doesn't happen overnight as children are well aware of the competitive nature of many school and out-of-school activities and this often influences their behaviour. Learning to work well in a group can be a slow process but there can be enormous benefits for the children both in terms of their learning and social development (see Doise *et al.*, 1975: Wodarski, 1973; De Vries, Edwards and Wells, 1974 and Johnson and Ahlgren, 1976). Ideas for moving from quite tightly organized collaborative activities like the one described above to much more open-ended ones across different areas of the curriculum (maths, science, language, music etc.) can be found in a range of materials for teachers and children some of which are listed below.[9]

Language involvement or language practice?

It might be instructive to compare the Snappy Lotto session with a totally different sort of activity in which a young second-language learner, Carlos, worked with his teacher[10] in the nursery. First of all they 'read' the *Bears in the Night*[11] together. They had looked at this book together many times before and Carlos almost knew it by heart. There follows an extract from the 'reading':

Reading	Text
T: What's that one? There.	
C: Under the bridge.	Under the bridge.
Around the lake.	Around the lake.
Through the rocks.	Between the rocks.
Through the rocks.	Through the woods.
T: Good.	
C: Up Spook Hill.	Up Spook Hill.
T: Up Spook Hill.	
C & T: Ooooh!	Whoooo!
C: Down Spook Hill.	Down Spook Hill.
T: Down Spook Hill.	
C: What's that?	
T: Through ...	Through the woods.
C: (Unintelligible).	
T: Betw ...	
C: Through the rocks.	Between the rocks.
T: Between the rocks.	
C: 'Tween the rocks. This?	
T: A ...	
C: Around the rocks.	Around the lake.
T: Around the lake.	
C: The lake.	

Carlos's pleasure in sharing this book with his teacher is quite unmistakable when one listens to the tape recording and the teacher is clearly enjoying the activity too. Notice how she echoes Carlos on more than one occasion. However a careful look at the transcription reveals

[9] See the teachers' notes accompanying the BBC TALKABOUT series (1979) and the Language for Learning Materials (particularly Unit 4, Listen, Discuss and Do) published by the ILEA Learning Materials Service. For collaborative activities related to reading see the 'Make-a-story' series of the Reading Through Understanding materials (ILEA, LMS) and an article by Studdert (1980).

[10] I am grateful to the teacher for allowing me to discuss this activity and quote from the taped material she collected.

[11] *Bears in the Night* by S. and J. Berenstain, Collins Picture Lions.

that Carlos is confusing through and between and also substitutes rocks for woods and lake. It seems fairly likely that there is a good deal of parroting going on here. Of course 'through' and 'between' are concepts which could easily be confused at this age (Carlos is four). The difference between them is very subtle and would need to be conveyed by means of a good deal of practical experience. They are not the sort of concepts you can learn from a book. Having said this, I would argue that there is almost certainly a lot of learning going on here: a taste of the pleasure to be had from books, learning where a book starts and finishes, how we turn over the pages, the relationship between marks on the page and speech, the sounds of English etc. Whether Carlos is learning English prepositions, which is what the teacher intended, is, however, highly doubtful.

After the story, Carlos and his teacher move on to a different activity. The teacher takes a pile of cards with a range of pictures on them. In the pictures people are engaged in different activities (walking, cooking, reading, etc.). The teacher lifts up a card and if Carlos describes it correctly, it is posted in a box. Another box is reserved for those he doesn't respond to and these are run through again at the end. All very familiar.

Cards in the box
T: What's happening there? (points to card)
C: The lady's cooking.
T: The lady is cooking. Yes. What's she using there Carlos?
C: ... Cooking.
T: What's this she's using to do some cooking?
C: ... the bowl.
T: Yes. A bowl. And what's this she's breaking into the bowl?
  What's that?
C: Lady ... the bowl broken.

As long as the teacher sticks to the procedure Carlos is used to, there is no problem. He's got it off pat, 'The lady's cooking'. But the moment the teacher moves into unknown territory Carlos flounders and one begins to wonder just how much he had originally understood. It would of course have been much better to support Carlos's understanding by using real objects and demonstrating the actions. This language could have been more appropriately learnt while Carlos was participating in the nursery cooking sessions.

A little later in the procedure Carlos attempts to make a personal contribution to the 'dialogue'.

Free discussion (?)
T: What's happening there? (points to card)
C: The man is brushing the dog.
T: Yes.
C: I got a brown dog.

T: A brown dog? Yes. Is it a big dog or a little dog?
C: A little dog.
T: Do you think that's a little dog?
C: Yes.
T: Is he little or big?
C: No. It the dog.
T: But he's bigger than what you were showing me.
C: I got 'morrow. I got dog big.
T: You're going to get a big dog tomorrow?
C: Yes. Tomorrow, big, big, fat dog.
T: A big fat dog?
C: Yeah —— and then my brother dog.
T: Who's going to bring you the big fat dog?
C: She's my brother.
T: Your brother?
C: Yeah, my dog.
T: You haven't got a brother. You've got a sister.
C: Got a sister dog.

One can really feel for both of them as they struggle to share meanings and make some sort of contact. To take one example of an issue that is quite impossible for them to resolve – the size of the dog. Size is relative so without some sort of referent (and a picture won't do as that will only further complicate the situation) there is no way Carlos can answer the teacher's question about the size of the dog. Young children's language is usually (but not always) grounded in the here and now, it arises from current activities and immediate pre-occupations. Therefore, it is even more important that the early stage second-language learner is given ample opportunity to learn the language through first-hand experience and interaction in natural situations. The activities themselves and the supporting visual clues in the environment will make clear the meanings. However tempting it is, we should be cautious about resorting to the sort of language exchange that Carlos's teacher (thankfully?) fell back on when she realized that 'sister dog' had got out of control:

Back to the cards
T: What's happening there?
C: The lady's washing.
T: She washing what?
C: The hands.
T: Her hands. Good boy.
C: The mummy is pushing the baby.
T: In.
C: In the car.
T: In the
C: In the car.
T: Pram.
C: Pram.

First and second language learning

In this context it is worth remembering that many of the traditional approaches to the teaching of English as a foreign or second language were virtually the opposite of the natural learning situation in which young children acquiring their first language find themselves. For example, we don't expect young children to get it right first time. We tolerate, even welcome, plenty of deviation from adult speech models, seeing such features as evidence of learning (see Gorbet, 1979). For example, young children often say 'mans' or 'foots' instead of 'men' or 'feet' which shows that they have learnt and are overgeneralizing the rule for the formation of regular plurals, noun + s. The exceptions to this rule will be learnt at a later stage. Most parents mercifully pay more attention to the meaning rather than the form of a child's speech. In fact, it's interesting to speculate on what would happen if they reversed this approach. It would presumably result in very little communication taking place at all. Children resent the constant correction of form as the following example shows:

Mother: What did you do at school today?
Child: I done apparatus and I done reading ...
Mother: Oh, you *did* apparatus and reading, *did* you?
Child: ... and I done writing, and I done painting ...
Mother: Did, darling, I did painting.
Child: Mummy, if you don't listen to what I'm saying, I won't tell you what I did at school today.

(The child is five years old)

Correction; does it work?

Children learn a language because they have a need to communicate and it is vital that we create environments for second-language learners that harness this natural urge. In addition we must learn to be more tolerant of the second-language learner's 'interlanguage' or 'transitional competence' (see Selinker, 1972; Corder, 1971; Nemser, 1971) as it has been called. Traditionally second and foreign language teaching has involved introducing and practising a particular language item until it has been fully learnt. Only then has it been thought appropriate to move on to the next language item. Stress has been put on grammatical correctness rather than adequate communication. We don't even know if focusing on errors helps to eliminate them. The persistent nature of many common errors that have been the focus of the teacher's attention over long periods of time would suggest that it doesn't. H. V. George (1972, p. 62) writes:

Tolerance of errors is indirectly a factor in their prevention. Many errors are the result of generalization from inadequate experience, and the total experience of the learners can be drastically reduced by (a) the actual time spent in correction, and (b) the attitude and feelings towards learning standard forms of English which excessive arbitrary-seeming correction may set up.

This would apply equally to the correction of dialect features of English and is certainly applicable to the young child's learning of his/her first language. Consider the following exchange which I recorded recently:

Child: She just left ... leaved them on the floor.
And Charlotte left them too.
Adult: Did she? (pause) You said 'left' and 'leaved' just now.
Do you know which is right?
Child: Why, don't you?
[the child is a 6 year old mother-tongue English speaker]

Children operate their own rule systems as they gradually approximate to the adult grammar of their environment. Attempted correction of these systems, in my experience, virtually always ends in failure. This will almost certainly be the case with young second-language learners. They are also generating their own rule systems as they move towards the target language. Their systems will contain rules which are influenced by their first languages but they will also be generating rules from the data in their new language environment. It will not always be possible, as I have argued in detail elsewhere (Wiles, 1979), to distinguish these different influences. With the young child they frequently overlap. A deviant language feature which could be seen as resulting from interference from the first language will also be found as a developmental feature in the speech of a young mother-tongue English speaker. What is important, is that young second language learners have ample exposure to the target language so that they can constantly revise their rule systems in the light of the data and feedback they are receiving. But more than simple exposure is necessary, and it is here that the teacher's role is crucial. S/he must organize the class so that communication is an essential part of the learning process, she must build on the support that children freely give each other (linguistic, intellectual and social) and most importantly s/he must present the learning tasks in such a way that the second-language learners are motivated to participate in the ongoing activities of the classroom.

Linguistic variation and the writing process

It is frequently argued that although 'errors' may be tolerated in speech, they are much less acceptable in writing. This anxiety about written work is understandable for at the back of all our minds is the thought that ultimately children will need to write adequately if they are to pass public examinations and have a range of career options open to them. But writing is almost certainly the most complex of the four language operations (listening, speaking, reading, writing). Most of us probably put it off for as long as we can, preferring face to face or telephone communication. Could it be that tolerance of 'errors' in writing might also be a factor in their prevention (cf. H. V. George above)? Many teachers of young children certainly take this line, believing it to be more important to get children going (and enjoying the process) than to insist (initially at any rate) on standards of 'correctness'. Just as it is important to focus cn the message when we talk with children, rather than allowing ourselves to be sidetracked by the form or surface features of the language used, the same is true with children's early writing.

School policy and school practice

But many schools, even though they may accept (and at times encourage) the use of dialect in speech (as in the example quoted at the beginning of this article), have a school language policy which urges the use of standard English in writing. It is not unknown for example for schools to state that they will not display writing in dialect on the classroom walls. In this respect schools are reflecting value judgements about the relative merits of standard and dialect forms of English which are widely held in society today. Individual schools will work out their own salvation in this respect but as a result of current linguistic knowledge this will almost certainly be a dynamic process. Whatever the school's approach it is crucially important that the children should have as clear an idea as possible of what is expected of them.

In practice however this presents something of a dilemma, for the separating out of standard from non-standard forms is not quite as straightforward as might be imagined. Recently, a teacher[12] who comes from a school which is anxious to encourage the use of written standard English from an early age was sharing with me the fruits of some of the children's (and teachers') labour in the form of a class writing book. On the cover of the book, and therefore in pride of place, was a piece of writing (reproduced overleaf) by a young girl who had only just celebrated her sixth birthday:

What are dialect features?

A very impressive piece of writing, but how did all those Caribbean dialect features tally with the teacher's insistence that they encouraged only standard written English? There are four classical dialect features

[12] I would like to thank Mrs Singh and Mrs Haddon of Pakeman Primary School for bringing 'Granny's Narrow Escape' to my attention and allowing me to discuss it in this chapter.

Wolf Frightens Granny
by Louise Bowbrick

There was a girl called Red Riding Hood One day Red Riding Hood said to her mother I going to see my granny said Red Riding Hood So a wolf was sleeping in granny bed granny was in the cupboard and Red Riding Hood said what big ears you has got and what big teeth you has got and a man comes to chopped down the wolf and the girl live happily after (see Edwards, 1979; Craig, 1969) as you will probably have noticed, (1) omission of the auxiliary 'am' ('I going to see my granny'), (2) omission of possessive marker 's' ('in granny bed'), (3) hypercorrection ('to chopped down'), (4) omission of past tense marker 'ed' ('the girl live happily'). When I raised this with the teacher she was surprised by my assumption that the young writer was of Caribbean origin. She was in fact a white Londoner. So how did these features come about? We discussed this. There were no Caribbean dialect speakers in her class so it wasn't a question of peer group influence. They weren't really consistent with London dialect features, so was it something to do with the writing process? The teacher felt that it was, and pointed out that they wouldn't have corrected these 'errors' in any case on account of the child's age and the fact that it was her first piece of extended writing. School policy as always is tempered by knowledge of the individual.

I asked whether the school would allow me to record the child reading her short story. This they readily agreed to, and there follows a transcription of Louise reading 'Granny's Narrow Escape':

> There was a girl called Red Riding Hood. One day Red Riding Hood said to her mother, 'I'm going to see gra ... my granny' said Red Riding Hood. So a wolf was sleeping in granny's bed. Granny was in the cupboard and Red Riding Hood said, 'What big eyes you have got and what big teeth you have got.' And a man came to chop down the wolf and the girl, and Red Riding Hood lived happily ever after.
>
> (My punctuation marks attempt to capture Louise's reading boundaries).

You will have noticed that all the 'Caribbean dialect' features disappeared as Louise read the text. And because she is reading for meaning and attempting to relate this rendering of the story to other book versions with which she is familiar she alters and embellishes the text in other places too.

Jumping to the wrong conclusions

This was a very instructive exercise for me because it showed that the linguistic conclusions I had jumped to on the basis of a piece of writing were quite wrong. The teacher was right to see these features as related to the writing process and it points up the need for extreme care when drawing inferences about a child's linguistic competence on the basis of written work. It is all too easy to see children's written work as adversely affected by dialect (or first-language) features when a careful analysis of the writing will show that many of the 'errors' have nothing to do with dialect (or first-language) interference at all. If Louise, a relatively standard English speaker, produces so many non-standard features in her writing, it is worth bearing in mind the relatively greater distance a more pronounced dialect speaker (or second-language learner) has to travel when attempting to write as the teacher expects. And most children do make considerable adjustment to the linguistic demands of school as we saw above in the 'Snappy Lotto' example and will see below with reference to more examples of writing.

To show that Louise was not an isolated case but typical of young writers, I would like to quote a few more examples. The omission of the noun plural marker 's' is said by V. Edwards (1979) to be a feature 'familiar to any teacher who has worked with West Indian children'. But this is a much more general feature due no doubt to a combination of inattention to detail and the fact that the -s suffix is often inessential if plurality has been marked in some other way. I remember seeing a young standard English speaker label a picture with infinite pains thus:

2 cat

She said the picture was of two kittens but as she couldn't write kitten she had put cat.

Other features that Edwards sees as 'exclusively West Indian' (due to Creole interference) are the use of the standard English active form of the verb to express both active and passive standard meanings, and the difficulty 'many West Indian children' have using 'the English sequence of tenses'. But consider the following written 'sentence' by Jane (seven years) who is not of Caribbean origin:

My day in the pet shop was hard there was dog's selling and cat's.
Jane

Here the active form has been used to express the intended passive meaning, 'there was dogs (and cats) being sold'. Now examine the sequence of tenses in the following examples from work by Jane's classmates:

Before the shop is open I got thing ready   *Ashok*
Before the shop is open I got things ready
Then I opeen the shop   *Ross*
Before the shop is open I get ready and the van came with the ...
Asad

Clearly the sequence of tenses in English is something that many children have trouble with. Two of the children quoted above have English as a second language, the third (Ross) is an indigenous mother-tongue English speaker.

A 'spot the dialect or second-language feature' approach. Will it work?

Whilst acknowledging that the situation is by no means as clear cut as earlier writers have made out, some teachers would still wish to argue that is a question of degree. Children of Caribbean origin, they argue, tend to make more 'errors' of a certain type. In this connection it is worth considering a piece of research conducted by Steve Landor at Sheffield University[13] into differences between the written language of secondary age 'West Indian' and 'Indigenous' children. In only two of the 76 categories of error analysed did the W.I. children make significantly more 'errors' (lack of past tense marker and omission of copula). In addition, the West Indian group fell into two subgroups, those who made a large number of 'errors' and those who made only a few. As Landor points out, the effect of this is to exaggerate the difference between the West Indian and Indigenous groups. He goes on to raise the question of whether those who use a good deal of non-standard features in their writing are doing this as a result of *'conscious choice'*, using them as distinct 'markers' of ethnic group membership. This is an important point because it indicates that the issue in all probability is not one of lack of linguistic skill. Obviously the older the children, the easier it will be to discuss such issues with them.

In an interesting article entitled 'Dialect features in mainstream school writing' John Richmond (1979) analysed in great detail all the 'errors' in a piece of writing produced by Pat, a third-year secondary school girl of Caribbean origin who did not find writing easy. Close scrutiny of the work revealed that by far the greatest proportion of 'errors' were those related to the writing conventions such as punctuation, spelling and organization. Caribbean dialect features were relatively few in number (less than 25 per cent of the total 'errors') and in some cases overlapped with London dialect features.

A colleague and I made a similar study of some writing undertaken by all the children in a second-year junior class in a North London Primary School. The beginning of the story 'The King of the Crocodiles'[14] was read to the class and they had to write their own versions of how it finished. Some superbly creative writing was produced as a result of this activity, much of it also beautifully illustrated. Children of Caribbean origin formed the largest cultural group in the class, so we analysed the individual scripts for three features said to occur frequently in the writing of such children: omission of 's' to show possession, omission of 's' to mark a plural noun and omission of the past-tense marker. There was no clear-cut pattern in our findings which are being written up in detail elsewhere.

[13] 'Morphosyntactic features in the writing of second-generation West Indians', unpublished MA dissertation 1979. Examples of twelve-year-old children's written work were collected in Sheffield and London.
[14] 'The King of the Crocodiles' from *Tales of the Punjab*, F. A. Steel, 1973. London: Bodley Head.

But to give some idea of the complexity of the linguistic situation, I will briefly describe the findings in relation to the past-tense marker. Thirteen out of the 20 children in the class had omitted the past-tense marker on one or more occasion where its use was called for in the text. However, included in the 13 were children of English, Irish and Caribbean origin as well as children for whom English was a second language. Ranking the children according to number of 'errors' made produces no clear pattern. Although two children of Jamaican origin head the list with 5 and 4 'errors' (out of 15 and 14 examples respectively), the two children with the fewest 'errors' (1 out of 19 examples, and 2 out of 39) are also of Caribbean origin. Of the 7 who had no 'errors' in this category, 2 were of Caribbean origin (one of these using the past tense 74 times without error), 4 were second-language learners (one of whom used the past tense 48 times without error) and one was indigenous English. Findings for the other two items considered were similar. Even where children were making 'errors' it was never the case that it was 100 per cent of the time. On the contrary the children got these items right more often than not. Once again it is clear evidence that children are making considerable adjustment to the language demands of the school.

It is obvious therefore that a 'spot the dialect' approach to children's language won't do. There is no clear linguistic demarcation between the different groups. On the contrary, there is considerable overlap. As we have seen, it is hard to point to any particular feature and say with certainty that it is due to dialect or first-language interference. More importantly, such an approach draws our attention away from the more significant aspects of writing: the ability to present information or describe a scene or event logically and coherently, the ability to marshal one's arguments, persuade, show evidence of creativity, match the style of the writing to the subject in hand and the intended audience and so on. One thing is certain, linguistically the situation is very complex. In such a situation it will not help to overgeneralize and look for group characteristics, for that way lies the dangerous territory of reduced expectation and failure to consider adequately individual children's contributions.

We must certainly attempt to be more analytical about our children's language competence. But it is equally important for us to be analytical about what we want from the children and how best to achieve this. Two crucial dimensions will be the extent to which we make explicit to children what we require of them (for example by means of models) and the extent to which we organize the classroom so that it gives them maximum space to extend their linguistic competence in a supportive environment (collaborative models of learning).

Supporting first languages other than English

I started this article by considering an activity which had allowed the children to display their knowledge of dialect. They had responded enthusiastically to this opportunity. It is equally important to attempt to make use of the other languages spoken by some of the children in our schools. This is easier said than done particularly if we have no personal knowledge of these languages. However, individual schools and teachers have made an effort to put into practice child-centred theories of education which encourage teachers to build on the knowledge and skills that the children bring with them to the classroom. The following practices have been found beneficial:

(a) the provision of books in a range of mother tongues in both class and school libraries
(b) the reading of stories in different mother tongues to the children by teachers, parents or community workers who have knowledge of the language
(c) the production of tapes and story books in a range of languages in conjunction with teachers, parents and community workers
(d) the translation of early readers into a range of mother tongues in conjunction with teachers and members of the community
(e) encouraging teachers who speak other languages to use them with the children where appropriate
(f) encouraging children (where they can) to produce written work in the mother tongue

Drawing on the wealth of cultural and linguistic knowledge in the local community

Clearly the support of the local community will be a vital factor if some of these 'events' are to happen. Such contact and mutual sharing can only be of benefit to schools and their children. Even modest overtures of the sort mentioned above can have exciting spin-offs for both teachers and children. One boy was able to transfer his newly acquired skill of reading English to his mother tongue just because his teacher had provided books in Turkish in the class library. Teachers with knowledge of other languages but who in the past had thought it inappropriate to use them in school, have been overwhelmed at the response from both the children and their parents when they have at last used them in the school context. A child who has heard a story in his/her mother tongue will find it easier to follow the story when it is presented in English. There is evidence to suggest that support for and extension of the mother tongue will only enhance the learning of a second language (Skutnabb-Kangas and Toukomaa, 1976) and not the reverse, as has been argued in the past.

But in the long run, these gestures will not be enough. British educationalists will have to come to terms with the multilingual nature of our society and recognize that in not making provision for bilingual education we are neglecting a crucial component of many children's social, intellectual and linguistic development as well as squandering a precious asset. Bullock made this point in 1975:

> Certainly the school should adopt a positive attitude to its pupils' bilingualism and wherever possible should maintain and deepen their knowledge of their mother-tongues.

The ILEA set up a Bilingual Education Project in 1977[15]. Other projects have been funded by the DES and EEC, but by and large the response from local educational authorities has been rather muted. For a full discussion of these issues see Khan (1980) and Tosi (1979).

A richer heritage

Teachers who have responded to the multilingual and multicultural nature of their classes in some of the ways mentioned above have found that there has been a positive gain in educational terms both for themselves and the children. To be sure, the classroom is a much more complex place, but by the same token it is a richer environment. Faced with a wide range of linguistic competence teachers have found it necessary to be more analytical about language development and the relationship between language and learning in general. In turn this leads to a reconsideration of the organizational framework that is required if all children are to gain maximum benefit from the time spent in school. A further dimension is the necessity to forge closer links with parents and the local communities. This cannot fail to benefit the school, for in the process it can only become more open and responsive to the community it serves.

References

BULLOCK COMMITTEE Report 1975: *A Language for Life*. London: HMSO.

CHOMSKY, C. 1969: *Acquisition of syntax in children from 5 to 10*. Cambridge, Mass.: MIT Press.

CORDER, S. P. 1971: Idiosyncratic dialects and error analysis. *International Review of Applied Linguistics (IRAL)* **2**, 147–60.

CRAIG, D. R. 1969: *An Experiment in Teaching English*. Caribbean Universities Press.

DE VRIES, D. L., EDWARDS, K. J. and WELLS, E. H. 1974: Team-games

---

[15] This project is based at ILEA's Centre for Urban Educational Studies (CUES). Bilingual materials intended for use in the mainstream secondary classroom are being produced. They will take the form of workcards.

tournament in the social studies classroom: effects on academic achievement, student attitudes, cognitive beliefs and classroom climate. Report 173, Center for Social Organization of Schools, Johns Hopkins University.

DOISE, W. *et al.* 1975: Social interaction and the development of cognitive operations. *European Journal of Social Psychology* **5**, 367–83.

EDWARDS, V. K. 1979: *The West Indian Language Issue in British Schools*. London: Routledge & Kegan Paul.

FATHMAN, A. K. 1976: Variables affecting the successful learning of English as a second language. *TESOL* **10** (4), 433–41.

GEORGE, H. V. 1972: *Common Errors in Language Learning: Insights from English*. New York: Newbury House.

GORBET, F. 1979: 'To err is human': Error analysis and child language acquisition. English Language Teaching (*ELT*) **43**, (1), 22–8.

HUGHES, A. and TRUDGILL, P. 1979: *English Accents and Dialects*. London: Edward Arnold.

JOHNSON, D. W. and AHLGREN, A. 1976: Relationship between student attitudes about cooperation and competition and attitudes towards schooling. *Journal of Educational Psychology* **68**, 92–102.

KHAN, V. S. 1980: The 'mother-tongue' of linguistic minorities in multicultural England. *Journal of Multilingual and Multicultural Development* **1**, 77–88.

NEMSER, W. 1971: Approximative systems of foreign language learners. *IRAL* **2**, 115–23.

RICHMOND, J. 1979: Dialect features in mainstream school writing. *New Approaches in Multiracial Education* **1**, 10–15.

SAPARA, S. *et al.* 1978: *Share-a-Story, Reading Through Understanding*. Edinburgh: Holmes McDougall with Learning Materials Service, ILEA.

SELINKER, L. 1972: Interlanguage. *IRAL* **3**, 209–31.

SKUTNABB-KANGAS, T. and TOUKOMAA, P. 1976: Teaching migrant children's mother-tongue and learning the language of the host country in the context of the socio-cultural situation of the migrant family. *Tutkimuksia Research Reports* **15**, Department of Sociology and Social Psychology, University of Tampere, Finland.

STUDDERT, J. 1980: Reading development: the use of cloze procedure as a small group activity in the classroom. CUES occasional paper.

TOSI, A. 1979: Mother-tongue teaching for the children of migrants. *Language Teaching and Linguistics: Abstracts* **16**, 213–31.

WILES, S. 1979: The Multilingual Classroom. In the OU Language Development Course PE 232, Supplementary Readings, Block 5 Milton Keynes: Open University Press.

WODARSKI, J. S. *et al.* 1973: Individual consequences contingent on the performance of low-achieving group members. *Journal of Applied Social Psychology* **3**, 276–90.

4

*Implications for curric of
Accepting bi-dialectalism* (handwritten)

Community language and education

Neil Mercer and Janet Maybin

Introduction

Children have already begun to communicate with the people around them before they learn their first word. And when they do begin to speak and listen, they do so in the context of existing social relationships which are vital for their developing self-identity. Learning to use language means using it to relate to the people who matter, and this means being sensitive not only to what is said, but how it is expressed and the effect it has on the people who hear it. In the earliest years of life, of course, relationships with parents and immediate family are the strongest influences on language behaviour; later on, relationships with others, like friends and teachers, may become important.

The acquisition of a first language is the acquisition of a particular kind of social experience. And even within one small nation like Britain this experience is open to enormous variety. Factors such as family's geographical and social background, the strength of different social relationships which are formed in the community determine the kind of English (or other mother-tongue) that we acquire, and the ways we will use it. What is more, such social factors not only determine the ways we speak, they influence our attitudes to the ways other people use language, and inevitably our feelings about the speakers themselves.

There is nothing new in pointing out that English is spoken in many different ways, or that 'it is impossible for an Englishman to open his mouth without making some other Englishman despise him' (G. B. Shaw). What is relatively new, however, is the realization that attitudes to language variation are a controversial educational issue.

If in the past there was very little educational debate about language variation, this was because interest in regional accents and dialects of English in schools was almost entirely concerned with how to eliminate them, and assert the supremacy of the 'Queen's English' which was assumed to be the only language appropriate for educational endeavours.

As this assumption, like many other conventional wisdoms, has been questioned now by many people involved in education, those concerned with classroom practice have had to ask themselves: if what was going on wasn't right, what should be done instead? Faced with this problem, the classroom teacher will find few ready answers. The less value-laden accounts of language variation offered in recent years by linguists like William Labov (1972) do not, in themselves, generate a school language policy.

In the gap between theory and practice which quite clearly exists in this area, enormous confusion has arisen. This reveals itself in many ways; in misconceptions about the nature of language variation, what it means in terms of children's experience in their school and elsewhere in their community, how it affects teachers' attitudes, and how it relates to justifiable educational aims and ideals.

One of our concerns in recent years has been to collaborate with teachers in exploring and classifying the practical classroom implications of language variation (see, in particular, Mercer and Edwards, 1979). Our intention in this chapter is to set out some kind of conceptual framework for handling the issues involved[1].

Our discussion in this chapter rests on the truth of certain statements about language and education which we feel have now been sufficiently well established to be taken as given. One is that there are no 'primitive' or 'inadequate' languages or language varieties – if the speech of any social group is regarded as 'inferior', this is understandable in terms of the social status of that group and the social values of society, not through linguistic analysis. The other is that educational values, and not least those implicit in the 'hidden curriculum' of daily classroom life, inevitably reflect the broader social values and established interests of the dominant social groups or classes of society. This does not mean that we think that education cannot be a force for social change, as we believe it can and should generate a basis for constructive social criticism. Any useful discussion of language variation and education, however, must take account of the real constraints within which teachers and schoolchildren operate.

What we intended to do here, working from these basic assumptions, is to look at the nature of language variation itself, to consider its implications for social life in and out of school, and to try to interpret these implications in terms of classroom practice.

The nature of language variation

The kinds of language variation which concern us most here are four: *language, accent, dialect* and *register*.

---

[1] The present authors wish to acknowledge the valuable work in this area performed by previous writers, and upon which the present discussion draws extensively. Interested readers are referred in particular to Trudgill (1975) and J. R. Edwards (1979).

Variation in terms of different *languages* is, of course, the most obvious of these to appear to present educational problems. If a child at home speaks a mother-tongue very different from the language at school, then a teacher might well expect this to create communication problems of a different order than for children speaking the same language in and out of school. Other writers in this volume focus directly on this matter (see in particular Chapter 3 by Silvaine Wiles), and so we feel we need not do so here. The problems of bilingual children are, however, relevant to us here in that these problems will not be entirely, or even predominantly, linguistic. The language of their home, and the culture of the ethnic group of which they are members, will itself have a status or value in society, and they will be aware of this. Although our discussion will mainly focus on variation within the English language, many of the points we raise will have equal relevance to bilingual children in British schools.

Accent refers to the different ways people pronounce the same language. (This may involve differences in intonation patterns and rate of speech, as well as the pronunciation of specific words.) Everyone has an accent of some kind; if we say that someone from Durham has 'lost his Geordie accent' we really mean that he has found another one – probably the non-regional 'BBC' accent known as RP (Received Pronunciation).

The term *dialect* refers to the natural variation in grammar and vocabulary that exists between local forms of the same language in different regions, or as spoken by different social groups. Of course, different accents and dialects do 'go together', but they are not inevitably and inseparable combined. The whole of a BBC news bulletin could be read out in a broad Geordie, Belfast or Cockney accent, while remaining in the same Standard English dialect in which it was written. Likewise, one could, in the pursuit of eccentric art, read out the dialect poems of Robert Burns or Linton Kwesi Johnson in an Oxbridge accent – they would still contain lowland Scots or Creole words and constructions.

The fourth kind of variation is that in terms of *register*. By this we mean the different kinds of language which are conventionally used in different kinds of social situations.[2] The relative formality of an occasion, for example, usually influences the kind of language used. In formal public meetings it is normal to hear people saying things like:

'With all due respect, Mr Chairman, I feel it is necessary to point out that this is not the case ...'

---

[2] We are using 'register' here to refer to what some writers have called 'style' (e.g. Trudgill (1975); J. R. Edwards (1979). We have avoided the latter term because of its individualistic connotations, i.e. the 'style' of a particular author or speaker.

In a discussion amongst friends in a pub, that kind of language would, to say the least, seem odd. You might, however hear someone say:

> 'What? You must be nuts if you believe that. Shut up and listen for a change ...'

Both of the above examples, are, of course, Standard English. They might well be both uttered by the same speaker in the same day, as we all vary our style of speech quite dramatically depending on where we are, who we're talking to, and our purpose in doing so. The examples represent different registers, and all speakers possess a repertoire of such registers or styles. This is really a kind of language variation that occurs within any one dialect. (Speakers may, of course, feel it appropriate to change dialects, too, according to social circumstances, but if they do they are making a rather different kind of linguistic choice – one more akin to choosing which language to use in bilingual company.)

We have tried to distinguish accent, dialect and register variation not for the sake of pedantry, but because the definition of educational policy on language variation has been beset by confusion about these kinds of variation. A teacher, concerned about 'language standards', might object if a pupil responded to the question 'What's wrong with you today, Mary?' with the statement: 'I'm bloody knackered, Miss!' If she did object, however, this would be an objection to the pupil's choice of register (one suited to informal conversations amongst familiar people of equal status) not to her dialect (which in this case, as Peter Trudgill has pointed out, is perfectly consistent with the rules of Standard English). If, on the other hand, a Cumbrian pupil replied:

> 'I's badly today, Miss'.

then the teacher's response would depend on whether or not she wanted to hear Cumbrian dialect spoken in her classroom.

Of course, register, accent and dialect changes may co-vary in practice to a large extent. For many children, the speech of their playground and community will not only be a regional dialect, it will involve registers in which language is less formal, less explicit, and no doubt more profane than in the classroom. And although it complicates matters somewhat, we have to recognize that children may choose to use a 'non-standard' dialect in class for the same reasons that they might deliberately choose an inappropriately informal register – to put 'social distance' between them and their teacher, to appeal to the solidarity of their classmates and to show disrespect for the formality of school. Speech in any dialect can, of course, be as explicit or formal as the occasion demands, as demonstrated by dialect poetry and by examples like the Northamptonshire teacher who gives complete lessons in the local dialect.[3] Children whose native dialect is Standard English all acquire informal registers, and even BBC newsreaders are reputed to be both casual and profane conversationalists on occasion!

Confusion about accent, dialect and register variation has not been confined to teachers, but exists where one might least expect to find it. The earlier writings of Basil Bernstein reveal that he wasn't sure which kind of variation he was concerned with, and the same applies to some of his critics. Eventually, however, it seems he decided he was definitely not talking about dialect variation, and was perhaps talking about register.[4] Although only recently published, the HMI Secondary Survey (DES, 1980) unfortunately seems to add to the chaos in this area. Consider the following paragraph from the survey report, headed 'Some general observations' on spoken language in the classroom.

> On the whole, there was a gap between the language of the teacher and that of the pupil, and this is not a new phenomenon. Most of the language of classroom talk and of textbooks was in standard English, and it was a part of the concern of teachers to help pupils to acquire this form of English through talking as well as through the related activities of reading and writing. The best teachers were sensitive to differences in language and led their pupils discreetly and by a variety of means towards a wider range of language use and a surer command of language itself. Very occasionally, a teacher adopted features of the language of pupils, and superficially this enhanced social relations. But there was ample evidence of pupils making it quite clear that they recognized this as a device, and that the cost of it in terms of setting a positive language example was high. Perhaps the most encouraging example to any teacher who was anxious to maintain linguistic standards came from a young teacher who intimated that her colleagues regarded her way of talking as 'posh'. Yet she conducted one of the most successful discussion lessons seen in that school, with a group of pupils generally regarded as difficult and uncooperative. She did so without abandoning her normal manner of speech, and the class was not in any way alienated.
>
> (Chapter 6, p. 99)

In these comments the inspectors confuse two entirely different propositions – that RP accented standard English should be promoted in schools at the expense of other dialects, and that a basic aim of education should be to develop 'a surer command of language itself'. But there is also a much more worrying hidden message here, which to expose fully we must consider the research of social psychologists Giles and Powesland (1975). They have commented on the fact that

[3] The prevailing climate of attitudes is still such, however, that this particular teacher wishes to remain unidentified.

[4] This does not seem an appropriate point to delve into the complexities of Bernstein's theory and related research. The interested reader is referred to Mercer and Mercer (1978), MacKinnon (1979) and J. R. Edwards (1979) for clarification on these matters.

people's accents and dialect (which together Giles and Powesland term *speech style*) are not entirely static; we may vary our accent depending on who we are speaking to and the kind of relationship we wish to establish with them. When two conversationalists are mutually concerned to establish a good social relationship, they often modify their speech style towards that of the other to some extent; this is called *convergence*, and can be seen as a dynamic paralinguistic method of expressing mutual respect. To avoid doing this, or to actually *diverge* from the speech style of a fellow conversationalist (i.e. make one's accent less like his than would otherwise be the case) is often used as a way of putting 'social distance' between one speaker and the other – perhaps because the latter, and his speech style, are perceived as unattractive or as having lower social status by the 'diverging' speaker.

The inspectors are clearly implying that teachers should avoid speech style convergence, but that pupils should be encouraged to converge on the style of their teacher. Look at the value-laden terms they use to describe this perfectly normal feature of conversational interaction; it only happens 'very occasionally', and it only 'superficially' enhances social relations. Moreover, pupils recognize it as 'a device', and it exacts a high cost 'in terms of setting a positive language example'. (one would be interested to see the 'ample evidence' for the pupils' dismissal of this in the way that the inspectors claim, as evidence of that kind is notoriously hard for social psychologists to gather, even under controlled research conditions.)

On the other hand, the teacher who steadfastly maintains her RP accent ('posh' even to her teaching colleagues) is applauded *simply for doing so*, and is singled out as 'the most encouraging example to any teacher'! We are not suggesting that this teacher should self-consciously change her natural accent towards the regional variety of her pupils (accent convergence is not, normally, a self-conscious act); patronizing histrionics of that kind would help no one. The distressing implication of the inspectors' comments is, however, that teachers should by their own speech behaviour and by their response to pupils' speech, seek to make their pupils feel they and the speech style of their community are of lower status and generally inferior to the teacher's own self and speech style as an 'educated person'.

In order to conclude this part of the discussion, and to prepare for a consideration of other, policy-related issues, we will try to make clear our own position on language variation and language development in school.

If a teacher who wishes to 'set a positive language example' and 'promote language development' means by this helping children learn how to convey ideas, concepts, facts and feelings in language which is clear and elegant as the occasion demands, then he or she is quite properly doing his or her job. This means making children more aware of the existing and potential range of their language skills, and must also involve some consideration of the attitudes and assumptions which different speech styles embody. If a teacher also feels that the business of the classroom is generally best conducted through language which is relatively formal, then this reflects a personal approach to teaching which can be justified perfectly well – though not in terms of language development *per se* (it may, for example, be part of a teacher's apparatus for maintaining classroom order, for ensuring that quieter, more hesitant children are not shouted down by others, and so on). However, promoting language development, 'maintaining language standards', and similar catch-phrases cannot in our opinion, be used with any educational justification for trying to eliminate 'non-standard' accents and dialects from children's speech, in or out of the classroom.[5] Neither is there any educational justification for trying to eliminate certain registers or ways of speaking (e.g. the 'catch-phrases' of peer group language) from a child's repertoire, as opposed to broadening that repertoire. Any teacher who tries to do this is not only wasting his own time and that of his pupils, he is arguably wasting a potential resource for language development present in the classroom. We will explain why we believe this, and what alternative courses of action exist, in the following sections.

The social significance of 'non-standard' speech varieties

In a recent article, Ellen Ryan (1979) asks 'why do low-prestige language varieties persist?' By 'low-prestige' varieties, she is referring to the fact that, in many languages besides English, one particular dialect has become the 'standard' form of the language, the one which is used to determine 'correct' usage in writing and formal speech. This standard dialect is typically based on the language habits of the social group who have historically accumulated most power, wealth and hence prestige in a society; in the British case, the upper and middle classes of southeastern England. Other language varieties, used by less prestigious groups, become defined as 'non-standard' and carry less prestige than the standard. In some countries of course, entirely different languages occupy these different status positions – e.g. the American Indian languages have lower status than Spanish in Latin America, while Spanish generally has lower status than English in bilingual regions of the USA.

Generally, research findings show that speakers of non-standard varieties recognize as well as anyone else in their society that their

[5] As the Bullock Committee (DES, 1975) put it, 'The aim (of education) is not to alienate the child from a form of language with which he has grown up and which serves him efficiently in the speech community of his neighbourhood.'

language is not well regarded (see Giles and Powesland, 1975). They know it is considered 'common' and 'broad', and that it may influence the way they are evaluated as individuals. As one Cockney speaker in the TV series 'Word of Mouth' said, 'you won't get on the Board of Directors with a voice like that!' Yet, as Ryan says, these 'low prestige' varieties do not die out. So well do they continue to thrive that

> the stubborn persistence of diverse language varieties within many societies demands an explanation. For example, despite the lure of social mobility and years of educational (and frequently political) efforts, there is no apparent move towards universal adoption of RP English in Britain, or of Standard English in the United States, of Castilian in Spain, or of European French in French Canada.
>
> (Ryan, 1979, p. 147)

The resolution of this paradox, of course, lies in the fact that 'prestige' is a relative term. It refers to the social standing that someone or something has *within a particular social group*. And for many people, the most important group as a source of prestige is not the whole of British society, or the middle class of southeast England, but their family and friends and the rest of their home community. Speaking 'posh' may impress some teachers, or the prospective employer glimpsed on some distant horizon, but it doesn't cut much ice in the playground and streets, in the club or on the factory floor. To be more precise it might well *impress* your mates, but it certainly won't endear you to them. A further point worth noting here comes from Howard Giles' 'matched guise' experiments on attitudes to regional accents (Giles and Powesland, 1975). As one might expect, he found that speakers were rated as being more intelligent, more reliable and more educated when they used RP than when they used regional accents. He also found, however, that regional speakers were often rated *higher* than RP speakers in terms of personal integrity and attractiveness (e.g. good naturedness and sincerity), thus indicating that a regional accent may convey positive social connotations even outside the speaker's immediate community.

In support of a bidialectal language policy in school

Trudgill (1975) distinguished three policy approaches to language variation in school – the 'elimination of non-standard dialects', the 'bidialectal', and the 'appreciation of dialect differences' approach. In accord with the present writers, he considers the 'elimination' approach both impractical and educationally dangerous; we offer our own criticism of this approach below. He puts his weight mainly behind the 'appreciation of differences' approach – i.e. that schools should concentrate on changing pupils' attitudes to their own and other dialects, rather than teaching them to use a second (standard) dialect. His support of the 'bidialectal' approach is limited; he sees the advantages of teaching children to write in Standard English as merely being those of placating prejudiced attitudes of examiners and employers and does not accept that the use of Standard English for writing is necessary to ensure readers' comprehension. As teachers are often quick to point out, however, he is very vague about the extent to which variations from standardized vocabulary, spelling and grammar could be permitted on all occasions without creating comprehension problems. While not dis-agreeing with Trudgill to any great extent, we would argue more strongly than he does for the value of developing children's awareness of the linguistic and social nature of their own and other dialects of English, for such increased awareness can assist the development of more liberal attitudes towards language variation. We also believe that the pursuit of bidialectalism (being able to speak and write in two dialects) is not so unrealistic as Trudgill insists. He writes:

> The point is that ... with a new dialect you have to retain some aspects of your native variety while rejecting others – and the big problem is to learn which is which. The two linguistic varieties are so similar that it is difficult to keep them apart. The motivation to learn, moreover, is much smaller. If an English speaking person learns French, then at least he can communicate with French people and read French books and newspapers. But no new communication advantages of this sort arise from learning a new dialect. (p. 78)

We would agree with Trudgill that if a pupil is not motivated to learn Standard English, then a teacher will not succeed in teaching it. The same problem, however, applies to the acquisition of foreign languages like French – as many a modern languages teacher will testify! Whether or not there are 'communication advantages' to be gained from acquiring a use of Standard English for formal writing, or for certain social encounters, depends on how narrowly one wishes to define 'communication advantage'. As for the difficulty an individual might have in distinguishing between two dialects, we feel that here that Trudgill is, surprisingly, perpetuating a traditional and peculiarly British attitude towards language learning which has not real educational or psychological basis. His position here reflects an un-necessary concession to the 'elimination' approach, as we hope to demonstrate below.

As mentioned earlier, the policy on language variation historically favoured in British schools has been that of attempting to eliminate all other than Standard English usages. Besides its demonstrable and inevitable failure, this policy is unfortunate because it may serve to alienate children from education itself. Referring back to our discussion of the social significance of 'non-standard' speech varieties, it can be seen that this policy offers many children an unfortunate and un-necessary choice; between retaining the loyalty and self-identity offered by their social group, and becoming an 'educated' person. They may well accept the validity of this choice, and decide that education, part and parcel, is not for them. The reality of this decision is well illustrated in Paul Willis's book, *Learning to Labour* (1977). Amongst the 'low-achieving' adolescents he interviewed, the choice was very clearly perceived as being either 'one of the lads', or an 'earhole' (a swot), and this was often symbolized in speech styles. William Labov (1972) has, of course, forcibly argued that the 'elimination' approach has contributed to the alienation of Black American adolescents from the school system, because children are more likely to reject school if their mother-tongue is treated as educationally worthless.

This is all the more unfortunate and unnecessary because the 'elimination' approach rests on a conception of language learning which is fundamentally incorrect. This view is essentially that the development of productive skills in a second dialect is assisted by, or even entails, the suppression of the first-acquired dialect. That is, for children to be able to write in such a way as to satisfy examiners, or to present themselves formally and favourably when they wish to do so in writing or in interviews, they must first be made to *forget* their original native speech style. This is a strange notion – rather as if learning French entailed forgetting English, or learning to play Rugby entailed forgetting soccer. There is no psycholinguistic or sociolinguistic evidence to support this view (see Mitchell, 1978), and in fact in many parts of the world being fluent in two or more dialects is common. The associated notion of bilingual or bidialectal 'overload' – whereby acquiring a second language or dialect is seen to place some kind of cognitive strain on the language learner, who will thus be educationally inhibited – is likewise unsubstantiated. Bilingual or bidialectal children do not suffer in educational attainment because of their additional skill (again, see Mitchell, 1978). We believe, therefore, that the pursuit of some form of bidialectal language policy which incorporates an 'appreciation of dialect differences' is a practical and acceptable teaching aim.

Using children's own language resources

We pointed out at the beginning of this chapter that children, from their earliest years, learn language within the context of social relationships. We would argue that it is essential to build on this out-of-school experience of language rather than to deny it, and to help children to develop not just fluent Standard English, but a whole range of language skills and resources through their work in school. We would argue further that this approach will not only give children a much surer command of Standard English, but it will strike at the base of those attitudes which suggested that this language variety was not theirs to start with.

How then, within the confines of one social situation – the classroom – and within the limits of one relationship – that between teachers and pupils – can children be helped to develop competence in all the language varieties they will want to use, and the experience to make appropriate language choices? Probably the richest resource teachers have at their disposal – and it is often an under-exploited one – is the children's own language, and their knowledge about how it works. There is evidence to show that children are sophisticated code-switchers from their earliest years (Shatz and Gelman, 1973). The following three examples of children talking about their language show clear understanding of the difference between talking to your peers and talking to your elders, of the social embarrassment that can arise from even a slightly inappropriate choice of register, and of the way language use in the classroom will vary according to subject area, and level of schooling:

'I'd speak freely to my friends, right, and when I go home I'd have more respect in my voice. I would speak to my parents the same as the senior staff you know.' (14 years)

'I was talking really nice and saying "Do you like jam?" and all this lot and she's going "Yea, 'course I do", so I felt really shamed up ... she was talking naturally and I was talking poshly to her.'
(14 years)

'Miss tries every time we come across a new Maths problem, if you say just an ordinary word like "add" or "take away", she'd say "subtract", she wants us to know the language for when we get to secondary school, not just "adding" and "taking away".
(10 years)

Children will compare the relative merits of using different language varieties in a particular context; one West Indian Londoner commented that

'A fel like a could lick yu, go 'weh!'

was a much more effective way of telling someone she was angry with them than:

'I feel like I could hit you, go away!'

And two twelve-year-olds, talking about the kinds of books they liked, had this to say:

Q: So what makes a book really interesting for you?
Diane: That's got kids in ...

> *Jackie:* Kids in it our age and crimes and everything
> *Diane:* And language like – and bad language, slang language
> *Q:* Why does that make it more interesting?
> *Diane:* Makes it more funnier
> *Jackie:* Makes it more realistic
> *Diane:* Yea 'cos you don't see people going up (assumes posh accent) "Hey you, do you want a sweet?', something like that, you say "Oi, you, d'yer wan a sweet 'ere?' You just have ordinary play language.

We might question the girls' labelling of informal dialogue as 'bad language', but we would support their enthusiasm for children's books where the characters speak in a language which is realistic in the context of the story.

In their written English, children will also, given the chance, show a sure command of different registers and dialects. The eleven-year-old boy who started his film review 'I suppose you think this film is all that usual sort of war rubbish, but fear not ...' knew exactly who his audience was going to be, while another eleven-year-old's use of dialect gives an added vitality to the beginning of his account of 'The Fight'.

> 'I was playing cricket with our Darren, I hit a wacker and it caught him in the gut. He started walking towards me with a rage on his face ...'

To look at a more extended use of dialect, who could fail to be drawn into this girl's account of a visit to her boyfriend in Brixton gaol?

> *Him:* How come yuh worry bout me an me nuh worry bout you?
> *Me:* Me never tell yuh fe worry bout me!
> I knew he was only trying to get me vex jus so he would know I care. But me nah gan get vex me can tek de insults just for now.
> (Supplied by John Richmond)

Children can often achieve a power through writing in the language variety most comfortable to them that they would otherwise lack. Some may also, incidently, show a command of Standard English which they hadn't been motivated to draw on before.

The children quoted above were able to make clear and confident choices of language style in their written work. The next extract is from the writing of a less fortunate pupil. Valerie was also classed as 'difficult' and in fact her English teacher had more or less given up any hope of her managing to get formal qualifications. She was fifteen. (Extract opposite.)

The direct, informal style of this piece is not sustained through the rest of the story, which drifts into a more formal narrative. The teacher's comments at the end include criticisms of the 'terrible presentation' of the piece. More specifically, her marking shows rejection of three different aspects of the pupil's use of language. Her corrections in the first line suggest that a conversational style like this is inappropriate to

FINDING A NEW JOB IN OTHER COUNTRY

Here I am, ~~me and~~ my wife and I ~~kinds() settl~~ It started at the airport in Kingston Jamaica. I was waiting for my flight for my flight number BOAC 24590 I was on my way to England, in case you wondering my name is Bill... The stewardess ~~speaks~~ "fasten your SEAT BELTS PLEASE". I didn't like the way the plain goes up, it gives my stomach there is a sinking feeling now my stomach a wave...

written work. Secondly, she rejects the use of dialect; 'the stewardess say' is changed to 'the stewardess speaks', and 'it gives my belly a wave' 'corrected' to the rather less colourful 'there is a sinking feeling in my stomach'. Thirdly she corrects spellings and other written conventions. We can sense a feeling of despair in the teacher's marking and comments. Many of the problems in this piece of work may have arisen from Valerie's lack of a sense of specific purpose or audience for her writing. She may be producing (with diminishing conviction), what she thinks is expected in response to a school task. Yet within these constraints, she still displays certain strengths, which might have been seen as providing some starting points for development.[1] The fact that Valerie is attempting a dialogue with the reader, which involves her in a skilled combination of present, past progressive and past perfect tenses in the first few sentences is probably not even noticed. The teacher's treatment of the use of dialect and informal register as 'errors' which are marked in the same way as spelling mistakes, denies the long-established tradition in the English novel of addressing the reader directly, and the more recent examples of literature written by Londoners with West Indian backgrounds, for example Samuel Selvon. This kind of response to a child's writing does, however, reflect the confusion which is present in many official educational statements about language variation. Further examples are easily found. The Assessment of Performance Unit, set up by the government to assess school children's language on an unprecedented scale, and in a way that may exert a powerful influence on practice in schools, emphasizes that the 'style' of a writing task should be appropriate to 'subject matter, audience and intention', but states that 'he done it' should be treated as a 'morphological error'. It may be a matter of dialect choice which a teacher should explore with a pupil, but to treat 'he done it' without qualification as a morphological error is to assert the existence of Standard English as an uncontroversial base-line for correctness rather than letting a sensitivity to subject matter, audience and intention determine the choice of appropriate language. This inconsistency is perpetuated in the differences between the contemporary approaches to language in inservice teacher training courses, and the 'Advice to the Examiner' of most English 'O' level and CSE boards. Children who sense the confusion and contradictions in educators' approaches to language work will not have the confidence to develop those language skills and resources they already have, which are too often regarded by the school as not really relevant to the English curriculum.

[1] For a more detailed discussion of working on pupils' strengths rather than their weaknesses to improve their written work, see Keen, 1978.

Language variation – classroom activities

In the last 15 years there has been a slow but significant increase in language activities, which draw on children's own resources to develop their skills. In the early 1970s, the Schools Council Oracy Project constructed listening tests designed to take account of 'addressor, addressee and situation'. They also produced their *Language in Use* materials, the aim of which was to develop 'an awareness of what language is and how it is used and, at the same time, to extend competence in handling language' (Doughty *et al.*, 1976, pp. 8–9). These materials treat language as behaviour rather than as an abstract system; for example:

> Explore, in discussion, whether people need to change their way of speaking when they take up different roles. Consider likely pairs of situations in which an individual would have to use different ways of speaking. Divide the class into groups and ask each to prepare a pair of sketches, which will show the difference. (Doughty *et al.*, 1971, p. 207)

Suggestions for possible contrasting situations include an employee explaining an accident to (a) the workmate's wife, (b) the foreman and (c) the manager.

These attempts to examine a wide range of examples of language use in an environment as restricted as the classroom tend to rely heavily on either role play and improvization, or the importing of video and audio tape recordings. Most English teachers are now familiar with ideas for activities like these:

> Collect examples of recorded speech from radio or TV. Compare the different registers employed and identify audience, purpose and subject matter. (BBC, 1980a p. 3)

> or

> Can you guess what the following bits of writing are *about* and who they are *meant for*? It might help if you can think of *where* you might see these bits of writing. (ILEA, 1979b, pp. 54–5)

(Eighteen examples follow.)

Most English teachers have also seen suggestions for examining the way English has changed over the years through looking at studies of place names, versions of old English, or the origins of words that English has 'borrowed' from other languages. Although the very fact that these sort of activities are even considered within a classroom may indicate the beginning of a change in attitude, it may be much more significant to look at whether they are taken seriously enough to question and inform the class syllabus in Standard English. If these activities are introduced to pupils as an 'extra' in an otherwise inflexible English curriculum, the work will obviously not have the same effect on their knowledge and attitudes as it would when carried out as an integral part of language work based on a bidialectal model. Many language activities on accent and dialect, for example, can quite easily be reduced to 'butterfly collecting'. In the Pupil's Notes for a current radio series for ten to twelve-year-olds, the children are asked:

> And have you ever ridden on a dicky? No, not a bird but a donkey – that's the old name for it in parts of Norfolk and Suffolk.
> Try asking around, especially amongst older people. You may be surprised at what a lot of dialect words there still are to be found. (BBC, 1980b, p. 9)

Children are asked later to discuss arguments for and against 'preserving dialects'. Dialect could be treated here as merely a miscellaneous collection of picturesque words and expressions, to be 'collected' from old people before it finally disappears with them into the grave. In some ways, an anthropological approach towards varieties of language that children may not be familiar with is healthy. But any implication that the languages 'out there', beyond the school gates, are of no more than peripheral importance to the children in the classroom is a denial of the linguistic diversity of Britain today, and, often, of the child's own language. Activities like making a slang dictionary, or examining a disc jockey's patter can lead, in some classrooms to real insights about the nature of language; in other classrooms, a teacher's treatment can reduce them to token gestures which do nothing to challenge the notion of there being one unchanging, correct form of English. If a teacher's model of language is a rigid one, then his handling of these kind of activities could render them ineffective, or confusing to his pupils.

The model of language underlying classroom activities determines their validity to the pupils, and their relevance to work in school. It is not enough to start with children's own language experience if the model is not genuinely bidialectal. The materials in 'Dialect and Language Variety' produced by the Ebury Teachers' Centre in London (ILEA, 1979a) argue convincingly for the worth and legitimacy of London children's own language; but rather than emphasizing the dynamic nature of language use they tend to use an 'us and them' approach, thus resurrecting the choice between in-group loyalty and educational participation, which was a product of the 'elimination approach' (see p. 85). For instance,

> The London Cockney accent is especially looked down on, sometimes by Cockney speakers themselves, but mostly by people who hold power; teachers, lawyers, employers etc. . . . Employers of non-manual labour would prefer it if working-class children tried to cover up their background so that they merged in with everyone else. (ILEA 1979a, p. 15)

The whole issue about the relationship of language use to power is not one that should be dodged, but whether it should be approached in this sort of way is another question. Activities such as 'Write a short play about two London children in which one accuses the other of stealing a pen. Now rewrite it as though the two characters were upper-class characters from a public school' must inevitably produce a very stereotyped version of upper-class language, the language of 'people who usually speak "posh"; and don't let outsiders in who speak differently'. Many of the activities suggested are admirable in that they encourage children to look not just at language, but at the social context in which it is used, and how context and language interrelate. The setting of this discussion of language variation within a simplistic class conflict model, however, reflects an attitude to language variation which is in some ways as rigid as that which sees only Standard English as acceptable.

The way forward

Classroom activities on language variation should raise questions about the nature and value of a lot of other language work that goes on in school; but the questions generated often do not seem to spread beyond the confines of that particular lesson, and 'today we're doing dialects' too frequently becomes just another self-contained exercise in the segmented secondary school curriculum. There seem to be two main reasons for this. Firstly, activities which ask children (and teachers) to analyse and discuss the ways in which language varies are calling on linguistic skills which most teachers have not been equipped with in their preservice training, and without which the discussion cannot go beyond a fairly superficial level. An exploration of anecdotal examples cannot on its own provide the analytical framework needed for real advances in understanding, which will produce an informed reassessment of classroom language work. A respect for, and confidence in, a bidialectal approach in school must depend on linguistic and sociolinguistic knowledge. The second reason for the limited effect of many language activities is the relative impotence of any changes of attitude in one area of school work unless they are supported by changes in other areas. With the increasing emphasis on 'basic skills', language work is marked as one of the most 'crucial' areas of the curriculum. At the level of the whole school language policy there needs to be a commitment to the principles of helping children develop these skills through language work which builds on the competence and resources they already have, and which takes into account the complex language choices they will need to make in the adult world. This official acknowledgement by the school of the worth of children's own language must be reflected in a reappraisal, at classroom level, of the ground-rules for language work. If discussion can be opened up about the criteria for evaluating work, and a real negotiation of ideas occurs between teachers and pupils, then the activities described earlier have a much better chance of being something more than a one-off exercise.

Many children's lack of confidence in their own language skills, and limited competence in Standard English (even after 15,000 hours' exposure to school), is the result of cultural barriers; if children can see their language work in school as valuable, and building on resources they already have, we may start to break those barriers down.

References

ASSESSMENT OF PERFORMANCE UNIT 1978: *Criteria for Assessing Writing.* London: Department of Education and Science.

BBC 1980a: *Resource Units 11–13 – English*, Teachers' Notes. London: BBC Publications.

BBC 1980b: *Web of Language, Teachers' Notes.* London: BBC Publications.

DES 1975: *A Language for Life* (The Bullock Report). London: HMSO.

DES 1980: *Aspects of Secondary Education in England: A Survey by HM Inspectors of Schools.* London: HMSO.

DOUGHTY, P., PIERCE, J. and THORNTON, G. 1971: *Language in Use.* London: Edward Arnold (for Schools Council).

EDWARDS, J. R. 1979: *Language and Disadvantage.* London: Edward Arnold.

GILES, H. and POWESLAND, P. 1975: *Speech Style and Social Evaluation.* London: Academic Press.

ILEA ENGLISH CENTRE 1979a: *Dialect and Language Variety.* London: Ebury Teachers' Centre.

ILEA ENGLISH CENTRE 1979b: *Languages.* London: Ebury Teachers' Centre.

KEEN, J. 1978: *Teaching English – a linguistic approach.* London: Methuen.

LABOV, W. 1972: *Language in the Inner City.* Philadelphia: University of Philadelphia Press.

MCKINNON, D. 1977: *Language and Social Class* (Unit 23 E202 Schooling and Society). Milton Keynes: Open University Press.

MERCER, N. and EDWARDS, D. 1979: *Communication and Context* (Block 4, PE232 Language Development). Milton Keynes: Open University Press.

MERCER, N. and MERCER, E. 1978: The nature of the theory of sociolinguistic codes. In *Supplementary Readings*, PE232 Language Development. Milton Keynes: Open University Press.

MITCHELL, R. 1978: Bilingual education of minority language groups in the English speaking world. *Seminar Papers 4*, University of Stirling Department of Education.

RYAN, E. B. 1979: Why do low-prestige language varieties persist? In

H. Giles and R. St Clair, *Language and Social Psychology*. Oxford: Basil Blackwell.

SHATZ, M. and GELMAN, R. 1973: *The Development of Communication Skills: Modifications in the Speech of Young Children as a Function of Listener*. Monographs of the Society for Research in Child Development **38** (Serial No. 152).

TRUDGILL, P. 1975: *Accent, Dialect and the School*. London: Edward Arnold.

WILLIS, P. 1977: *Learning to Labour*. London: Saxon House.

WILKINSON, A. 1974: *The quality of listening: the report of the Schools Council Oracy Project*. London: Macmillan.

5

Classroom modalities: black and white communicative styles in the classroom*

Thomas Kochman

Introduction

In November 1914, Monroe Trotter led a black delegation to the White House to protest against the segregation of federal employees that had become widespread for the first time during Woodrow Wilson's administration. President Wilson indicated that the reason for the segregation was to avoid friction between black and white clerks. Trotter disputed this, saying that white and black clerks had been working together for 50 years in peace, harmony and friendliness and that it was only after Wilson's inauguration that segregation was drastically introduced in the Treasury and Postal departments by Wilson's appointees. Following Trotter's rebuttal, Wilson and he and the following exchange:

> *Wilson:* If this organization is ever to have another hearing before me it must have another spokesman. Your manner offends me.
> *Trotter:* In what way?
> *Wilson:* Your tone with its background of passion.
> *Trotter:* But I have no passion in me Mr President, you are entirely mistaken; you misinterpret my earnestness for passion.[1]

In another more recent meeting between community representatives and university faculty, members of each group were similarly distracted from the issue – in this case a proposal for a graduate study programme in Urban Education – because of the way disagreements were expressed. For example, the university faculty regarded the behaviour of the community people as not meeting their requirements for rational discussion. One faculty member characterized the heated session as a 'Baptist Revival meeting'. Another called it a 'pep rally'. The community people likewise regarded the behaviour of the faculty as lacking 'sincerity' and 'honest conviction'. Some considered it 'devious'.

This last meeting, which I attended, and the earlier encounter between

---

* Also to be published as a chapter in *Black and White Styles in Conflict*, by T. Kochman (1981) Chicago: University of Chicago Press.

[1] 'Mr Trotter and Mr Wilson', *The Crisis* January 1915, pp. 119–20.

Trotter and Wilson, are indicative of what often happens when black and white Americans engage each other in public debate of an issue: divided not only over content – the issue itself – but more fundamentally, over process: how disagreement on an issue is to be appropriately engaged.

What I propose to do here is account for the different views that blacks and whites have on how properly to engage an issue in public. This account will consider the meaning and value that blacks and whites attach to their own and each other's behaviour. It will also consider more fundamental aspects of black and white culture and communi- cation in order to explain why the patterns should have the meaning and value that they do.

The data for this chapter come from several sources: from public meetings such as the one cited above, and from examples in the literature. Principally, the data come from my own classes, which over the years, have typically drawn a heavy enrollment of black and white students. This has given me numerous opportunities to observe the consistently different patterns of behaviour that blacks and whites display in such contexts, to inquire about their meaning and value, and to reflect upon their larger social and cultural significance.

Modes of behaviour

The modes of behaviour that blacks and whites use and consider appropriate for engaging in public debate of an issue differ in their posture (stance) and level of spiritual intensity. The black mode – that of black grass-roots community people – is high-keyed: animated, inter- personal and confrontational. The white mode – that of the middle-class – is relatively low-keyed: dispassionate, impersonal, and non- challenging. The black mode, characteristic of involvement, generates heat, loudness and affect. The white mode, characteristic of detachment, is cool, quiet and without affect.

Argument and discussion

Blacks and whites both classify the black mode as that of argument. But this agreement on classification is misleading, concealing as it does, deeper formal and functional differences.

For example, blacks distinguish between argument that is used to debate a difference of opinion and argument that is used to ventilate anger and hostility. Formally, both modes consist of affect and dynamic opposition. However, this resemblance is only superficial. In the first form of argument – argument for persuasion – the affect that is shown is expressive of debaters' relationship to their material. Its presence indicates that people are serious and sincere about what they are saying.

However, the affect that is present in the form of argument that is a ventilation of anger and hostility, on the other hand, is more intense: passionate rather than earnest. Also, it expresses less a positive attitude towards one's material than a negative attitude toward's one's opponent.

This same formal and functional distinction applies to dynamic opposition. Within argument for persuasion, blacks assume a challenging stance with respect to their opponent. But blacks are not antagonists here. Rather they are contenders cooperatively engaged in the pursuit and creation of truth.

Dynamic opposition within the framework of argument that is a ventilation of anger and hostility is again more intense than in argument for persuasion. Opponents are viewed as antagonists, givers and receivers of abuse, not simply contenders engaged in the creation of truth.

Because the two kinds of argument function differently in black culture, blacks are also alert to those formal elements that distinguish them: not simply the presence of affect and dynamic opposition but their degree of intensity and the direction of their focus.

Whites on the other hand fail to make these distinctions because argument, for them, functions only as a ventilation of anger and hostility. It does not function as a process of persuasion. For the latter, whites use discussion that is devoid of affect and dynamic opposition. Consequently, whites feel people are not engaging in persuasion when affect and dynamic opposition are present. Their mere presence, regardless of focus or intensity is seen as the onset of a mode whose function is to ventilate anger and hostility. In their failure to make the same distinction as blacks, whites belie black intentions: not believing that blacks are acting in good faith when they say they wish to resolve disagreement.

The negative attitude of whites towards argument as a process of persuasion is only partly influenced by the function of argument in their own culture. For even were they to be convinced that the black mode was intended as a persuasive mode and not as a ventilation of anger and hostility – this happens after black and white students have interacted with each other for a while – whites still regard it as dysfunctional because of their view that reason and emotion work against each other: that the presence of the latter detracts from the operation of the former. This explains why the white truth-creating process, discussion, is devoid of affect and why its presence to whites automatically renders any presentation less persuasive to the extent that affect is present.

Discussion also hopes to avoid dynamic opposition. This is because whites see confrontation as leading to intransigence: a hardening of opposing viewpoints, with the result that neither opponent will listen to, let alone concede, the validity of the other's viewpoint regardless of its merit. This explains why whites equate confrontation with conflict. The goal of whites is to have an 'open mind': to be flexible in one's approach and to recognize that no one person has 'all the answers'. To realize these aims whites place their faith in a truth-creating process that weakens or eliminates those aspects of character or posture – affect and dynamic opposition – that they feel keeps people's minds closed and otherwise makes them rigid and unyielding.

Blacks do not feel that the presence of affect and dynamic opposition leads to intransigence. Quite the opposite. Blacks often use formal argument as a means of testing their views. Thus, they speak their mind with the expectation that either their views or those of the opposition will be modified as a result of a successful challenge: a point against which one or the other opponent has no effective reply.

Struggle

Black and white concepts of intransigence derive from their opposite views on the relevance of struggle in the persuasion process. Whites attempt to minimize dynamic opposition within the persuasion process because such confrontation, or struggle, is seen as divisive. Blacks however, see such struggle as unifying, as operating within, not outside, the persuasion process. It signifies caring about something or someone enough to want to struggle with it. Blacks, in turn, regard inflexibility and intransigence as a refusal to contend: a rejection of the crucible (struggle) through which truth is created and reconciliations are effected. It means as one student put it, 'you'll stay your way and I'll stay mine'.[2] The withholding of affect – the presence of which blacks view favourably – also has this meaning. As the same student put it, 'When blacks are working hard to keep cool, it signals that the chasm between them is getting wider, not smaller.'

Relationship to material

The element of struggle for blacks is primarily communicated through dynamic opposition. But it is also communicated by the way people relate to their material. Blacks present their views as advocates. They take a position and show that they care about the position they take. This stance is characteristic of the mode of predominantly oral cultures like that of present-day black community people and white society of an earlier era. There, as Walter Ong has pointed out, a scholar was taught to defend a stand he had taken or to attack the stand of another. The orator's stance: passionate involvement in his material and a feeling that there was an adversary at large, was standard equipment provided by formal education for man's confrontation with the

[2] Joan McCarty, conversation.

world.[3] This perspective survives in such general expressions as 'taking a stand' which still retains its positive connotation in white usage. It reflects a time when whites also regarded passionate involvement in one's material favourably.

Present-day whites relate to their material as spokesmen, not advocates. This is because they believe that the truth or merits of an idea are intrinsic to the idea itself. How deeply a person cares or believes in the idea is considered irrelevant to its fundamental truth value. The truth of the matter is in the matter. This view – the separation of truth and belief – is heavily influenced by what whites understand of the scientific method, where the goal is to achieve a stance of neutral objectivity with regard to the truth that is 'out there': a truth that is not to be possessed or created, but rather discovered. Whites believe that caring about or believing in one's ideas, like scientists becoming infatuated with their own hypotheses, would make them less receptive to opposing ideas, consequently preventing them from discovering the truth that exists. In light of this view they are taught to present ideas as though they had an objective life, as existing independent of the person who happens to be expressing them. This accounts for the impersonal mode of expression that whites use, which, along with the absence of affect and dynamic opposition, establishes the character of detachment to proceedings in which white cultural norms dominate.

Black community people do not strive for neutral objectivity, but to have a position and take a stand on it. As one of my black students put it – herself a teacher of black students – 'I've personally found it difficult in my classes to get people to just discuss an issue. They invariably take sides. Sometimes, being neutral is looked upon with disdain.'[4]

Roles and responsibilities

Because blacks deal from a point of view, they are disinclined to believe whites who claim not to have a point of view, or who present their views in a manner that suggests that they do not believe themselves what they are saying. This explains why blacks often accuse whites of being insincere.

But blacks have another reason to misinterpret (and distrust) the dispassionate and detached mode that whites use to engage in debate. It resembles the mode that blacks themselves use when they are *fronting*: that is, self-consciously suppressing what they truly feel and believe. As one black student put it: 'That's when I'm lyin''. Fronting generally occurs in black/white encounters when blacks perceive a risk factor

[3] Walter J. Ong, S. J. *The Presence of the Word*, p. 225.
[4] Joan McCarty, conversation.

to be present and where they judge it to be more prudent to keep silent than to speak. As one black woman put it, 'When in the minority, only a fool shows the anger that he feels.'[5]

Both black views underlie the way blacks initially interpret and respond to white silence in the classroom. For example, blacks do not believe that whites do not have a position on an issue but rather that whites are reluctant to reveal the position that they have. Their attitude towards white silence, consequently, depends upon their assessment of the risk factor for white students. If the ratio of the class is mostly black, blacks are likely to be sympathetic towards white silence, they often being the silent minority themselves. But when the black/white student ratio is about 50/50, then blacks are not inclined to interpret (or forgive) white lack of participation as due to a risk factor, but either as intransigence: a refusal to engage in the struggle through which truth is created, or as deviousness: an unwarranted concealment of what they really think and believe – 'unwarranted' because they perceive no risk factor to be present. At this point blacks often comment, 'How come black people are the only ones doing the talking?' Should whites still remain silent after that invitation to talk, blacks will either start to question individual white students directly, or make deliberately outlandish statements to provoke whites into speaking. Thus, one black female becoming impatient with the wall of white silence, finally said, that she thought 'white men couldn't handle it sexually'. She knew 'by the way they walked and talked'. The black person who reported the incident, Joan McCarty, thought the remark was intended to get the white students to talk. But they still remained silent. The white men turned red and the white women looked down to the floor. The black students just looked at the white students, amazed that such a remark would go unanswered. Moreover, until the black female who made the remark got a response, she indicated that she would just 'go on talking'.

The white students are typically bewildered and chagrined when this happens because they don't see themselves as being intransigent or devious by being silent. One white female student said, 'I hardly ever talk in class', thereby hoping to convince the black students that her quiet, passive, receptive, posture was her *customary* mode of classroom behaviour.

But whites resent being called upon to justify their silence. They do not consider talking in class as something that can be demanded. It is after all their 'right' to remain silent if they so choose, just as it is their 'right' not to have to answer direct personal questions ('I don't see why I have to answer that'). Such questions to white students are seen as outside the boundaries of 'class discussion'.

Blacks however, do not agree that silence is a 'right' since it runs directly counter to what they regard as obligatory behaviour for

[5] Delores Williams, conversation.

engaging in debate. For truth to be created, all parties must engage in the truth-creating process. To refuse, especially if one should disagree with what has been said – silence signifies agreement – is 'cheating'. It withholds from the group a viewpoint that might cause the prevailing view to be modified, and is thus considered subversive of the truth-creating process.

Blacks also disagree with the white view that probing an individual's personal viewpoint is outside the boundaries of class discussion. This is because blacks feel that all views expressed and actions taken derive from a central set of core beliefs which cannot be other than personal. As Carolyn Rodgers put it, 'ultimately a person's life-style is his point of view.'[6] Consequently, blacks often probe beyond the given statement to find out where a person is 'coming from' so as to clarify the meaning and value of a particular behaviour and statement.

In view of this perspective, I regularly indicate in my opening lecture on black and white racial, cultural and speech differences what my personal position on such differences is so that students will know that when I talk about differences it is not with the idea of reinforcing existing prejudices towards them. Without this clarification of 'where I am coming from', it would be difficult to continue discussing the subject, since differences have typically been used as evidence of group inferiority – biological and social – and members of ethnic and minority groups are particularly sensitive to the possibility that a discussion of differences will have these kinds of implications.

Certifying knowledge

Blacks and whites also disagree on what establishes the authoritativeness of an idea. White students regard authoritative ideas as those which have been published or otherwise certified by experts in the field. For blacks, the fact of an idea having been published is not sufficient to establish its authoritativeness. Blacks consider authoritative ideas as those whose truth value has been certified by the crucible of argument. These conceptions directly affect the different ways that blacks and whites define their role and responsiblity when engaged in debate.

For example, whites debate an issue impersonally. Theses are advanced to the group as a whole. Those who agree or disagree with one or another thesis are expected to present their views in the same impersonal manner. Individual people are not directly addressed; ideas are. The relative merits of the ideas are assessed independently with only minimal regard to how they were presented or who originally introduced them into the discussion.

Blacks, however, debate issues by engaging those who initially advanced the thesis in personal argument. This is because blacks see

[6] Carolyn Rodgers, 'Black Poetry – Where it's at', p. 345.

debate to be as much a contest between individuals as a test of opposing ideas. Because it is a contest, attention is also paid to winning, consequently, to performance, for to win requires that one out-perform one's opponents, to out-think, out-talk, and out-style them. It means to be concerned with art as well as argument. Also because it is a contest, no one else may redirect its focus until the outcome has been decided. This usually occurs when one or the other contender is unable to come back with an effective reply. At that point other participants may enter the debate to test and develop the truth value of the opposing ideas further.

Blacks and whites define their roles and responsibility in terms of these conceptions. For example, because white students consider an authoritative idea to be one which has been published they see their role and responsibility as limited to representing the idea and its source accurately and showing its relevance to the topic under consideration. They do not see themselves as personally responsible for the idea itself. Nor do they see that they must necessarily agree with the idea they are presenting, or have a personal position on it.

Blacks however, consider authoritative ideas to be those that have been tested and certified through argument. Thus, they consider it essential that individuals take personal positions on issues and assume full responsibility for arguing their validity. For without that, they feel individuals would not care enough about truth or about their own ideas to want to struggle with them. And without such struggle, the truth value of ideas cannot be ascertained.

Because of these differences, black and white debate of an issue typically produces the following scenario. White students will make statements that they believe are authoritative by virtue of who said them and where they were published. Black students will cast the statement into the framework of personal argument and challenge the white students directly on one or another point with which they disagree. Because the white students did not intend their statements to be cast in the form of an argument they see the challenge as inappropriate. Consequently, they respond with 'Don't ask me, ask McLuhan', or, 'You ought to be arguing with McLuhan. He was the one who said it.' But this response is also convenient, because not having thought about the validity of the idea as idea, they also have no intellectual ammunition with which to contend.

The black students consider these responses to be irresponsible and evasive: a way to say things without allowing oneself to be held accountable. Thus, should white students continue to cite authorities in their presentations, blacks will say, 'Never mind what McLuhan says. What do *you* say?' Only statements that an individual will assume personal responsibility for in argument are admissable in debate.

Turn-taking

Collisions between black and white students in the classroom are also caused by different procedures for turn-taking, or claiming the floor. The white classroom rule is to raise your hand, be recognized by the teacher, and be given a turn in the order in which you are recognized. An individual's turn generally can be as long as the number of points they have to make that are related to the topic under discussion. The black rule on the other hand, is to 'come in when you can'. This means to wait until a person has finished their point – it would be rude to attempt to claim the floor before at least one point has been made – and then come in. Coming in, generally means to engage in argument on one or another point that has been raised or to introduce a new point entirely. Should two or more people want to come in at the same time, it is usually negotiated by the principals themselves ('Let me just get this one point in'). Deference is often shown to the person who feels their point is the most pressing ('I just have to say this!'). That person may or may not acknowledge the courtesy by keeping their point concise, so that the one who conceded the turn can go next. Consideration may also be shown to a person because of greater status due to age, experience, occupation, or general reputation. Because there is competition in claiming the floor individuals are favoured who have the greater capacity for self-assertion, or who can better manage to keep track of the pulse of the interaction so as to insert themselves a split second before someone else. Also helpful is sheer forcefulness in commanding the attention of others. Also, because of the competitive nature of black turn-taking, occasionally two or more people end up talking at the same time, though not necessarily to the same audience. Each speaker claims their group of listeners, so to speak, even if it is only those within the immediate vicinity. Listeners have to decide whom to attend to. Sometimes several conversations go on and are attended to at once. This pattern resembles closely the one Karl Reisman described for Afro-Antiguans.[7]

If someone is trying to get into the debate but is having difficulty getting their turn and can get other more assertive members to notice, the latter will often intervene on their behalf. The person has to be seen as making the effort however. Within one's own group, people who do not make the effort are not generally asked why they did not. It is assumed that those who feel they have something to say will be sufficiently moved by what they want to say to enter the debate. In class with whites the same black attitude prevails initially until blacks become conscious that it is predominantly they who are doing the talking. As we already indicated it is at that point that the silence of whites itself becomes an issue.

[7] Karl Reisman, 'Contrapuntal Conversations in an Antiguan Village', p. 113ff.

Because the framework of argument governs black interaction, a black turn rarely consists of more than two points if the issue is controversial. This is to allow others to answer the points that have been made if they so choose. Should someone use their turn to make several points, those blacks who want to comment will object, saying 'By the time you get through with all of your points, I will have forgotton your first point on which I wanted to make a comment.' The issue here however, is not only that those who wanted to get in will have forgotton their comment, but that the pattern and pulse of the interaction: the point and counterpoint of argument, as well as the spontaneous impulses to speak that the black pattern allows, will have been defeated by the manner of the presentation and the number of points made.

A nice example of this occurred at a meeting consisting mostly of black community people. The talk centred on male-female relationships. During the question and answer period people were allowed to give their opinions. In one such case, a man was giving his opinion when a woman said (after a point had been made, but before the man had finished), 'That's not true, that's not true. . . .' At this point the black moderator, whom the person who reported this account considered acculturated to middle-class norms said, 'I just won't listen to any of you. You have to raise your hand. There's no debate and you cannot ask the question to the person who made the statement.' As a result, according to her report, 'the heat level went down so low that it actually became boring to the people there, despite the fact that the issues were exciting.'[8]

Blacks and whites also differ in the conditions they set for taking a turn. For example, the white concept of turn-taking limits its authorization to the order of individual assertion. It hopes, but does not require, that a turn be contingent upon people having something valuable to contribute. But a person can nonetheless be granted a turn even without saying anything important or relevant, such as when others show 'democratic' concern that 'everyone should have a turn'. Black self-assertion within the framework of turn-taking is more strongly regulated with respect to content. Thus, if people insert themselves out of turn, but nevertheless say something significant ('on time'), then their self-assertion will be accepted. Conversely, if someone whose turn fitted within the prescribed order didn't say anything worthwhile, then others may challenge the person's self-assertion with 'What did you come in with that for?' Within the black conception, the decision to enter the debate and assert oneself is self-determined, regulated entirely by individuals' own initial assessment of what they have to say. It is only validated or not by the group afterwards based upon what the individuals said. Within the white conception, the individual decision to

[8] Joan McCarty, conversation.

enter the debate does not immediately translate into self-assertion. The impulse to assert oneself and speak must be checked. A turn first has to be requested and granted from an authorized person. Once the turn is granted however, it is not seen as needing to be further authorized by audience validation of the content of what was said. The content might also be positively or negatively evaluated but that has no bearing on the person's right to take the turn. The two are independently validated.

White turn-taking is authorized from without. Consequently, it is seen as an entitlement, to be granted only to one person at a time, and to be surrendered only by themselves or by the person empowered to grant turns. Whites are chagrined therefore, to have their turn preempted 'before they are finished', or infringed upon by other unauthorized conversations. A turn claims the floor and preempts other goings-on.

One reason that whites often find themselves preempted when interacting with blacks is they don't cast their presentation within the framework of personal argument. Thus, they may wish to make several points relevant to the topic. This blacks consider inappropriate since according to the rules of argument, the truth value of each point has to be ascertained as best as can be realized by those present before new points can be addressed. Moreover, all who want to are entitled to have their say before new points can be considered. Because blacks consider turns to consist of fewer points than whites, they often come in to argue a point before whites 'have finished'. This whites consider rude. However, blacks believe a turn is over when a point has been made that others wish to comment on. Consequently they consider whites to be selfish for 'hogging the floor' or for disallowing the process of argument to be activated. It is then that blacks will attempt to take the floor feeling that the white claim to undivided and noncompetitive attention has been forfeited. If they are unsuccessful in this, they may alternatively start another conversation, with whomever's attention can be obtained.

Capacities

When the white student responded that 'she hardly ever spoke in class' to the black request to 'hear from some of the white students in the room', she was attempting to convince the black students that her classroom mode of behaviour was normal for her and consequently that her silence did not mean that she was necessarily withholding or concealing something. The black students were reluctant to accept this. We have already mentioned two reasons why: one is their disinclination to believe that she (and white students generally) would not have a position on a topic that everyone could be expected to have a position on (e.g. racism). The second is the general black rule within argument: that if you disagree with the view being expressed then you are obliged to speak up. This rule becomes internalized as an 'impulse towards truth': that if people disagree they will be sufficiently moved by that impulse to enter the debate. Silence therefore signifies agreement, but since it was unlikely that the white student agreed with everything that was said, they felt her silence had to have another explanation. But the black students' view was also influenced by what they assumed were the capacities of the white students to voice their disagreement if they did disagree. For example, blacks feel that the constraints against speaking up are caused by external factors that create risk: rules and regulations against speaking, or people being in the minority. They do not see constraints against speaking as due to internal factors, e.g., psychological inhibitions. Consequently, blacks feel that once external prohibitions against speaking have been lifted – that it is 'safe' to speak – then everyone should feel equally free to speak. This view implies that the capacities and inclinations of whites and blacks to assert themselves are equivalent. They are not.

The reason for this is that black culture allows its members considerably greater freedom to assert and express themselves than white culture. Black culture values individually regulated self-assertion. It also values spontaneous expression of feeling. As a result, black cultural events typically encourage and even require individuals to behave in an assertive/expressive manner, such as in the black speech events, *rapping, signifying*, and *call and response*, to name just a few, and, as we are claiming here, in *argument* also.[9]

White culture values the ability of individuals to rein in the impulses that come from within. Consequently, white cultural events do not allow for individually initiated self-assertion or for the spontaneous expression of feeling. Rather self-assertion occurs as a social entitlement, a prerogative of one's higher status, or, as with turn-taking, something granted and regulated by an empowered authority. And even when granted, it is a low-keyed assertion, showing detachment, modesty, understatement. Even play in white culture reflects the same norms. It is serious, methodical and purposeful. 'Showing off', which would represent individually initiated (unauthorized) self-assertion and more unrestrained self-expression, is viewed negatively within white culture. Black culture, on the other hand, views showing off – in black idiom: *stylin' out, showboating, grandstanding*, positively.[10]

[9] For a discussion of rapping and signifying, see Thomas Kochman, 'Toward an Ethnography of Black American Speech Behavior', Claudia Mitchell-Kernan, *Language Behavior in a Black Urban Community*, and Roger Abrahams, *Talking Black*. For *call and response* see Jack Daniel and Geneva Smitherman, 'How I Got Over: Communication Dynamics in the Black Community'; for *argument*, see Karl Reisman's analogous discussion for Afro-Antiguans in 'Noise and Order'.

[10] Grace Holt, 'Stylin' Outta the Black Pulpit'.

Because white culture requires that individuals check those impulses that come from within, whites become able practitioners of self-restraint. However, this practice has an inhibiting effect on their ability to be spontaneously self-assertive. Consequently, white students find themselves at a disadvantage when engaging in debate with blacks. Not only is it easier for blacks to assert themselves – they can follow through on their impulses without having to wait for external authorization – but the level of energy and spiritual intensity that blacks generate is one that they can manage comfortably but which whites can only manage with effort.

As a result, whites find it difficult to establish the dynamic balance necessary to achieve parity for their opposing viewpoint.

Blacks initially don't see this relative mismatch because they don't see their normal animated style as disabling. This belief is intensified on those occasions when white students of the counter-culture are in class. Their style like blacks, is animated, interpersonal and argumentative. This reinforces the black belief that their classroom mode is the standard way of engaging in public debate of an issue and makes them suspect those white students even more when they claim that their quiet, unobtrusive behaviour is their customary classroom style.

Self-control

Whites are not only constrained by the higher level of energy and spiritual intensity that blacks generate which makes it difficult for them to establish parity for their views. They are worried that blacks cannot sustain such intense levels of interaction without losing self-control. The reason for their concern is that whites conceive and practice self-control as repression: checking those impulses from within before they are released. Once released, whites feel they no longer can be contained: that self-control has been lost. Because whites feel they are losing self-control when engaging in highly energetic and animated argument – the kind that functions for them as a ventilation of anger and hostility – they feel no one else can successfully manage such intense exchanges either. However, blacks do not conceive or practice self-control as repression. Rather – consistent with their cultural value towards assertive/expressive behaviour – blacks conceive and practice self-control as 'getting it together': harmonizing the internal and external forces in the mode that black cultural events activate and release.[11] Internal forces are therefore, controlled by the structure of the mode through which they are released. And as Paul Carter Harrison said, 'An emotion is never out of control when it fits the modality it is released in'.[12]

[11] Paul Carter Harrison, The Drama of Nommo, p. xv.
[12] *Ibid*, p. 157.

Other disabling factors

Two other factors also interfere with the way blacks and whites initially relate to each other in the classroom. One is the rule among blacks, generally activiated when they are in the minority or when the ratio of blacks to whites is about even, not to disagree with each other in front of whites. The white students, who typically do not organize themselves that way, feel like isolated individuals pitted against a united black front when this occurs. In conjunction with the more animated and energetic style of blacks which whites feel already somewhat disables them and their concern over blacks' ability to manage inter-action at the higher levels of spiritual intensity, this unified front only has the effect of inhibiting white participation further. Of course, this only increases black impatience with the white students' lack of partici-pation – which blacks interpret as intransigence – which leads to increased pressure by blacks to get whites to talk, which only intensifies white reluctance to speak, and so on. It is not long in this process of escalation before whites begin to interpret the black pressure as deliberate harassment and think about dropping the class – a few white male students indicated that they were ready to fight at this point, the intensity of the interaction having reached a level that they considered provocative.

It is usually at this time that I explain to the black and white students what effect their behaviour is having on each other. This is often immediately confirmed by the students themselves. One white student remarked that he would disagree more with things that have been said since he's used to talking a lot in class, but that here he felt that he was 'outnumbered'. The risk that the student took in making the statement openly to the class – frequently white students make such statements to me privately – raised his classroom stature to blacks who appreciated the public admission of something honest and personal, and strengthened his own sense of personal security in class. It also effectively dissipated much of the impatience, frustration and anger that blacks had begun to feel generally over white lack of participation.

A second factor adding to white silence is the fear of whites that they will be chastised by blacks for personal views that they might reveal in response to requests to 'hear from some the white students in the room'. This makes them reluctant to respond to topics such as racism when it is brought up – racism is usually the first subject that blacks and whites seriously interact over – thus producing silence on the topic and causing blacks to address whites individually as to their personal viewpoint, with little success. What whites miss here is that blacks do not want to elicit a personal admission from white students that they are racist so as to condemn them – which whites believe – but rather to get whites to acknowledge the extent to which racism has affected *everyone* in this country. Paradoxically, those who *admit* the effects of racism on themselves are perceived more positively by blacks than those who would deny its effects. Thus, one white male student got a lot of credit from black students when he said openly 'I know I'm a racist. I grew up in Belmont-Craigin [an all-white working-class area in Chicago]. I'm working on it.'

Changes

All that I have said here applies to blacks and whites interacting with each other during what I would call the initial phase of their coming together, the length of which I would estimate between at least one and perhaps two academic quarters. During the first quarter the full force of cultural ethnocentrism is at work. The meanings and values that members of each group attach to the others' behaviour are those of their own culture. How potent this ethnocentrism becomes in creating conflict also depends on how much forgiveness is present. Thus, the disruptive potential of ethnocentric judgements is also a function of the general political climate of the times. The late 1960s and early 1970s were especially unforgiving and some of the more contentious scenes described here were taken from this period. Even then, however, changes in behaviour and attitudes became apparent after blacks and whites interacted with each other for a while. For example, white students began to revise their initial views that the more animated black mode was an attempt to intimidate them and dominate the proceedings. They did not come to the point where they accepted the argumentative black mode as an equally valid means of getting at the truth, but they did come to see that blacks were not merely attempting to ventilate anger and hostility. Experiencing greater comfort, white students started to speak up more, thereby more nearly satisfying black expectations for greater verbal participation from white students.

In turn, black students began to concede that the dispassionate and detached white mode did not necessarily signify concealment or deviousness. On the other hand, they did not come to consider the impersonal presentation of ideas as an acceptable alternative to argument as a truth-creating process. Also blacks began to disagree with each other more, apparently, no longer feeling the need to present themselves before whites as a united front on all issues.

In accidental or unmediated encounters the initial phase is the only phase that blacks and whites typically experience. Thus, in the meeting between community representatives and university faculty, members of the two groups held the same ethnocentric views of their own and each other's behaviour at the end of the meeting as they held at the beginning: each one accusing the other of negotiating in bad faith; of introducing behavioural elements into the process that did not belong while simultaneously refusing admission of those elements that members of each group considered essential if anything constructive were to be accomplished.

Functionality and dysfunctionality of black and white classroom modalities

In practice, the ways that black and white truth-creating processes are rendered dysfunctional is consistent with their other respective areas of cultural development. For example, in black cultural events generally, those with greater ability tend to dominate the proceedings as well as offer themselves as contenders against whom others can test their skills. Likewise when engaging in debate. Those who can more successfully assert themselves or who possess greater debating skills tend to dominate class interaction. While those who possess such skills generally can be counted on also to have more meaningful things to say, this is not always so. Yet in the latter case, I have observed that their dominance of the discussion is not always challenged, notwithstanding the black turn-taking rule that establishes that self-assertion is supposed to be regulated by an assessment of the content, which also allows people to take the floor away from those who aren't saying anything worthwhile. The reason they are not always challenged is that blacks don't just debate an idea, they debate the person debating the idea. Consequently, individuals in the group assess their own debating skills relative to others in the group and if they feel they cannot generate the kind of dynamic balance necessary to establish parity for their view, they don't contend. The competitive aspect of claiming the floor and contending the opposition within the black mode favours the more energetic, confident, assertive and skillful individuals. The reluctance of the less skillful individuals to contend defeats the ideal purpose of the group to get the maximum truth value that the entire collectivity present is able to produce.

The white mode tends to debate the idea rather than the person debating the idea. This allows those who disagree to enter into the discussion without having to match the forcefulness of the opposition, since they are not in direct contention. This mode would seem to allow the greatest possible involvement since it doesn't make participation dependent upon having acquired strong debating skills. And in practice, whites (and blacks) who do not enter the debate when it is governed by black norms have participated when white norms prevail. Nonetheless, even within the less competitive and intense white framework, some individuals are still reluctant to assert themselves. And they cannot be made to do so if they choose not to. It is interesting to note that an individual's decision *to* assert himself can be overruled by the empowered authority but not the decision *not* to assert himself. Yet, in some ways the latter more severely disables the truth-creating process than the former. For instance, as a teacher, it is easier to suppress irresponsible self-assertion in the class than it is to overcome irresponsible non-assertion.

The rationalization that whites use when pressed to account for their silence is that it is their 'right' to do so, just as they have a 'right' to their own opinion. Herbert Marcuse and Trevor Pateman have argued that the latter is a corruption of the free-speech idea and I consider their arguments to apply equally well to the 'right' to remain silent.[13, 14]

Marcuse and Pateman base their arguments on the concept of free speech adopted by John Stuart Mill in *On Liberty*, namely, that free speech is to be governed by the impulse towards truth: that people should be granted free speech so as not to be afraid to speak the truth. It was not intended to allow people to protect their views from being challenged under the rule that they have a *right* to their opinion regardless of its irrational or inhumane content.

> One could even claim that the fundamental right in classical liberal theory (as in Mill) is the right to dispossess people of their irrational ideas ... not just to express an opinion, but to contribute to a debate ... aiming at a positive outcome, in terms of the acceptance and application of one opinion rather than another.[15]

Similarly, a right to vote in a democracy becomes subverted by a claim for its converse: a right not to vote, which American citizens also hold, despite its weakening effect on basic democratic processes. The right to remain silent is the same corruption of the free speech concept as the 'right to one's own opinion'. The goal for which freedom of speech was obtained – the pursuit of truth – becomes subverted by the right to remain silent. In Herbert Marcuse's terms, tolerance that was promoted as a means to an end, in becoming an end unto itself, has become repressive of the goal it was originally intended to promote.[16] By individuals insisting upon the right to remain silent during a debate they also withhold the inclusion of another idea and thus work against the realization of a better collective truth. By way of contrast, the black view that one is obliged to contribute to a debate, especially if one disagrees, is consistent with the Millian ideal: in satisfying the impulse towards truth that was the goal for which tolerance of free speech was originally obtained.

The white cultural idea that individuals should approach an issue with an open mind is based on the conception that one side in a disagreement is not likely to have a monopoly on the truth. But the idea of 'keeping

[13] Herbert Marcuse, 'Repressive Tolerance'.
[14] Trevor Pateman, *Language, Truth and Politics*.
[15] Pateman, p. 92.
[16] Marcuse, p. 82.

an open mind', like free speech, was conceived as a means of arriving at a better truth. It was intended as a mode of inquiry, a stance to be taken when people do not as yet feel they have sufficient information to form an opinion, and here it functionally works to advantage. Where it becomes dysfunctional is when it becomes an end in itself, a state of indefinite mental suspension, to be maintained without regard to the relative merits of the different views being advanced. Yet this is often what occurs.

That it does is not surprising. It is the logical consequence of a process of schooling that typically asks students simply to research and report information on issues: to present the views of *both* sides but not to develop a personal position with respect to either one. Thus teachers take a required Philosophy of Education course which basically asks them to read and feed back the ideas of John Dewey and others. But they are not also asked to consider let alone debate which of the views they have read are more persuasive to them, and why. *Their* ideas don't 'count'. Credit is given only for knowing 'authoritative' ideas.

Where this process becomes dysfunctional in satisfying the impulse towards truth is that it doesn't encourage the activation of independent thought processes. Consequently, a group doesn't benefit from the different intellectual capacities of its membership except in so far as one or another is better able to grasp and articulate the authorized viewpoint. This defeats the truth-creating process that presumes that the collection of individuals engaged in debate will be sufficiently independent-minded so that qualitatively *different* views will be debated, and produce a better truth. Everyone engaged in producing only authorized viewpoints will produce – with only slight variation – authorized viewpoints. Similarly, by students not being given the opportunity to put their ideas to the test, they do not develop their own ideas because they are not confronted with situations that require that they have them. Nor do they see creating a personal position as the logical end result of an exhaustive inquiry into different sides of an issue.

The black notion of accepting personal responsibility for the views that one presents requires that individuals develop a personal position. In doing so, it at least compels blacks to activate their own thinking on any idea that has been presented that has not already been tested by them and passed as received truth. This posture contrasts with the posture of whites when engaging in debate in ways that I have already mentioned. But it also affects the way black and white students respond to questions asked by the teacher. As one of my students observed:

> I've noticed that when an instructor asks a question of white students, they tend to give him back what he has just said on the subject. Black students, on the other hand, tend to give their own opinion.[17]

[17] Allen Harris, conversation.

References

ABRAHAMS, ROGER D. 1976: *Talking Black*. Rowley: Newbury House.

DANIEL, JACK L., and SMITHERMAN, GENEVA 1976. How I got over: Communication dynamics in the black community. *Quarterly Journal of Speech* **62**, 26–39.

HARRISON, PAUL C. 1972: *The Drama of Nommo*. New York: Grove Press.

HOLT, GRACE S. 1972: Stylin' outta the black pulpit. In T. Kochman (ed.), *Rappin' and Stylin' Out*, Urbana: The University of Illinois Press.

KOCHMAN, THOMAS 1970: Toward an ethnography of Black American speech behavior. In F. Whitten, Jr. and F. Szwed (eds.), *Afro-American Anthropology*, New York: The Free Press.

MARCUSE, HERBERT 1969: Repressive tolerance. In *A Critique of Pure Tolerance*, pp. 81–123. Boston: Beacon.

MITCHELL-KERNAN, CLAUDIA 1971: Language Behavior in a Black Urban Community. *Monographs of the Language-Behavior Research Laboratory* **2**. Berkeley: University of California Press.

ONG, WALTER J., S. J. 1967: *The Presence of the Word*. New York: Clarion.

PATEMAN, TREVOR 1975: *Language, Truth and Politics*. Nottingham: Stroud and Pateman.

REISMAN, KARL 1974a: Contrapuntal conversations in an Antiguan village. In R. Bauman and J. Sherzer (eds.) *Explorations in the Ethnography of Speaking*, London: Cambridge University Press.

—1974b. Noise and order. In W. W. Gage (ed.), *Language in Its Social Setting*, Washington DC: The Anthropological Society of Washington.

RODGERS, CAROLYN 1972: Black poetry – where it's at, In T. Kochman (ed.), *Rappin' and Stylin' Out*, Urbana: The University of Illinois Press.

6

British Black English in British schools

David Sutcliffe

In the poetry and drama produced by black children we glimpse language ability which is clearly not being exploited to the full in British schools. *Jennifer and 'Brixton Blues'*[1] provides just one example of this ability, an all too rare example of its use in a school setting. The play, devised by several girls at Vauxhall Manor School, London, in 1977, was subsequently videotaped and then transcribed by the actresses themselves. The central character, 'mum', is a Jamaican woman beset with troubles brought on by her husband's desertion. She battles – mainly with her tongue – to preserve her family, and her dignity. Jennifer's virtuoso performance in this role is admirable, but not exactly unusual. Labov, Abrahams and many other writers have commented on the fostering of fluency in a variety of speech styles or speech events in black American and Caribbean cultures, and a similar emphasis on verbal fluency is found in the black communities in Britain. Jennifer has drawn upon the repertoire of speech styles which real life black 'mums' command, and she role-plays her way through them with a dramatic facility which is also culturally based. As we shall see *performance* is an important element in black culture.

John Richmond, Jennifer's teacher, describes her as not generally very successful at school: her reading was poor, her written English was 'awkward, laborious and full of technical errors', and her behaviour led to frequent clashes with the staff (Richmond, 1979). This too, un-fortunately, is hardly an unusual pattern. There is a widespread feeling amongst teachers, supported by the findings of a number of recent, mostly small-scale studies,[2] that West Indian pupils are on average performing less well than those from any other ethnic group.

---

[1] An unscripted Jamaican dialect play now available as *Jennifer and 'Brixton Blues'; language alive in school* by John Richmond, in Supplementary Readings for Block 5, PE232 Language Development (Open University Press, Milton Keynes, 1979).

[2] Little (1975); Ewen, Gipps and Sumner (1973); Walkerdine (1974); Redbridge (1978) see also Essen, J. and Ghodsian, M. (1979) and Coard (1971). It is deplorable that, up until now, so little notice has been taken of these research findings and observations.

Together with similar fears expressed by many black parents this has led, finally, to the setting up of the Rampton Committee to look into the performance of ethnic minority children, with especial reference to West Indian children.

The Assessment of Performance Unit of the Department of Education and Science, which measures scholastic performance, is also planning to carry out separate nationwide monitoring of black West Indian children to provide much needed authoritative information.

There is near universal acceptance that language is somehow bound up with this issue of academic underachievement, though not necessarily in the sense that the (non-standard speaker's) language directly *causes* the underachievement. Many educationalists agree that the best educational practice should begin 'where the child is' and that includes starting with the child's language. Yet this all too frequently does not happen. In the work of Rosen, Ashworth, and Barnes (amongst others) there is a clear articulation of the advantages of encouraging pupils to use their own expressive language to 'make meanings' as they struggle with the curriculum. However, some of the most prized and most developed black speech is celebratory, an enjoyment of words and voice for their own sake. This means that rather than being used to pin down meaning, such speech *is* the meaning. Can it or the abilities presupposed by it be used more in school, and to what end? Later in this article we shall be looking at the importance of this type of speech in language development, oral and written, and recognizing that the best examples of it achieve the status of literature. Furthermore the encouragement and exploitation of this type of language/language ability could play an extremely important part in combating the vicious circle of black alienation.

A Rastaman quote in Cashmore (1979, p. 83) states:

> It is inevitable that we, as black people, were never and can never be part of this country where we do not belong; like a heart transplant it rejects us.

Many other black people in Britain would not be so uncompromising, but would express similar feelings of rejection.

Anxiety, rejection and counter-rejection, unconstructive hostility, none of these form a good basis for progress in school. The Redbridge enquiry into the performance of West Indian pupils in an East London Borough (1978) came to the conclusion that alienation, which it characterized as problems of self-identity in a hostile society, constituted the most powerful factor in inhibiting progress. If only they could make use of pupils' ability with black styles of language, schools would not just be practising good economy in exploiting a ready resource, they would be restoring confidence – in some cases it would be the pupils' confidence in themselves, and in others it would be their confidence in the school. Very many thousands of the black younger generation in Britain are seeking a point of emotional stability and a means of self-development, which is why so many are turning to the Rastafarian faith. In such a situation, for such young people, what a school does, in terms of curriculum and teaching styles, becomes more, not less, relevant.

Educationalists and educational policy-makers clearly need to be familiar with the distinctive linguistic background of young blacks in Britain. Let us begin by sketching one view (from the outside) of this complex picture.

Black people have complained that slavery robbed them of a distinctive culture, and pointed to the lack of a 'proper' language or history of their own. Yet there is a strong cultural identity (or range of such) available to them, finding expression in their speech, music and gesture, dance, cooking, hairstyles and so on – and of course in their 'world view'. This cultural heritage may have even greater significance for British-born blacks, seeking a positive identity in a society they perceive as hostile, than for their West Indian-born parents. Creole is bound up with the construction of this cultural identity – one could almost say that it generates it.

Broad Creole and its derivation

Every part of the West Indies has its local Creole with its own distinctive flavour. There are, however, striking similarities between all of them, particularly in terms of grammar. Even French-based Creoles have much in common with English-based Creoles in this respect. In fact, there is a thought-provoking similarity between all the Caribbean Creoles, the West African Pidgins and the Sudanic languages of West Africa.[3] I would argue that all New World Creoles have grammatical systems which derive at least in part from African languages, and that this is true even for black American varieties to some extent. Let us try to reconstruct the history and beginnings of the Creoles, particularly Jamaican, to explain how this could have come about.

Before Europeans moved into West Africa to trade and then to obtain slaves, a great many West Africans must have been bi-, tri- or multi-lingual. There are still something over 400 languages spoken in West Africa and only eight or nine of these have more speakers than, for instance, Welsh.[4] Mobile, active or enterprising members of any community therefore mastered several languages. In this they were helped by the considerable similarity between the grammars (and idioms) of all West African Sudanic languages.[5] A kind of consensus grammar

[3] See for instance the work of John Holm (1978) and Pauline Christie (1979).

[4] This is not intended as a slight on the Welsh language, which I take to have around 900,000 speakers including those outside Wales.

[5] See Dalby's comments in Todd (1974).

remained constant while the vocabularies of various languages were learnt to be used with it.

In the fifteenth and sixteenth centuries first Portuguese and then English were adopted as trading languages in the area. Once more the grammar which the speakers used with the new vocabulary was a version of the West African consensus. By the middle of the seventeenth century when New World slavery began in earnest, English Pidgin had largely superseded Portuguese. Amongst the millions of Africans who were enslaved and shipped to the Americas there must have been thousands of Pidgin speakers. Since speakers from the same linguistic stock were split up deliberately, the early slaves were confronted with a desperate language problem in which a common language had to be found or forged. Under these conditions Pidgin expanded rapidly. This process was aided once again by the consensus of West African grammar which many blacks had learnt through their culture – that is through learning more than one West African language. Just how quickly this expansion happened may be judged by the case of Surinam (formerly Dutch Guiana). English plantation owners left the country in 1667 after a stay of some 40 years, but the languages of the people have remained English-based Creoles to this day, despite the fact that Dutch has been the standard language there for over 300 years.[6] There is some documentation of a similar rapid expansion of the new Pidgin/Creole in Jamaica. As early as 1734 a writer remarked that all blacks born on the island spoke 'English', regardless of the diverse African tongues of their parents. And from the close of the eighteenth century onwards we have a written record of what contemporary Jamaican Creole (JC) was like. Moreton noted down this song in 1790:

(*Leader*)	(*Chorus*)
If me want for go in a Ebo	— Me can't go there
Since dem tief me from a Guinea	— Me can't go there
If me want for go in a congo	— Me can't go there
Since dem tief me from my tatta, (father)	— Me can't go there
If me want for go in a Kingston	— Me can't go there
Since massa gone in a England	— Me can't go there
	(*Cassidy 1961*)

The weight of evidence for the African nature of Creole grammar(s) is substantial. There is room here for one example: the personal pronoun system. All New World Creoles distinguish between the singular and plural of the second person. This distinction (between *thou* and *you*) was dropping out of Standard English when JC was being formed at the turn of the eighteenth century and so *unu* was borrowed from

---

[6] Sranan and Djuka are (very largely) English-based Creoles. Saramaccan is part English- part Portuguese-based. All three languages are strikingly like Jamaican Creole in many respects.

Ibo to preserve a distinction which is made in African languages. Other Creoles have also borrowed this word or formed their own paraphrases (see Table 1, below). Even Black American English Vernacular (BEV) has *y'all*, which it could have borrowed from Southern White dialects – though probably the reverse is true. On the other hand few West African languages indicate pronominal gender or case distinctions;[7] in other words there is generally one pronoun covering the English *he*, *his*, *him*, *she*, *her*, *it*, *its* and so on. The same is true for the languages of Surinam, and for broad JC which may have *im* for all forms of the third person pronoun:

> ... mi sista stay upstairs a play wid *im* dolly
> (my sister stayed upstairs, playing with her dolly –
>
> Patricia, Bedford-born Black girl)

Table 1 Unu – The second person plural

Belize	unu, all a unu	St Vincent	a'yu
Jamaica	unu, all a unu, yu	Barbados	yu, yu all a'wuna
Nevis	a'yu, yu all	Grenada	amongs yu, among yu
Antigua	a'yu, yu	Guyana	yu all
Nicaragua (Miskito Coast)	unu, yu	Sea Islands (Georgia + South Carolina)	unu, y'all
Surinam (Saramaccan)	un, unu	Surinam (Sranan)	un

Dynamism and stability of Creole

Creoles are essentially not written languages, and since their earliest days have coexisted with their respective standard languages. Interplay with English (in the case of Jamaican, for instance) has created a spectrum of different shades of dialect known to linguists as the *Continuum*. In such a situation almost every word has a range of pro-

---

[7] There is a *trace* of case distinction in several of the major languages however. Yoruba has (lightly marked) case distinctions throughout its pronominal system. For a more detailed presentation of evidence for African influence see Sutcliffe (forthcoming).

nunciations, and constructions are reassembled, camouflaged or monitored out as the speaker changes dialect. The verb system itself has to undergo drastic modification, which produces a high degree of variability. As John Richmond puts it (Richmond 1978, p. 26), Caribbean Creoles '... possess a plastic, innovatory and organic quality which offers to those privileged to be fluent in them particular opportunities for exploration and experimentation'. Beryl Bailey, who produced the definitive *Jamaican Creole Syntax* (1966) writes in her introduction that speakers often shift back and forth between Creole and something very similar to standard 'within a single utterance'. We might well characterize this linguistic situation as unstable. The unexpected fact remains that Moreton's eighteenth-century Creole looks very much like modern Brixtonian or Bedfordian Creole. The broad form of the language is still very much with us and has changed little in 200 years.

To explain how this could happen we must assume a kind of Creole Standard which is almost as definable as Standard English, exerting an influence and attraction on Jamaican speakers equal and opposite to that of Standard English.

The tapes we have made with black Bedfordian children, and the transcripts of Jamaican language drama such as *Brixton Blues* show that young black British speakers spend much of the time ranging back and forth along the Continuum in a very uninhibited way, so that the indentifiable syntax of Creole is constantly merging and re-emerging (cf. Richmond, 1979).

Yet they can also focus on a particular dialect, including broad Creole. Note how Jennifer as 'Mum' in *Brixton Blues*, focuses on broad Jamaican Creole on several occasions in order to assert her formidable authority in typical Jamaican style, or express powerful emotions. In this example she is reacting to her estranged husband and her wayward sister who have dared to come and ask for money after setting up home together:

> ... Yuh tink seh me ah go give yuh money me? !!!
> fi go dig down inna my purse go seh mi a go gi' yuh money mi?
> You would a mad. An' yuh, yuh tink se mi forget yuh 'months
> pass all years and whatever you want call it pass, me nah
> give unnu a 'apenny ...
> (You think *I* am going to give you money? *I* should
> dig down in my purse and say that *I* am going
> to give you money? You must be mad. And you, you
> think that I've forgotten you? If months or even
> years and whatever you want to call it have passed,
> I'm not giving you two a ha'penny.)

while in church her public utterances are delivered in what is virtually Standard Jamaican English:

Now I will say this prayer for you young youths,
the young sisters and the young people. Now I
would like to represent one of my old friends
that come from Jamaica.
Would you stand up Sister Wright. Well the Lord bless her and keep
her and I don't know why she come to church this Sunday but she come
in her own way. The Lord said come to church, she came, she came to bless
us. Now she's not gonna say a prayer for us but she's gonna give us all her
thanks. Would you kneel and we pray for you. (Richmond, 1979)

Another factor in the retention of broad Creole forms is the apparent
law of minimum change and maximum retention of Creole features
when a speaker shifts from Creole towards English. It is true that some
grammatical features must disappear at a certain point on the
'Continuum' – that is, when a certain degree of Englishness is reached.
For instance:

Wa mek yu a waak?

has to be dropped in favour of:

Wai yu waakin?
(Why you walkin'?)

But often however the underlying principle remains the same: *y'all*, for
instance, is not broad Creole but it fits a broad Creole grammatical
slot. Similarly it often happens that a sentence can be interpreted as
either Creole *or* English – the modulation between the two being
achieved by subtle pronunciation difference on the part of the speaker,
or perhaps left entirely to the listener. For instance the last line of the
chorus to *Brown Girl in the Ring* can be taken as:

'She look(s) like a sugar in a plum'

which is a rather nonsensical English line – or it can be interpreted as
Creole:

Shi look lakah sugar i-na plum
(She looks like sugar in plums/in any plum)

where *lakah* is a conservative Creole word meaning 'like' (in comparison) and *in* swallows the indefinite article to become i-na. The indefinite article is not now needed before *plum* which has become generic
(i.e. plums in general) by means of a Creole rule which reflects a rather
similar rule in many African languages.[8]
    Remodelling of this nature retains 'African' grammar under the guise
of English and 'smuggles' it into places where it is not anticipated:
pronounce the phrase *in a plum* and it is acceptable in an international
'hit'; pronounce it the other way and the 'African' grammar comes to the

[8] Ibo, Yoruba and Mende have similar rules for instance (cf. Welmers, 1971, p. 220).

surface. The linguist's term *Continuum* is too pedestrian and unilinear to capture this order of language dynamics. Such a process means that some more or less disguised features of Creole appear in what the listener (and perhaps the speaker too) would take to be English. One good example would be the tenacious African particle *se* and the rules for its use. It resembles the standard English word *say* and has a similar, though wider, meaning in broad Creole. One of its African uses survives the shift towards English, where it still often is pronounced *se*, does not show tense or the third person -s inflection, and appears not to fit with the English syntax of the sentence:[9]

> And then again you can't say that, you can't go to your friend *say* 'Talk proper English' because you don't even know what proper English really means yourself.
>
> Angela Copeland (Richmond, 1978)
> (Angela, a pupil of Vauxhall Manor school, is discussing her use of and attitudes towards Jamaican Creole, Standard English and Cockney)

A time and place for creole?

Apparently some teachers feel the need to teach their black pupils about appropriateness: the way in which different dialects and registers are acceptable (or not acceptable) in different contexts. Yet black people are well aware of their patterns of language use and have explicit views on what constitutes appropriate choice of dialect. So this would be a topic for discussion in class rather than instruction. This may seem to contradict what has been said earlier about the extreme variability of black language. Briefly there are times when focusing on one dialect or another is called for by the community and times when it is not. I have witnessed long discussions by black children on dialect choice. Despite the complexity of the situation – all the experimentation and the grammatical *double entendres* we have mentioned – there seemed to be some ground-rules commonly agreed upon by the pupils with whom we talked. The following comments from fifteen-year-old girls – Caribbean and British-born – are quite typical:

Q: When you can really speak in a West Indian way, and really speak an English way, how is it that you don't get mixed up? Is there one place where ...

Angela: We can speak English when we're working and talking (in school). But sometimes when we're outside we start talking Jamaican. Or sometimes when a teacher goes mad with us and we ain't done anything we get in a real temper.

Peggy: Waa! Dem still so stupid sometimes. Yeah. For instance a few black of us can't, a few coloured people of us can't stay

[9] Interestingly the same use of 'invariant' *say* survives in urban Black American dialects.

	together in the playground. They think you're goin' round makin' trouble. (...)
Q:	What do you talk at home?
Angela:	English, *pli-en Inglish*.
Peggy:	English ... and sometimes Jamaican.
Q:	Sometimes Jamaican, depends on your mood.
All:	Yeah/yes.
Q:	You say it's when you get angry you talk Jamaican. Any other kind of moods?
Angela:	No.
Peggy:	No.
Q:	Say you're at home. What kind of thing will make you start talking West Indian?
Peggy:	My grandma, when I'm talking to my grandma 'bout school and soma dese teachers.
Q:	And you get more and more West Indian?
Peggy:	'Course!
Q:	You can't just speak it now and again or you wouldn't know it properly. So you must speak it quite a lot. You say your mum and dad don't speak to you like that? (Vehement contradiction from the girls).
Peggy:	When we have company at home, you see? Jesus! You can't ... there's no English word that they say.
Angela:	I've got this uncle. When he comes to our house I always stay downstairs 'cause I want to hear what he's sayin'. When he's speakin' Jamaican, mate, he start drinkin' tea and everything, and they *talk*? Man? They really can talk. They stop all night. All night they got something to talk about. (...)
Angela:	And my big sister says I'm not to speak Jamaican because it's bad: I'll soon get worse and worse.
Q:	You think it's bad?
All:	No.
	'Cause I don't speak it all the time.
	It's your language.
Q:	Who says it's bad? Other Jamaican people say it's bad, don't they?
Angela:	Well the older folks. They don't want us to learn it.
Q:	Why not?
Peggy:	Don't know ... Bad for your education.
Angela:	(laughing) Nat gud fo yu ejikieshan!

These girls' conception of language is diagrammed below in Figure 1. This diagram is misleadingly clear-cut. There is abundant evidence of black children talking freely amongst themselves, and *not* using broad JC or not using any kind of broad Creole at all. Angela (above) recognizes this in her use of the word 'sometimes' in her opening remark. Home certainly does not emerge as the 'Creole-only' zone which perhaps most teachers imagine. To gather information on two

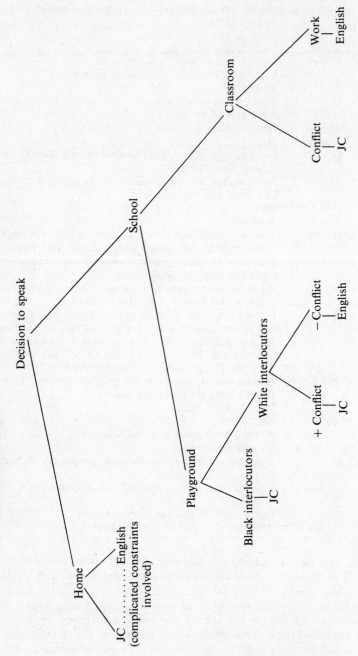

Figure 1 A version of dialect selection in the young black Bedford community at home and at school

domains (playground and home) a questionnaire which could yield quantifiable results was administered. The domains were broken down into four speech settings:

Home
1. To brothers and sisters
2. To parents
3. From parents
Playground
4. To black friends

This may seem rather a naïve procedure, not least because of the different shades of dialect involved. However, the questionnaire took for granted that there was some general consensus in the community over what Creole was and where the cut-off point for Creole was located on the Continuum.[10]

The pattern which emerged from the questionnaire findings was surprisingly clear cut and insistent. The black children whom I questioned thought that they used a low amount of Creole when talking to their brothers and sisters at home, and when talking to their parents. They saw their parents however as using a high amount of Creole to them, so there was an asymmetrical exchange of English and Creole as they envisaged it. The only context in which they thought they used a high amount of Creole was in the playground to black friends. The pattern was similar for both Caribbean-born and British-born, younger (age 8–11) and older (12–16).[11] Nearly all claimed to speak some Creole in at least one context, and over three-quarters claimed to use broad Creole at least sometimes, equivalent to:

mi aks di man fi put mi money iina him packit.
(I asked the man to put my money in his pocket)

The findings were not exactly what we had expected. Why did they see themselves as using comparatively little Creole to their mothers and fathers, in contrast to their high use in the peer group away from home? Was this a distortion of what actually happened? We had one conversation recorded in a Jamaican home which illustrated the reported pattern rather well. In this Patricia K. chose to speak in focused English throughout a conversation with her mother lasting several minutes. All the other recordings of Patricia – several hours of them – show her talking with her black friends in a mixture of dialects with 'purple passages' in broad Creole and practically no focused English at all.

There are two other tapes of talk in West Indian homes available to the writer, one recorded in Bedford, the other recorded by Rosemary Thomas in London. In these the pattern of dialect choice is much more

[10] There seems to be justification for this assumption. See Sutcliffe, 1978.
[11] Surprisingly, in this sample, age did not radically affect the amount *or* the pattern of Creole spoken.

varied, and would repay more study, though in both the broadest Creole is spoken by the mother in her role as organizer and (censorious) parent.

There is practically no literature on Caribbean language use and linguistic culture in Britain. Abrahams's book *Talking Black* (1976) does however describe black American speech behaviour in detail, and sees the Caribbean situation as corresponding in many ways. The inference is that there is an overall design to New World black language and culture, modified by local conditions. He states that it is widely accepted amongst black Americans that home is a place for less flamboyant behaviour where speech is moderated, and silence is valued, especially around 'momma'. If the same is true for Jamaica and its British outposts, the questionnaire finding that a limited amount of Creole was reportedly used by children to their parents could then be explained as a form of deference. After all, in parts of the Caribbean, to 'mek noise' is to speak in Creole.

In that case why are parents seen as using a high amount of Creole in the home? The answer again could lie in the style of parental control described in *Talking Black* (Abrahams, 1976) where the alternately sweet- and tough-talking momma is seen to control those around her by adroit use of language. Here, *tough* means, among other things, vividly non-standard.

> The essence of this negotiation (of role as a respected mother figure) lies in a woman being both sweet and tough depending upon her capacity to define and reasonably manipulate the situation. Ideally she has the ability to *talk sweet* with her peers, but *talk tough* or *cold* with anyone who might threaten her self-image. (p. 63)

This evidence is American, admittedly, but the same figure of a tough-talking, powerful mother emerges from two of the three British home recordings mentioned above, and emerges perhaps even more clearly from Jennifer's portrayal of Mum in *Brixton Blues*. From this (and other) data we can piece together a picture of language use, simplified, but recognizable to most black people. Broad Creole is, or was, the natural language of many Jamaicans but for the majority it is part of a 'co-structure', as Bailey calls it, of English and Creole interwoven. The interplay of English and Creole prefigures the never-ending debate between 'African' and European values in Caribbean life. We can also now say that a move towards English may mean deference or respect ('manners' as West Indians term it). Creole may be used by superiors in age or status as a means of control; amongst equals it tends to indicate very relaxed in-group behaviour, and used to superiors it may mean defiance. This kind of demarcation of Creole may be found even amongst brothers and sisters within the family, whereby one can speak in Creole to anyone younger but expect to be answered in (near)

English.[12] Audrey's comment below supports this, in so far as she describes the use of Creole for control of what is probably a younger sister:

> When I speak to my sister in a proper English voice and tell her to behave it don't seem to do much good but if I raise my voice in a Jamaican accent it certainly does wonders.

Audrey in Richmond 1978

Such a schematization does not however allow for dropping into Creole when chatting with Grandmother, when quoting someone else, or when identifying with mother or father in a family dispute.[13] Nor does it explain why English, perhaps tinged with Creole, seems to be much used by the young people I have recorded in peer group conversations.

Education, language, and Caribbean culture

Clearly it must be an advantage for the teacher to know more about Caribbean language and culture, not least because it should bring him/her closer to what are often alienated and dispirited pupils. But is there a way in which such knowledge can directly affect the organization or content of the curriculum? More specifically, can we begin to answer the thorny question of how to enable black children to transfer to school work language ability developed in other social milieux? Part of this problem is caused by a direct clash in straight grammatical terms between the required Standard English of written school work and the dialects of black speech. While teachers, examiners and employers continue to believe that there is only one 'proper' English, red ink will continue to disfigure much written work. Viv Edwards has also shown that interference from Creole may be causing subtle oral and reading comprehension problems for some (V. Edwards, 1979). Aside from this it is also clear enough that black language, not just as a grammatical system but as a carrier of social values and identity, may clash with language in this larger sense in school. The work of both Torrey and Labov emphasizes that American schools tend

(1) to undervalue black dialect, characterizing it as 'sloppy' or 'illogical';
(2) to be incapable of valuing the ongoing concerns and values embedded in the vernacular of lower-class black students.

Taking up the second point it is equally clear that certain well-developed styles of British black street talk would be judged by many teachers as highly inappropriate to the classroom. The following is a

[12] I am indebted to Mr Delroy Salmon of Bedford's Language and Resources Centre, and himself a Jamaican, for confirmation of this as a common pattern, in his experience.

[13] Where use of Creole to 'superiors' would certainly *not* indicate defiance.

short example from a heated peer-group conversation between two twelve-year-old boys:[14]

> *Peter* (shouting): shet up Monkey, wha' Nigo then, Breh
>   Monkey
> *Roy:*   you shu' up. Fox, Breh Fox (laughter)
> *Peter:*   Pigstripe (...) the Dulash (Girls' nickname)
>   wi-wi on his foot.
> *Roy:*   wha' bout you, you   need a kick in you backside.
>   You need some good lash. At that time you will
>   get licks in you skin, you see? When the Dula
>   come she give you púm-púm.

Similarly, many black pupils would regard such language as inappropriate to the classroom. However I believe we have to look for a more fundamental mismatch between school and background culture than that represented by the opposition between school language and peer group language, taboo words and all. There is a whole range of varied speech styles developed by black children in the peer group *and* elsewhere. Many black children, perhaps more girls than boys, prefer to extend their verbal talents in other directions than – or in addition to – what one black girl called 'Jamaican swearing'. Some of these typically are attracted to the thoughtful reasoning of Rastafarianism. Others become regular church-goers. In either case they are involved in milieux where 'cooler', more predictable behaviour is cultivated, and oracy, literacy and study encouraged. It seems reasonable that young blacks with these affiliations should be more motivated and successful in school. What also seems very likely, unfortunately, is that they still 'operate optimally' in the black rather than the (white-dominated) school situation. They may well be more fluent speakers, debaters, reasoners and even writers in the Rastafarian or black church settings.

Certain researchers, with a practical commitment to improving the lot of minority pupils, have pointed to cultural mismatch as an insidious source of educational failure. Barre Toelken, who has worked on the problems of American Indians in higher education (Toelken, 1975), describes how fundamentally their world-view can differ from that of Anglo-Americans. Indians see time quite differently, almost akin to space 'with the individual in it, rather than with the individual on a ribbon of it'. They tend to conceptualize in terms of the circle – whereas Caucasians tend to think in terms of lines and grids, imposing order on nature in this way. The white concern with individuality, competition and 'amounting to something' is also alien to Indians, who tend to think rather in terms of adjusting. Toelken recognized that such basic differences in outlook compounded the problems which Indian students experienced at the university where he taught – almost all of

[14] This and the transcript of Martin G. (below) are from the Bedford Survey – the research basis for Sutcliffe (1978).

them dropped out after their first term. Accordingly, after consultation with the students, he and his colleagues started a special course in freshman composition for Indians only. The class convened on 'Indian time', that is, when everyone was ready. Topics which the students found puzzling or alien were dropped and everyone sat round in a circle. This arrangement generated a great deal of talk and work. Attendance remained at nearly 100 per cent – except for an interlude when a classroom with grid-pattern seating had to be used, which caused a drastic, temporary fall-off in numbers. It is worth quoting Toelken's observations at some length:

> The particular directions and precautions taken in the case of this class are ... patently the sorts of concerns which might well be applied to any ethnic group, including the whites. Especially today when many youths of all cultural backgrounds are speaking out on behalf of interaction, negotiation, ecology, and ethnic awareness, when many educators are trying to rid the school of meaningless grid patterns, it is no accident, it seems to me, that the circle rather than the line or grid can be seen as a viable conceptual pattern for today – that 'straight' is a negative term while 'groovy' (as with a circular phonograph record?) is a positive one. Nonetheless, it is still in the schools that we continue to impose physical order by the use of a grid system. (p. 282).

'Straight' and 'groovy' have both been adopted from Black American slang – again no accident. Commentators have noted the strong *dynamic* element in black slang in America, and we have repeatedly used the word *dynamic* to characterize Caribbean language and culture. Rhythm, movement, debate, 'interaction' and performance pervade Caribbean life styles, but these are elements which are inhibited in the classroom, particularly in the secondary school with their stress on solitary written work. It seems that there is at this point a dysfunctional clash which must affect virtually all pupils of Caribbean origin, no matter how well motivated. For the last part of this paper let us concentrate on just two of these cultural elements, *interaction* and *performance*, since they underpin the others. Performance as we shall use the term refers to a speaker's (or singer's) ability to hold the listeners' attention and be positively evaluated by his audience not only for what was said, but how well it was said. As such it is the application of the theatrical sense to everyday language use. In black communities this cultural trait of performance runs very strong.

Interaction

Many cultivated black speech styles require some kind of continuing interaction between speakers and listeners. Quite often the effect seems chaotic to European ears. Abrahams (1975) describes the communication pattern on St Vincent in the Caribbean as:

dominated by an overlap of voices and other 'presence' indicators; this overlap signals a kind of interlock between the participants as active members of the performance. Each person in the performance environment is part of – and yet playing apart from – the focal interaction. The result is richly textured, vibrating interchange, but one which might be regarded as noisy and chaotic by Western norms.

Our sample of excited speech from Roy and Peter on page 128 shows exactly this kind of noisy voice overlap. This is 'mekin noise'. There are many degrees and varieties of West Indian group interaction, however, and not all seem as chaotic. Interactive behaviour is not necessarily *rude* either (the community's term for deliberately disruptive behaviour). Vibrant interaction is an essential feature of black church services – settings for social and academic learning which ought to be given careful consideration. Often, however, there is a competitive element which may be more, or less, mock aggressive. Most importantly, in the kind of culturally typical interaction being discussed, there is often a feeling of striving after some kind of excellence, of carrying off a good performance as a group, in or of a group. The following example is a transcript of a recorded joking session between two ten-year-olds – one from an Eastern Caribbean family, the other from a black American one. This becomes a competitive interactive performance, a scarcely disguised verbal duel. The distinctive use of what might be termed 'Black Voice' is striking. This is the use of the voice in an attention-holding way, with (amongst other characteristics) an increased tonal range, increased volume, and a skilful avoidance of hesitation and stumbling:

Gregory: Hey, Simon look, I heard something about you, you know. When you was two years old. I heard that, when you was small, that if you put a piece of cheese on the floor, near to your big toe, a rat would come and eat the piece of cheese and your big toe with you.
You know that?

Simon: uh-uh.

Gregory: I heard that from your mother.
I heard that when you was sitting on your bed, one day when your mum came inside the room with your bottle, you were so overjoyed that you fell off the bed.

Simon: One day, um, I heard from my sister, when she was riding down Clarendon Street that you....er....you.... walking along the road when you were two years old and you had very, very bony legs. And with all your bony legs there was this dog come along and he chases for all your bony legs. I remember that.

Gregory: Now you listen to me, mate. I don't find that funny. What about when you came out this taxi when you was about seven years old? Yeah, you're sorta you're sorta rich, and you drop about all your coppers on the floor. And now, there was this boxer dog, following all your coppers along the floor, and he come and see you, with a hole in your trousers, and he got hold of your thing and bite it off.

Simon: Rubbish! I remember you, when you were walking along the road, and you were trying to get into the park, and you were smashing down the gate. And then when the man comes he say 'It's open, sonny, you can walk in.' Remember? You were so embarrassed, that instead of walking in the park, you walked home again, remember?

Certain teachers have already seen the possibilities of performance-orientated and interactive black speech and found ways of using it in school work – Steve Hoyle, for instance, teaching at Santley Primary School, Brixton. Initially his approach was to highlight Jamaican Creole and the 'roots' background culture with, for instance, the production of a Natty Dread ABC colouring book featuring words such as mumma (mummy) mash up (destroy) and magga (skinny). Encouraged by the freedom to use highly distinctive vernacular language and idiom, his pupils (mostly black) have written poems and stories for the magazine produced at the school, the *Santley Lookout*. Much of the success of Steve Hoyle's approach, however, comes from the way in which the performance features of black language have been capitalized upon. He has encouraged his pupils to use playground rhymes and jokes, verbal duelling and improvization on black music (dubbing and toasting) as the basis for oral and written classwork.

A good example of oral improvization: after hearing the line 'Me seh she come from Jamaica and she daddy is a baker' from a song by Dennis Alcapone, a group of children developed this rhyming:

Me seh she come from Guyana
And she nyam off [ate up] banana

Me seh she come from Jamaica
And she daddy was a baker

Me seh she come from Spain
And it never, never rain.

Me seh she come from the Congo
And she play upon the Bongo

Me seh she come from France
When dem happy dem a prance

Me seh she come from Jamaica
And she daddy was a baker

(V. K. Edwards 1980)

Certain teachers in London who have been working along these lines with black children, are associated with the Language in Inner City Schools movement, a very fruitful collaboration between teachers and the English department of the London Institute of Education. For example the West Indian writing group has been looking at relationships between black pupils' speech and writing. A list of publications of the work done by this and other groups within the movement is given at the close of this paper.

It is perhaps role-play and drama above all which allow pupils of Caribbean origin to give free rein to joyous interactive noise which can then be as 'rowdy-rowdy' or emotion-charged as they like without the teacher feeling threatened or the pupils feeling that they are being disrespectful. This in itself goes a long way to explaining the exuberant (but effective) talents of young black actresses such as Jennifer. Acting perhaps comes easily to those black children who are fluent users of black speech styles, because they enjoy performing with words – and playing the part of someone else in the black community involves taking on that person's repertoire of socially recognized speech performances. It becomes relatively easy to take on, for example, *Mum's* roles as tough-talking parent, sweet-talking friend, outraged woman scorned, effusive church-goer, and so on.

Drama of this kind is so successful in tapping community-developed talents with language that many teachers – and many black pupils and parents too, for that matter – dismiss it as 'not really school work'. Child X cannot do schoolwork, Child X *can* do Y, therefore Y is not proper school work – that is the implied syllogism. This is where we need to re-examine our conception of language development, and to arrive at a new working definition, wide enough to be applicable cross-culturally and yet retaining its discriminatory power. Armed with this we can counter with a syllogism of our own: Language development forms a central part of school work, Y is an example of language being developed, therefore Y is school work.

Oral narrative performance

We have already hinted at a *hot* versus *cool* dimension to West Indian speech. Let us now look at narrative, a genre which is generally *cool*, that is it requires little participation from the 'audience', little interaction, heated or otherwise, but which is still a performance since it *does* require a degree of 'artfulness' to be effective, and this is evaluated more or less consciously by the listeners. Clearly oral narrative could fairly easily be introduced into school work to take its place alongside written narrative which forms quite an important element in the curriculum. Despite the fact that oral narrative is a production in time with the speaker 'thinking on his feet', the end product may differ only fairly subtly from written narrative on the same subject – and as we shall see speakers as well as writers take the opportunity of polishing and improving style. I take it that written narrative forms part of work in English because:

1. It assists writer to 'structure' his world – to make sense of it and celebrate it.
2. It is (therefore?) entertaining and satisfying to writer and reader.
3. It encourages effective use of words – language development if you will – including effective construction of discourse so that sentences fall coherently into place.
4. It is a practical exercise in the mechanics of literacy: handwriting, punctuation, spelling and paragraphing.

Many children signally fail to produce coherent written narratives:

A boat race
Chapter 1
It was a cold day and the sky was a dull colour with specks of blue. I was staying in an English hotel in the south near Portsmouth. I was getting prepared for a race in sailing boats. It was to be a ten-mile race for amateurs. I certainly wasn't an expert at handling boats. I was going with a friend for fun. We were entering just because we wanted to, not because of winning.

We had the sailing boat on hire for seven hours so before the race, with an hour to spare, we spent testing the boat out. We checked our clothes and provisions. The race was to start at two o'clock in the afternoon.

We stocked up with food and drinks. Our clothes needed to be warm and if possible waterproof, if they weren't then we would need a mack that would cover us completely.

Incoherence or awkwardness is not easy to remedy: it is often difficult to show exactly what is wrong, and that aside, improvement will mean messy deletions. More probably the teacher's red ink will be the only correction made. Speech may actually be a better channel for rehearsal and reordering of a story, since evaluation is immediate, with no need for a waste-paper basket. Let us look at the orally-produced narrative of a Jamaican boy whose written work would be much *more* unacceptable than the example above:

The Aunty Katie a transcript of a tape.
(. . . .)
I fix the chokey [*trap*], man.
and me sit-down
and me sit-down underneath the tree
and I set a lot of chokey on the tree-dem ... apple tree and mango tree
and all those lot
and sit down
and I walk come go look lime
and pick coconuts

and drink jelly ... water
and when I come down back I see a big Aunty Katie [Golden Oriole]
    into the tangerine tree
and me take me time come down out the coconut tree
me never let the coconut drop
me pick it up
me hold it in me hand
and a-come down slide out the tree
and when me come down and go, me put-down the coconut
and me see the bird neck in the thing you know
and me draw i
when me draw the bird I tie the string onto the other piece of limb down
    at the bottom
and then me go up there
and me catch the bird
but the bird didn't dead
the bird pick me on my hand
But me didn't let it go
Me run home quick a-shout out
'Heeey! I catch a bird
I catch a bird!
I catch a Aunty Katie, Aunty Katie'. (*Martin G.* 1974)

This *communicates* (despite the dialect). We feel we are there in the world created by the storyteller. There is no incoherence; instead we have the measured unfolding of a story leading to a climax. Note the deliberate slowing of the action from the sighting of the big Aunty Katie to the drawing of the string. Repetition here is part of the speaker's matured style – not verbal fidgeting – and this is true even of all the *and*s which would be anathema in Standard English writing. The reason for Martin's success is that he has already, probably, told the story to other listeners, or at any rate had opportunity to tell similar stories and develop his style. Also he has an immediate audience – in the case three young friends, one researcher and a tape-recorder.

Before leaving oral narrative let us make mention of what might be called a 'hotter' form of the genre, the sort of high-flown narrative style similar to black American 'rapping'. Angela D. recorded a sample in 1974: the dramatic account of a fight which took place after school. It was a highly rhetorical piece, fluently delivered to a group of friends. Its fluency derived from the use of occasional formulaic 'fillers' such as 'mek mi tell yu' (let me tell you) and a trick of parallel phrasing, which provided emphasis and maintained the flow of words:

Mek mi tell yu one time: Dem start a-fight yu see?
One piece a fight....

They started to roll pan a ground yu know. Roll!
Let mi tell yu when they roll they really roll!...

Four years later I went to see Angela, now aged nineteen, and asked her to repeat the performance. The resulting narrative this time was much longer and correspondingly looser in construction, less rhetorical, but still possessing impact:

> Mi reach inside school and one teacher come up and grab mi by di shoulder and tell mi: *Get over deh!* I seh: look 'pon him, mi seh: look 'pon him. Mi walk over by di wall where everybody was standin'. And mi look and mi notice all dese people dat was at di fight. And mi seh: what is dis dough? And den mi seh to mi friend: Wha gwine on yah? Wha gwine on? Wha' yu standin' up here for? And shi seh *ssh!* And next minute, big headmaster come. Him big yu see, big and stiff! And he ordered us out into his office: ALL A UNU GET INTO DI OFFICE!'

Angela explained that this later style arose in conversation with groups of friends, in college common-rooms for instance. It is easy to see how either style could be developed into the entertaining short stories of a dialect writer like Jennifer Johnson. This extract from Jennifer Johnson's *Ballad For You* tells how the four 'heroines' of the tale make their presence felt at a party:

> Well it so happened dat one a di gal ina di college a have party pan di satdey nite an' she invite di gal dem. From di time dem hear 'bout party, dem all a plan whey dem a goh wear, because is nothing but pure style a goh cut dah nite deh.
>
> Well di satdey nite come an' is one piece a t'ing gwaan. Man, you shoulda did dey deh fi see it, but seen as you wasn't, I a goh tell you 'bout it. Lightening, Chalice, Charlie an' Granny Roach arrive 'bout twelve o'clock an', as dem step all di man dem ina di room lef' whey dem a dhu fi come eyes dem up an' fuss roun' dem, like fly roun's ..., because when dem gal dress, dem sharp. Is not'ing but suit an' tips wid gold dis an' gold dat.
>
> Well di addah gal dem nevah like it but dem nevah seh not'ing. But one certain set start pass remark an' a stare pan dem. Now Granny Roach noh like anybody look pan she. Soh she stop dance an' look ina one a di gal dem eye. Di gal look whey an' Granny start dance agen.
>
> Nex' t'ing she feel eye pan she agen; soh dis time she spin roun', lif' up she skirt an' ask di gal if she see enough yet. Di gal shame soh till she turn she back an' start talk. Same time in bounce Squeakey ina she swade pants suit. Man, she look hot an' all eyes deh pan she. Di addah gal dem all bundle roun' she fi fill her in pan di situation. She smile an' pap two move. (...)
>
> Jennifer Johnson (1978)

Version in standard English:
Well it so happened that one of the girls in the college was having a party on the Saturday night and she invited the four girls. As soon as they heard about a party they were planning what they were going to wear, because on that night they were going to cut nothing but style (i.e. they were going to show off their high-living style).

Well the Saturday night came and things really happened! You should have been there to see it, but as you were not I shall tell you about it. Lightening, Chalice, Charlie and Granny Roach (cockroach) arrived at about twelve o'clock, and, as they stepped in, all the men in the room left what they were doing to come and give them the eye and fuss round them like flies round s... because when these girls are dressed up they are sharp! There is nothing but suits and (gold) tips with gold this and gold that.

Well the other girls did not like it but they did not say anything. But one group started to pass remarks and stare at them. Now Granny Roach does not like anybody to look at her. So she stopped dancing and looked one of the girls in the eye. The girl looked away and granny started to dance again. The next moment she felt eyes on her again; so she spun round, lifted up her skirt and asked the girl if she had seen enough yet. The girl was made to look so ridiculous that she turned back and resumed talking. At this moment in bounced Squeakey in her suede trouser suit. She really looked hot and all eyes were on her.

The other girls bunched round her to fill her in on the situation. She smiled and performed two movements (i.e. began to dance) ...

From oral to written narrative in school

Such narrative writing – and indeed any style of written work with a distinctively black flavour – could be cultivated in school, once certain conditions were met:

1. The connection between oral and written work would need to be developed.
2. School and pupil would need to understand why such work was being done, going beyond the poignantly obvious reasons already given for accepting the strengths of the vernacular. We have already listed several reasons for 'ordinary' written narrative in school. These are equally applicable to any narrative writing which draws more directly on a pupil's vernacular.
3. Teachers would have to be willing to re-examine their attitudes. We have already touched on the need to arrive at an understanding of progress in language regardless of its non-standardness.

It would be quite wrong to believe that by introducing distinctively black styles of writing into the classroom teachers would be going for a 'soft option' in which standards and progress became irrelevant. As we shall see from the following example this is a quite unrealistic view, even if we are considering only the business of mastering the mechanics of literacy. Viv Edwards (1980) provides an instance of the spoken narrative style of a black speaker in Britain being transferred to written work. Jenny, of Bajan descent, told a humorous story of her new neighbours and also made a written account. The results underline the possibilities and certain difficulties:

The New People Next Door – Oral version
It was Saturday morning and Hilda come and knock on our back door.
  'Morning, Mrs Small', she said.
  'Morning, Hilda', said my mum.
  'Anyway, I see you've got some snobby neighbours next door.'
  'How do you know?' said my mum.
  'Oh, I just been looking through my curtains', said Hilda.
  'You always looking through your curtains', said my mum. 'Anyway, they're still out there?' said my mum.
  'Oh, yes,' said Hilda.
  We went outside to meet our snobby neighbours.
  'Oh mind my furniture', said the woman.
  'Mind my goldfish', said the man.
  'Mummy, mummy, mummy that boy pull my ponytail!'
  'Naughty little boy!.... I told you let's go to America. But no, you insist let's go to Reading. "Nice people round here", you said, "nice fashion people. Oh, they so lovely!" But now we surrounded by this scruffy lot and unkind.'
  'How dare you call us scruffy lot! We nice people round here. We are nice and good people round here. What are you talking about? You the unkind and scruffy lot. You come round here making trouble about our street.'
  'Alfred, do something!'
  'Yes, don't insult my wife!'
  'Is that all you have to say? Is that all you have to say?'
  'Now I'm going. I'm not going to stand here to be insulted by this woman. Come on Sally, let's go.'
  Me and my mum and Hilda we went inside and we laughed about that the whole day.

In one sense the written account, reproduced in facsimile on the following pages, is a failure. But this is the case only if we (a) regard it as an end product (b) score it or judge it in the traditional way, arriving at a global mark that merges points for technical merit (spelling and punctuation) with points for style and content. On such a marking procedure it is doubtful whether Jenny would be left with any marks out of 20 at all, since she makes some 95 technical errors in this fairly short piece. Even if the teacher does not put '4/20 very careless' at the end of the work she might form an impression of a pupil with too many problems ever to be very successful at school. Jenny was in the remedial stream of her school at the time she wrote the piece, at the age of thirteen. If however, we remove the 'noise' from the communication, by correcting spelling and punctuation, and altering the few non-Standard features in the piece which are not part of the dialogue, we are left with a very different impression, one which is conveyed by the language itself:

  It was Saturday morning. Nosy old Hilda knocked on our back door.
  'Morning Mrs Small. How are you today?'

The new people next door

I was Saturday morning. Nosy old hilda knok on our back door. "Morning Mrs. small. how are you today" "alright" said my mum. "by the way I see you have new neighbor" "how do you now" said my mum. "I was happen to be looking through the curtains."

"you are always looking through the curtains" say my mum. "They look a snooty looking lot" said hilda. "are they sit their" said my mum. their yes said hilda. we went out to see them. "they do look rather snoty" said my mum. "I told you so" said hilda. "mind my tumter" said the lady. "mind my Gold fish said the man by the lady." my best was said they broke my little out he pulled my bone fall.

"mummy, mummy"

Part 2

" naughty little " . said the woman. " I told " " I told " you
more than I time we should Gone to America for our
holiday O no he said ' O no let go to Let go to
reading .. reading and here we are surrounded by scruffy
people " " no! " " how, dear she " said " hilda " " how dear she "
" how, dear you call us scruff " " but but " . no but's from you,
no horriable selfish ungratefull unkind woman ". Said hilda
" how dear you call me a unkind, horriable woman you
should not had said that " " " don't stand they Alfred and
let this woman call me name. " yes " don't called her name "
" is that all that you can say? well I an leaveing; come a
long sally ". my mum hilda and I laughed ^ the hole day.

'All right' said my mum.

'By the way, I see you have new neighbour.'

'How do you know?' said my mum.

'I was happen to be looking through the curtains.'

'You are always looking through the curtains' said my mum.

'They look a snobby-looking lot' said Hilda.

'Are they (still) there?' said my mum.

'Yes' said Hilda.

We went out to see them.

'They do look rather snobby' said my mum.

'I told you so' said Hilda.

'Mind my furniture' said the lady.

'Mind my goldfish' said the man.

'Try to don't broke my best vase' said the lady.

'Mummy, mummy,' said the little girl, 'he pulled my pony tail.'

'Naughty little ...' said the woman, I told you more than one time we should gone to America for our holiday. "Oh no" he said "oh no. Let's go to Reading." And here we are surrounded by scruffy people!'

'No!'

'How dare she?' said Hilda, 'how dare she? How dare you call us scruffy!'

'But, but ...!'

'No buts from you, you horrible, selfish, ungrateful, unkind woman!' said Hilda.

'How dare you call me a unkind, horrible woman? You should not had said that! Don't stand there Alfred and let this woman call me name.'

'Yes, don't called her name.'

'Is that all you can say? Well I am leaving. Come along Sally.'

My mum, Hilda and I, we laughed the whole day.

An analysis of the 'noise' (or errors, miscues and confusions) in Jenny's written piece is itself revealing of the way first impressions can be wrong and indicative of the need to separate out the various areas of difficulty such a learner.

Dialect features

There are just two non-standard features which occur outside the reported speech

knock (SE knocked) line 1
say   (SE said)   line 7

The major part of the piece is taken up by dialogue – where most teachers would allow at least a sparing indication of dialect. Note the following forms, occurring in the dialogue, which could confirm a Standard English speaker's view that West Indian language is often just a 'word salad':

try to don't broke my vase.' line 16

This is a perfectly legitimate Bajan construction. The broad Jamaican form will be: 'try fi no broke mi vase'. Actually in Jamaican as well as Bajan *don'* can be used as a negative before any tense (or person) of the verb. Compare the use of 'no' in Italian and Spanish. And *broke* interestingly is not a past tense in West Indian Creoles. It is one of a small set of verbs where the stem of the Creole verb derives from the English past tense. Other such verbs include 'lef' (leave, cf. *Ballad For You* on page 135) and 'los' (to lose). The verb 'full' (to fill, be full) is obviously connected.

We should gone to America. line 19

Again this is a legitimate construction in many if not all (English-based) West Indian Creoles. *Gone* is probably to be included in the above mentioned set of verbs: it is the stem form/infinitive form and means 'be gone' 'have gone'.

don't called her name. line 28
should not had said that. line 26–7

These are rather more ad hoc results of the meeting of Creole with English. The former is a hypercorrection – a case where a speaker or writer adopts a feature from the target dialect, but uses it incorrectly through lack of precise knowledge of its distribution, or through imprecision under pressure. The feature here is of course the Standard English -ed ending. The latter example is an (unusual?) blend of Standard English 'shouldn't have said that' and Bajan/Jamaican vernacular 'shouldn't did say that'./shudn did se dat/

Removing dialect features from standard

John Richmond (in Sutcliffe, forthcoming) suggests that most black pupils want and need the ability to produce invariantly Standard English for some purposes (examinations, for instance). But he argues that it is necessary to wait until such pupils reach a certain stage of their development, perhaps during the third or fourth year of their secondary education, before consciously working on this. Neither Richmond nor I would wish to underestimate the enormous importance of the acquisition of Standard English for success in examinations, for obtaining white-collar employment, and for keying into mainstream culture. The argument still stands that it is both ideologically desirable and pragmatically essential[15] to accept the language of the child. The act of abstraction involved in separating Standard English as a system from the whole range of dialect forms available to a black speaker, is a difficult task, (of a sort which few teachers are required to under-

[15] This phrase, a neat summing of two complementary issues, is taken from Richmond.

take) and it seems that the steady drip drip of red ink on 'grammar' mistakes throughout a child's schooling practically never has the desired effect. Adolescents who are becoming sharply more aware of the two different worlds they live in, and the possibility of polarizing their dialects to express this, are probably in the best position to perform the abstraction, but only provided that they are secure and well-motivated learners.

This proviso in turn depends on their past school experience, and their expectations of acceptance by mainstream British society.

I have already mentioned the black writer/speaker's sense of appropriate dialect shift. It is significant that although Jenny uses non-standard forms in her written narrative, her spoken version is markedly more non-standard, as shown in Table 6.1.

Table 6.1

		Standard	Non-Standard	%	Hyper-correction
Simple past tense inflection	written	19	2	9.5	2
	oral	14	4	22.8	0
Other grammatical features	written		6		2
	oral		12		0

Spelling and punctuation

The enormous number of mistakes in punctuation and spelling in the written account are quite enough to daunt pupil and teacher alike, provoking a flood of red ink. Paradoxically it is a hopeful sign that Jenny could have corrected most of the mistakes herself – that is, they could be labelled 'careless'.

She demonstrates that she knows how to use speech marks and does not put them in the wrong places, though she quite frequently opens them without closing them, or vice versa, or even misses them out altogether. She shows that she knows what a sentence is, and indicates this with full stops or capital letters, or by closing or opening speech marks – though seldom combines all these operations appropriately. In this way she indicates the end of a sentence correctly in 88 per cent of necessary cases, only twice wrongly indicating the end of a sentence. It would be too glib to dismiss Jenny's inconsistent use of these punctuation conventions as slipshod. Many people learning to write a foreign language find it taxing to remember to insert all the inflections for number, gender and perhaps case, slot unfamiliar vocabulary into the language's syntax, and spell properly, all in one combined operation. These concerted demands, coming at once, tend to overwhelm the student so that mistakes can only be avoided by going over the exercise painstakingly, more than once. Jenny is *not* writing a foreign language, and she may or may not be worried about dialect differences. She is, however, trying to carry through a use of language which is creative or recreative of actual experience, and typically oral in origin, but yet at the same time coordinate the different technical skills of writing which she has only just mastered (punctuation) or is still in the process of learning (spelling). The creative input (the narrative style) is outrunning the technical capacity. Rather than stem the flow it would obviously be better to encourage such writers to go back over their work afterwards. Briefly, a closer look at Jenny's spelling mistakes suggests that she has already learnt a great deal. She is capable of spelling the core words of English correctly as well as outrageously unphonetic words such as 'neighbour' and 'naughty' (but not *vase*, where her attempt 'vas' hints at the influence of Bajan pronunciation.) She remembers double consonants throughout, except in 'snobby' (but retains double 'l' in -full in her attempt at 'grateful'). The evidence here suggests that she is on the road to becoming a good speller despite some trouble with homophones – in Standard English, in Bajan, or both:

dare/dear
they/their/there

Together with the other errors and unintentional dialect forms however, there is a distinct danger that the spelling mistakes will contribute to the teacher's impression of failure. As Viv Edwards writes:

> It is easy to imagine how the poor presentation and technical weaknesses of this work could result in its very real strengths being overlooked, particularly with other essays to mark at the end of the day. (V. K. Edwards, 1980)

End note

The possibilities for fostering the language skills of black children in education have only been touched upon in this paper. It seems to the writer that teachers should seek to set up more opportunities for performance and interaction for black children in school, and to that end look carefully at the community's settings for language development and associated styles of learning – perhaps giving special attention to narration, Rastafarian reasoning and black church worship – not least to clarify our notion of what language development really is.

However, none of this work can be carried out effectively without quite a radical change of attitude in the majority of schools. Secondary schools tend to have what amounts to an overt policy that when language is the subject, the language is Standard English.

Primary schools tend to have a more child-centred approach, but here too, prejudicial attitudes to language can be educationally disabling, because individual teachers 'know' which pupils are going to succeed, in the long run, by the culturally dictated way in which children talk and act. It is recognized just how difficult it would actually be for schools to change their traditional orientation so that, at least in the earlier years, non-standard speech and speech styles might be accepted alongside standard as distinct but parallel, holding similar potential for development. This difficulty has to be weighed against the continuing failure of schools to engage successfully with the language, lives and cultures of non-standard speaking pupils, black or white.

Here again, we need to rework our understanding of language development, so that proficiency with language is not equated with proficiency in Standard English alone.

Without such an understanding, whatever piecemeal efforts are made to accommodate black dialect and speech styles into school, the school will not be able to meet the needs of the vernacular-speaking West Indian child. This understanding is something which schools will have to hammer out as a new policy for themselves – perhaps in conjunction with universities and colleges – and it will not be easy. But, whether we talk about language work *per se*, literacy, creative work, or work across the curriculum, language is the key to education, and as an African proverb has it:

The key that opens is also the key that locks.

References

ABRAHAMS, R. 1972: The training of the man of words in talking sweet. *Language in Society* **1**, 15–29.

—1976: *Talking Black*. New York: Newbury House.

BAILEY, B. L. 1966: *Jamaican creole syntax*. London: Cambridge University Press.

CASHMORE E. 1979: *The Rastafarian Movement in England*. London: Allen & Unwin.

CASSIDY, F. 1961: *Jamaica Talk*. London: Macmillan.

CHRISTIE, P. 1979: *Assertive 'No' in Jamaican Creole*. Occasional paper 10, St Augustine: Society for Caribbean linguistics.

COARD, B. 1971: *How the West Indian Child is Made Educationally Sub-normal in the British School System*: London: New Beacon Books.

EDWARDS, J. 1979: *Language and Disadvantage*. London: Edward Arnold.

EDWARDS, V. K. 1980: *West Indian Verbal Skills*. London: Commission for Racial Equality and Routledge & Kegan Paul.

ESSEN, J. and GHODSIAN, M. 1979: The children of immigrants: school performance. *New Community* 7 (3), 422–9.

EWEN, E., GIPPS, C. and SUMNER, R. 1973: *Language proficiency in the Multi-Racial Junior School*. Windsor: NFER.

HOLM, J. 1978. *The Creole English of Nicaragua's Miskito Coast, its sociolinguistic history and a comparative study of its lexicon and syntax*. Unpublished PhD thesis, University College, London.

LITTLE, A. 1975: Educational achievement of ethnic minority children. In G. K. Verma and C. Bagley (eds.) *Race and Education across Cultures*. London: Heinemann.

REDBRIDGE 1978: *Cause for Concern: West Indian Pupils in Redbridge*. Redbridge: Black People's Progressive Association. Redbridge Community Relations Council.

RICHMOND, J. 1978: *Dialect*. ILEA, London English Centre.*

—1979: Jennifer and 'Brixton Blues'; language alive in school, *in Supplementary Reading for Block 5*, PE232 Language Development. Milton Keynes: Open University Press.

—(forthcoming) Recognizing and using dialect in the classroom. In D. Sutcliffe, *British Black English*. Oxford: Basil Blackwell.

SUTCLIFFE, D. 1978: *The Language of First and Second Generation West Indian Children in Bedfordshire*. Unpublished M.Ed. thesis, Leicester.

—(forthcoming) *British Black English*. Oxford: Basil Blackwell.

TODD, L. 1974: *Pidgins and Creoles*. London: Routledge & Kegan Paul.

TOELKEN, B. 1975: Folklore, worldview and communication. In Ben-Amos and Goldstein (eds.) *Folklore, Performance and Communication*.

WALKERDINE, V. 1974: *West Indian Children in Schools*. Research report, University of Bristol (School of Education Research Unit).

WELMERS, T. 1971: *African Language Structures*. Berkeley: University of California Press.

Language and inner city schools: a reading list

BOOTH, R. 1978: *Talking and Working. A comparison of the efficacy of two learning methods in fifth year commerce*. Looking at language at Vauxhall Manor School No. 4. ILEA: English Centre.*

BOOTH, R. 1979: The effect of the Situation on the Language Production of Working-Class Children. *Looking at language at Vauxhall Manor School, No. 6*. ILEA: English Centre.*

MCLEOD, A. (forthcoming) *Writing, Dialect and Linguistic Awareness*. Available from the English Dept., University of London Institute of Education.

SAVVA, H. 1979: Reading Development in a Fifth-Form Girl. *Looking at language at Vauxhall Manor School No. 7.* ILEA: English Centre.*

RICHMOND, J. and MCLEOD, A. 1980: Art and craft of writing. In *English Magazine*, No. 6. ILEA: English Centre.

RICHMOND, J. 1979: Progress in Pat's Writing. *Looking at language at Vauxhall Manor School, No. 7.* (Produced in association with the West Indian Writing group at the University of London Institute of Education). ILEA: English Centre.*

ROSEN, H. and BURGESS, A. 1980: *Languages and Dialects of London School Children: an Investigation.* London: Ward Lock.

*Obtainable from Stephen Eyers, Lambeth Teachers Centre, Acre Lane, London SW9.

7

Ethnicity and the supplementary school

Liz Mercer

Although the notion of Britain as a multicultural society is a relatively new one, ethnic minority groups in Britain have, for many years, maintained their own cultural traditions and institutions. In the field of education, this cultural diversity is exemplified in the existence of 'supplementary schools', run by minority group members for the benefit of their community's children. Thus, evening classes involving mother-tongue teaching, religious instruction, traditional dance and other cultural activities have long been an important part of the life of some well established ethnic communities (for example, those of East European origin, such as Polish and Ukrainian). More recently established groups, such as those of Asian origin have, in the last decade or so, begun to do likewise.

The purpose of this chapter is to draw attention to the existence of supplementary education,[1] to suggest some reasons why such provision exists and to consider its relation to state schooling. Although I intend to exemplify the discussion by reference to the provision of 'ethnic education' among the Asian communities in Leicester, many of the issues raised will be of relevance to minorities in general.

In Leicester the Asian community has ten formally organized schools, although it is known that more informal teaching takes place in private homes. Approximately 2,000 children attend the schools once a week, or more frequently, either in the evening after a normal school day, or at weekends. The oldest school in Leicester has been going since 1964 and is run by the Indian Education Society for the Hindu Gujarati community; its pupils are between 6 and 14 years old. Classes are held on Friday and Saturday evenings in school buildings and approximately 600 children attend. The classes are run along very traditional lines – children are encouraged to respect the authority of the teachers and stand whenever the head teacher enters the room. This school is unusual in that attempts are made to give assistance to the

[1] For further information about supplementary schooling in Britain, see Saifullah Khan, 1976, 1980.

Table 7.1 Asian Supplementary Schools in Leicester

	Number of pupils	Age range of pupils	Date school founded
Hindu Temple School	60	5–14	1975
Indian Education Society, school one	450	6–14	1964
Indian Education Society, school two	150	6–14	1964
Bengali Language School, Bengali Youth Association	90	No Restriction	1976
Madrissa Islamic School, Leicester Muslim Society	450	5–12	1967
Guru Nanak School, Sikh Temple	20	9–14	1967
Gurdwara Guru Tega Bahodur School	70	5–12	1967
Sikh Welfare and Cultural Society	110	6–16	1974
Ismailia Jamat School	57	6–13	1975
Shri Sanatan Mandit School	160	5–12	1973
Madrissa, The Islamic Centre	260	5–16	1967

Times of classes	Content of courses	Reasons given for holding classes
Sunday, 10:00–12:00	Gujarati	To promote and retain culture and language
Friday, 19:00–21:00	English, Maths and Gujarati	Advancement of child in day school; study in the mother tongue
Friday, 19:00–21:00 Saturday, 18:00–20:00	English, Maths and Gujarati	Advancement of child in day school; study in the mother tongue
Sunday, 10:00–12:00	Bengali language, culture and heritage	To keep culture and language alive
Monday to Saturday, 17:00–18:00	Religious instruction, Arabic and Urdu languages	Religious reasons, and Urdu teaching
Sunday, 11:00–12:30	Basics of Punjabi, and the Sikh religion	To teach Punjabi, enabling pupils to read traditional literature and to know their cultural heritage
Sunday, 10:00–12:30	Punjabi, Gurmika script, religious instruction	To give children knowledge of religion and culture
Sunday, 13:30–15:30	Punjabi, Sikh religion	To teach the mother tongue, develop children's person-ality and aid communication with parents
Friday, Saturday and Sunday, 1 hour each day	Religion and mother-tongue	Self-help scheme for the mother tongue
Sunday, 10:00–12:00	Religion and mother tongue	To teach religion, folk dances and song, and the mother tongue
Weekdays, 17:00–19:00 Saturday, 9:00–11:00	Arabic and Urdu, religious instruction	Education in social and religious values

Adapted from a table compiled by Delia Hemmings, Leicester Teachers Centre, 1978 pupils in their day-school subjects (particularly English and maths) in addition to instruction in the mother tongue and aspects of traditional culture. The school does not teach religion as such, but classes begin with a religious assembly. The pupils are mainly Hindus although there are a small number of non-practising muslims who also attend.

The aims and objectives of the Indian Education Society with regard to this school and its more recently established second school are as follows:

1. To promote and provide for the educational advancement of Indian children;
2. To teach and improve Indian children's performance in such subjects as English, maths and science;
3. To make them know their own language by the medium of the mother tongue;
4. To acquaint them with the Indian culture, civilization and values of life so as to integrate with other societies with grace and confidence;
5. To encourage them to take higher studies and so give them better prospects;
6. To prepare a ground for them to become more educated, civilized and disciplined.

The aims of this organization are, thus, ambitious. Its educational programme is intended to supplement basic state education as far as possible, recognizing that Gujarati children may have special problems with ordinary subjects as they are not working in their first language. However, in addition to this, a primary aim is to instruct the children in their own traditional language and culture – a task which is virtually not attempted in state schools.

The remainder of the Asian supplementary schools in Leicester do not interpret their role so broadly, but concentrate all their attention on teaching the minority language and culture. As can be seen from Table 1, most are attached to a religious institution and place a considerable emphasis on religious instruction. There are two schools attached to Hindu temples which teach the Hindu religion and Gujarati language, three schools attached to Sikh temples which teach the basis of the religion and the Punjabi language, three schools for Muslim children, two of which teach the languages Urdu and Arabic and one which teaches the Gujarati mother tongue, and a school organized by the Bangladeshi Youth Organization which teaches the Bengali language, culture and heritage. The schools are well attended, and it is claimed by their organizers that the demand for such teaching is greater than present attendance suggests – they are simply unable to accommodate more pupils. None of the schools receives any state financial support (although some are allowed to use school facilities free out of school hours) and they rely on donations from parents and the community. Many of the teachers in the schools are voluntary, although some schools pay their teachers a nominal sum to cover expenses. The head teacher of the school of the Indian Education Society comments that his teachers are highly committed, and willingly give up their free time in order to be of service to the children and ultimately the community.

How can the existence of these schools be explained? Joshua Fishman (1966) who has studied ethnic schools in the United States argues that:

> By and large, the ethnic school is a product of dislocation wherever it is encountered throughout the world. Most folk cultures in which ethnicity thrives do not provide formal schooling, since literacy is either unknown or restricted and ethnicity itself is unconcerned with either formal occupational training or formal ideological indoctrination. (p. 92)

In such folk cultures, the extended family and the wider community adequately socializes children without threats from different cultures and value systems.

Although this gives the impression that ethnicity[2] is a rather exotic characteristic, of concern only to simple folk societies, and is handed down through agencies other than school, this is an oversimplification of the case. An ethnic identity is available to people living within complex industrial societies, and in such societies, school plays a major role in the transmission of ethnic awareness. Members of the British majority are, however, unlikely to be concerned about their ethnicity because their right to know about it, its importance and value are never called into question. Transmission of such knowledge is automatic. However when Britons go to live in other countries, they do not necessarily assume that they should 'become' Brazilian, or 'become' Norwegian – it is in such circumstances that, for some, ethnicity becomes of critical concern, and one way to ensure that children raised outside of their 'home' country are aware of their distinctiveness might be to organize ethnic schools. Thus, it is when a minority are living among a powerful majority and feel the continuation of their own culture to be threatened that members of the minority are likely to try self-consciously to keep ethnicity alive.

The educational situation of an ethnically distinct community in society is particularly problematic when the majority and minority groups concerned have very different cultural traditions. The Asian

---

[2] A social psychological definition of ethnicity has been attempted by Fishman (1977) who argues that there are three interrelated aspects. *Paternity* refers to a line of descent and is reflected in both surnames and personal names e.g. Donal O'Brien, Indira Pandya, Michel Vaytet, Carol Jasilek, Anne Brown, etc. *Patrimony* refers to a way of living which reflects the group's cultural and historical development, and which includes such things as style of dress, method of food preparation as well as the predominantly accepted moral code. *Phenomenology* refers to the experience of living the ethnic lifestyle and the importance any individual attaches to it.

community value their way of life, their tradition, religion etc. and these are intimately bound up with their traditional languages. Concern exists that the language and traditions will disappear as the children are educated in the English language in state schools and exposed to western influences through school, friends, television and so on. Living within such a majority society means that the children, exposed to two languages and two different sets of values, will not be automatically socialized into traditional ways. This problem is particularly acute when the minority community has little power or status *vis-à-vis* the majority and its cultural traditions are afforded little attention or respect. To gain status in the wider society some Asian children may feel that they must abandon the traditional language and cultural practices and become more like members of the host community. Some of the organizers and teachers in the supplementary schools clearly see their task as being to counter such westernization, particularly the loss of language. Others accept some changes as inevitable but feel that whatever lifestyle the young Asian eventually chooses s/he should be aware of and proud of the achievements of her/his ancestors – in other words be aware of his/her ethnic heritage and have the choice of an ethnic identity.

British state schooling offers little reassurance for the Indian parents concerned that their children will lose touch with their mother tongue and culture. Although the EEC directive on mother-tongue teaching specified that steps must be taken to provide linguistic minorities with specialized language facilities, little has been done towards this end. Although in Leicester there is some opportunity for Asian children to take 'O' levels in some Indian languages, this option is certainly not available to most children in city and county secondary schools. For most British Asian children today, home and school remain different language worlds and by the time they reach secondary school they may understandably have come to the conclusion that the language of their community is of no relevance to education. Although the mother tongue may be used almost exclusively to communicate with family and friends in home and community, school life requires that they rapidly become competent in English. There can be little doubt that many Asian children are made to feel as though their Indian language, the language of their ancestors, intimately tied up with traditional religion and custom, is second-rate, unworthy of educational attention. Teachers have even been overheard admonishing Asian children speaking Gujarati to each other at break-time to 'stop jabbering'. It is worth noting that Asian culture embodies a great respect for education and most Asian parents wish their children to succeed at school; these parents must reconcile a conflict in that school is an institution which they admire, yet their language (and ultimately their ethnicity) is denied within the school.

Apart from one or two localized projects in Britain, very little progress has been made with regard to mother-tongue teaching in state schools. A number of reasons can be suggested. Firstly, the minority groups themselves do not have sufficient political influence to achieve this. Secondly, besides the enormous costs such provision would entail (in the context of a period of educational cutbacks) account must be taken of an educational establishment whose attitudes regarding language tuition are, to say the least, conservative. In general the British do not see themselves as a nation of linguists – the world importance of the English language and the geographical isolation of the British Isles has fostered an uninterested attitude in other tongues. Standard curriculum languages, like French and German are taught formally, and few children take them seriously. Even Britain's own indigenous minority languages (Welsh and Gaelic) have historically been given little or no place in the school curriculum and a policy of standardization towards and within English is maintained.

There is also a common belief among British teachers and parents that multilingualism is not to be encouraged as it creates for children some kind of 'cognitive overload' which will hinder the course of cognitive growth and the development of academic ability. Yet there is good evidence from psychological research (Peal and Lambert, 1962) that this is not the case, and many societies exist where bi- or multilingualism is a natural and normal part of social life.

Apart from the language issue, British schooling generally relies on a highly ethnocentric curriculum, and makes few concessions to minority perspectives or interests. History is taught from the British point of view, most literature studied is European or American, religious studies often focus on an examination of the Bible, the arts and music curricula reflect western interests. What possibility is there for the Asian child to learn anything about the history of India, the artistic and cultural contributions of her ancestors, and to develop any knowledge of or respect for her background in the context of the British school? The most likely outcome is that the child will feel a misfit – her own background ignored or rejected by white society. In addition white children in the same classrooms will find it easy to learn and justify the idea that Indian culture is inferior, and that Indian languages are not 'real' languages, because they are denied educational status.

What do Indian parents think of the education offered to their children in state schools? Information on this is scanty although more research is currently being done. A survey carried out in 1979 by the Indian Workers Association in Wolverhampton intended among other things to investigate (1) the present situation in local schools as a result of the 1977 EEC directive on mother-tongue teaching, (2) to what extent the curriculum in local schools meets the needs of Asian children (3) whether the parents wished to retain the mother tongue for academic as well as humanistic purposes. With respect to the first question the investigators found that no progress had been made on this matter.

With respect to the other two questions, 1,000 parents were interviewed; their responses indicated a considerable degree of dissatisfaction with the curriculum of local schools, feeling that it did not reflect the interests of a multicultural community. More specific findings of most interest were that 95 per cent would like their children to learn about their own religion and culture at school, 81 per cent would like them to learn their mother tongue as part of the normal school curriculum, 90 per cent wished to see more Asian teachers in local schools, and 94 per cent would like their children to have the opportunity to play Asian games in school time.

However, a more in-depth study carried out among Punjabi parents by Ghuman (1980) found that of the 40 parents interviewed all 40 families wanted their children to learn Punjabi, but only 45 per cent thought that it should be taught in schools and saw such language tuition as the responsibility of the community (in particular of the Sikh temples). Parents who thought that it should be taught in schools supported this view by commenting for example that if it was possible to teach French then arrangements could surely be made to teach Punjabi, or that some English children might opt for it and that this would help community relations.

The question of whether the mother tongue should be taught in state schools is a complex one. There is scope for much debate about exactly what form it might take.[3] One suggestion is that as many minority languages as possible be available as curriculum subjects. In this case the language options would be available to native English-speaking children too. Another proposition is that minority children should receive at least some instruction through the mother tongue, either only in the early years of schooling as a way of increasing the children's initial confidence at school but being gradually phased out, *or* continuing throughout their school life. Although there are some strong arguments in favour of teaching through the mother tongue for young children, whose competence in English may be poor due to predominant use of the mother tongue at home, there are also problems, which would become particularly acute if such a policy were practised throughout the children's school life. The most obvious and serious consequence is that it is difficult to imagine how such a policy could be pursued without extensive ethnic group segregation. With reference to mother-tongue teaching, Shirley Williams has been quoted as being concerned not only about the cost of such a step, but also that to provide specialist education for minority cultures was not the way to an integrated society, (Education, 8 July 1977). It seems that, at the moment

[3] See Mitchell, 1978, for further discussion of relevant issues.

at least, any advantages gained such as the increased continuity between home and school would be more than outweighed by the disadvantages of increased separation of children into ethnic groups at school as well as in the community.

It is clear that the issue of mother-tongue teaching is of more than linguistic importance relating as it does to ethnic heritage and to ethnic group maintenance. Language is often one of the prime symbols of ethnic identity, and as such attitudes towards language are related to more general cultural orientations. A survey conducted recently among young members of the Gujarati community (Mercer, Mercer and Mears, 1979) revealed widely differing aspirations *vis-à-vis* the majority British society. Some felt that their ethnicity was of crucial importance to their identity and saw their future as being very much bound up with the ethnic community. Their hopes were that the community would stay distinct from mainstream British society, as reflected in such comments as:

> I like the Indian way of life, the atmosphere, our religion. Being British means not caring if your neighbour is living or dying. Indians help each other and it seems that the British don't.

> We are different and in some ways we should stay different. Why should everybody be the same?

Such comments reflect a positive attitude towards cultural pluralism – a desire to be equal but different. Such respondents also felt strongly that the mother tongue should be maintained at all costs, feeling that it plays a crucial role in the continuation of the distinctive culture. A typical comment was that 'If everyone spoke English, the (Indian) culture would die out.'

On the other hand there was a significant number of Gujaratis who did not see their futures as being bound up with the ethnic group and who wished to integrate into British society. Such respondents felt that they would avoid using Gujarati if at all possible, and although they did not mind if other Gujaratis carried on using the language, felt it had little place in their lives.

> I was at polytechnic in London and a year passed before I spoke any Gujarati. Even when I met a Gujarati from Leicester we got to know each other in English and wouldn't dream of speaking anything else.

Thus, Gujarati is seen as a symbol of ethnic group membership, and depending on the individual's attitude towards this membership, Gujarati becomes more or less important to her or him. It is thus clear that not all Gujaratis would be interested in utilizing state provision of mother-tongue teaching, depending on their orientation towards minority/majority society.

However, for those Gujaratis who feel that their ethnicity is of vital importance to them and who wish their children to develop a knowledge of and a sense of pride in their background, it can be seen that the ethnic schools exist to bridge a gap in the education of Asian children, and that these schools become necessary to a sector of the minority community most committed to their ethnic heritage because the ethnic group can no longer, in the face of mass British society, adequately socialize the young in an informal way. The continuity of the ethnic group cannot be guaranteed in the same way as if it were living in 'home surroundings'. It is no longer a case of just living the ethnic experience and being without any possible alternatives. Ethnicity becomes self-conscious – something to be taught about in special schools. Ethnic schools in British cities are thus a product of the encounter between the ethnic minority and British society.

Although some of the ethnic schools may aim to supplement the education of their children in basic curricular subjects like maths and English, it is clear that their most unique contribution to minority children's education is to develop, through formal study, greater awareness of and interest in the distinctive language and culture of the community. That this opportunity exists is important at both individual and group levels. The individual child is encouraged to understand and respect community interests and values; given the lack of opportunity for this during normal school work, they may be able to achieve a more balanced perspective on majority and minority cultures and relationships. If sufficient interest in the ethnic group can be sustained in the context of western society, the ethnic group increases its chances of survival as a viable community with a vital language and culture. The ethnic school, therefore, represents one of the community's supportive institutions, legitimizing and developing its pupils' positive identities as members of their ethnic group in a way state school education does not begin to attempt.

The role that the state school can play in the life of an ethnic community will inevitably be very different from that played by a school run by the community itself. At present, however, only a small percentage of minority group children attend weekend or evening supplementary classes. A recent estimate, provided by Jennifer Wilding of Leicester CRC, indicates that only 11 per cent of local Asian children currently attend supplementary schools. For this reason alone, state schools cannot justifiably leave the educational treatment of an important area of their pupils' experience to voluntary institutions.

References

FISHMAN, J. A. and NAHIRNY, V. C. 1966: The ethnic group school and mother tongue maintenance. In J. A. Fishman (ed.), *Language Loyalty in the United States*, The Hague: Mouton.

FISHMAN, J. A. 1977: Language and ethnicity. In H. Giles (ed.), *Language, Ethnicity and Intergroup Relations*. London: Academic Press.

GHUMAN, P. A. S. 1980: Punjabi parents and English education. *Educational Research* **22**(2), 121–30.

MERCER, N., MERCER, E. and MEARS, R. 1979: Linguistic and cultural affiliation amongst young Asian people in Leicester. In H. Giles (ed.), *Language and Ethnic Relations*. Oxford: Pergamon.

MITCHELL, R. 1978: *Bilingual Education of Minority Language Groups in the English Speaking World: Some Research Evidence*. Stirling Educational Seminar Papers, No. 4.

NOOR, N. S. and KHALSA, S. S. 1978: *Educational Needs of Asian Children in the Context of Multiracial Education in Wolverhampton. A survey of parents' views and attitudes – 1977–78*. Wolverhampton: Indian Workers Association.

PEAL, E. and LAMBERT, W. E. 1962: The relation of bilingualism to intelligence. *Psychological monographs* **76**, 1–23.

SAIFULLAH KHAN, V. 1976: Provision by minorities for language maintenance. In CILT Reports and Papers **14**, *Bilingualism and British Education: the dimensions of diversity*.

— 1980: The 'mother-tongue' of linguistic minorities in multicultural England. *Journal of Multilingual and Multicultural Development* **1**, 71–88.

WILLIAMS, S. 1977: Education, 8 July.

Part III
The language curriculum; research, planning and practice

In this final part of the book, the four authors each show how recent research in different areas of language study – into linguistic structure, language development and the social content of children's literature – can be utilized to plan language work which is systematically related to children's broader language experience.

In Chapter 8, Pam Czerniewska writes about teaching children about the English language in a way that relates meaningfully to their own usage. She contrasts the possibility of a coherent language policy based on an understanding of the nature of language which is provided by modern linguistics, with the loose collections of assumptions and *ad hoc* methods which have for so long provided the basis of much English language teaching. Her contribution is particularly valuable for attempting the difficult task of translating knowledge about the structure of language into guidelines for teaching children about the language they use.

Sally Twite's aim in the next chapter is to show how research into the acquisition and development of a first language can inform teaching practice. This is done through examples from three well researched areas: the development of children's ability to use connectives in writing, the development of word meaning, and the growth of children's metalinguistic awareness (i.e. their ability to treat language itself as an observable entity). Her discussion of this last topic will be particularly encouraging for teachers who wish to capitalize on the natural interest in language so often observed in young children.

Mary Hoffman's chapter is a careful examination of the content of children's reading, both voluntary and as 'enforced' in school. Her concern is with the ways social values are presented – and hence promoted or condemned – in such literature. This is done in relation to three major social variables; social class, race and sex. She very usefully relates this discussion of literary content to readers' broader experience of the same social values – as experienced by children in their social lives in and out of school, and as encountered by the teacher selecting reading material for his or her classroom. This chapter and that by Katharine Perera, in which the *structure* of reading materials is scrutinized, provide an excellent basis for a critical examination of any school's reading materials, and would usefully inform any discussion about school policies on such matters.

American Black English dialects have been at the centre of a great deal of educational controversy in recent years. This has largely involved attempts to establish their status as 'equal-but-different' varieties of the English language, attempts which have had to face the opposition of entrenched racial and elitist attitudes about what kind of language should be used in schools. As a result, many issues have been raised which are equally pertinent to the educational status of other 'non-standard' dialects on both sides of the Atlantic. In Chapter 11 Robert Berdan discusses the implications of this debate for the teaching of reading. Dismissing the possibility of 'dialect-free' instruction, he argues for the use of 'dialect-fair' methods which utilize the inherent flexibility of the English writing system. After illustrating the ways in which traditional instruction methods have helped to reduce black children's participation in education, he shows how a dialect-based phonics can provide a more appropriate basis for teaching children to read. He thus outlines an approach to reading instruction which is compatible with the kind of bidialectal language policy discussed in other chapters (notably Chapter 4).

8

Teaching children language

Pam Czerniewska

Most teachers would agree that language is something which needs to be included in the curriculum. Under the heading 'language' one would include talking, writing, listening and reading and few would dispute that the development of abilities in these four aspects of language is part of the responsibility of the educational system.

Given this initial agreement, the practising teacher faces the problem of deciding what should be taught and how it should be taught. Concerns about language teaching will range from those at the level of school policy such as, 'should one teach formal grammar and if so which grammar and for which age group?' or 'should one ensure that the use of Standard English is enforced in all written work?' to those at departmental level such as 'whose responsibility is it to teach spelling?' or 'what should one say to the modern language teachers when they complain about English teachers' failure to teach grammar?' to those concerns about individual pupils' language skills such as 'how am I going to persuade pupils to end a sentence with a full stop?' 'Why won't pupils learn to spell *their, there* and *they're* correctly?' or 'how can I stop pupils beginning every sentence with *and*?' The list of concerns is endless, and in every staffroom one will hear many such questions raised about the nature of language instruction.

The recent reports on language provision in primary and secondary education (DES 1975; 1979) have shown how varied language teaching is in terms of its quantity and quality. The conclusion that seems to be reached by such reports is that, while much excellent language teaching is carried out, there is a lack of a coherent language-teaching policy in many schools. Decisions about the what and how of language instruction tend to rest on an *ad hoc* set of principles. For there to be coherence in the language curriculum it seems important for teachers to step outside their classrooms, so to speak, to establish the aims and objectives of language teaching and to investigate the value of different

* Much of the material for this article is based on Gannon, P. and Czerniewska, P. (1980) *Using Linguistics.*

language-teaching methods. The need for such a review is not a new idea. In 1906, Hoyt pointed to the value of a scrutiny of grammar instruction:

> It is of course recognized that the present curriculum is largely the result of an evolutionary development and must continue gradually to adapt itself to the demands of society. But, unfortunately, in the process of development, it is often difficult to get rid of excrescences arising from past misconceptions of the purpose of education and to slough off practices now no longer adapted to existing needs. It would seem advisable and essential to the best welfare of our schools, therefore, that instead of leaving the revision and amendment of our curricula entirely to the slow process of experimentation under the ordinary schoolroom conditions, we should subject each study in the curriculum to the most careful consideration and, so far as may be done, to exact scientific investigation, and to determine its relative value as a means of education and the best methods of causing it to contribute to the preparation of youth for their places in society. (Hoyt, 1906, p. 2)

By tracing the main approaches to language teaching in the past and present this article hopes to highlight such 'excrescences' and inappropriate practices and, thus, to identify the nature of future language-teaching approaches.

Language teaching has not always been seen as a major component of the curriculum. During the last century, while skills in reading and writing were taught, any study of language beyond the basic two R's was given secondary status. Where English was a curriculum subject – and it became an examinable subject in the latter part of the nineteenth century – the aims and methods differed from those found in most contemporary classrooms. The 'rules' of the English language would have been instilled in children through drills and exercises and, perhaps, be committed to memory for later recall to a visiting inspector. Many teachers might have been sceptical of the value of such lessons. Trained in the classics, they would have drawn examples from Greek and Latin and the 'rules' of English would, in effect, be translations from a Latin grammar. The aims of such lessons, if stated at all, would be the disciplining of children's minds for rigorous thinking and strengthening of character. The aims which were not being met were the equipping of pupils with knowledge about, and fluency in, their native language.

The low status of English language teaching was noted in the Newbolt report of 1921:

> in many schools of all kinds and grades that part of the teaching which dealt directly with English was often regarded as being inferior in importance, hardly worthy of any substantial place in the curriculum, and a suitable matter to be entrusted to any member of the staff who had some free time at his disposal. (Board of Education, 1921, para. 6)

This report advocated that English be given a central role in the curriculum, considering it to be 'the one indispensable preliminary and foundation' for all other branches of education. Great emphasis was placed on the need for language study in order to develop the mind and character of pupils, but in addition, teaching language was seen as a means of promoting fluency:

> a lack of language is a lack of the means of communication and of thought itself. Moreover, among the vast mass of the population it is certain that if a child is not learning good English he is learning bad English, and probably bad habits of thought; and some of the mischief done may never afterwards be undone. (Board of Education, 1921 para. 6)

Over and above the goals of English teaching to develop communication and thought, the report also gave as aims the unification of social classes and the instilling of the 'right kind of national pride', through a shared appreciation of the English language and of English literature.

Thus, 60 years ago, a knowledge of English and an appreciation of English literature were promoted, by this report, to a dominant position in the curriculum. A direct relationship was drawn between the teaching of English and the development of communicative skills.

If one compares the aims put forward in the Newbolt report with those more recently stated, one finds considerable overlap. Rosen (1978) paraphrases the UNESCO Institute for Education proposal for the responsibilities of mother-tongue teaching as:

(i) the skills of creative, interpretative communication
(ii) the study of the objective aspects of language
(iii) the study of literary heritage
(iv) social and individual development (Opitz, 1972)

The parallel between those responsibilities and those proposed by the Newbolt report are many. Both emphasize the need for pupils to learn to communicate, both emphasize the need for pupils to study language and literature and, despite the difference in words, both focus on the role of language teaching for developing social and individual skills. The UNESCO proposal only seems to have omitted as a responsibility of mother-tongue teaching the development of national sentiments.

But while the aims of language teaching appear to have changed little over the last 50 or so years, the translation of such aims into classroom practice have been subject to much revision. Agreement about *why* language should be taught does not necessarily imply that there will be agreement about the *how* and *what* of language teaching. There is, and has been, wide variation in the ways in which language instruction is organized. Both the topics covered and the methods used vary greatly from classroom to classroom. As Rosen (1978), commenting on the UNESCO proposal, notes:

But amongst those who would subscribe to such goals (or some of them) will be some who believe that 'skills' are best developed by carefully graded drills and others by a total commitment to the pupil's expressiveness. Teachers will differ violently about the criteria for the effective use of language. Some will regard vernacular speech as a kind of disability requiring almost surgical remedies and others that it constitutes the most powerful equipment a child possesses. Some will strive for linguistic conformity and decorum and others for diversity and originality. Some will put grammar study at the centre of the syllabus, others at the periphery or banish it altogether. (Rosen, 1978 p. 54)

Diversity is very much the order of the day. In one classroom, one might find pupils spending their language lessons working through teacher-made worksheets or textbook exercises on vocabulary, spelling, past-tense forms, comprehension and so on. In another, children might be looking at a collection of autumn leaves and writing imaginative accounts of the changing scenes in nature. In a third, there may be an improvised drama lesson in progress, with children discussing the types of language used in different situations. And, given the eclecticism of most language teaching, all three types of language lesson might take place in the same school during one week.

Behind a list of aims there are assumptions made about the nature of language and the nature of the learning process; and these assumptions will determine how an aim is realized in classroom practice. In order to decide what to teach and how to teach it is these underlying assumptions which need to be examined. With a slight risk of caricaturing, the major approaches to language teaching and the premises on which they are based can be looked at and evaluated.

The approach predominating 30-odd years ago and still prevalent in many schools (see DES, 1975, Chapter 11) is one in which children work their way through a series of English textbooks. The traditional grammar book, still familiar today if wrapped in more attractive covers, provided pupils with drills and exercises in the 'rules' of the language with the objective of providing children with a knowledge of their language. Such exercises would probably have in mind the components of a language curriculum suggested by the Newbolt report:

first, systematic training in the sounded speech of standard English, to secure pronunciation and clear articulation: second, systematic training in the use of standard English, to secure clearness and correctness both in oral expression and in writing.

(The third and fourth components recommended were concerned with training in reading and literature but these aspects will not be discussed here.) The approach would, thus, be one in which children would be presented with a model of 'good' English, and class work would require children to emulate that model.

The actual 'rules' presented often lacked linguistic validity. Some rules have been passed down from the early Greek scholars. For example, the 'parts of speech' usually given for English can be traced back, with only minor changes, to the classification of Greek made by Dionysius Thrax in the first century BC. The categorization of the Greek language structure was mapped almost directly onto the Latin language and this classification was later transferred to other continental languages. English, despite its very different nature, was also analysed according to the rules of Latin. Describing English according to Latin rules produces many curiosities. For instance, one finds the Latin case system (nominative, accusative, dative, ablative etc.) applied to English even though English words are not inflected for case. In Latin, there are inflections which mark the relationship holding among words such that whether one writes, *Petro dixit Iohannus* or *Iohannus dixit Petro* or even *Dixit Petro Iohannus* one knows that John told Peter something. In English, on the other hand, *John told Peter* cannot be altered to *Peter told John* without completely changing the meaning. The relationships holding among the words in English are marked by word order not, on the whole, by inflections. Thus, calling *John* in *John told Peter*, the nominative case, and in *Peter told John*, the accusative case, even though the form of the word does not change, is neither helpful nor informative. The Latin grammar, while having some similarities to English grammar, was written to account for the Latin language and cannot simply be mapped on to English. The fallacy of mapping a grammar for one language on to another can be seen in familiar injunctions such as 'one must say *It is I* not *It is me*'. In Latin, it so happens that speakers would use the nominative form of the pronoun after constructions like *It is* or *That is*, but if one tries to apply this rule to English one produces unacceptable utterances such as

Is it she you are looking for?[1]
Who's the girl in the picture? That's I.

The teaching of Latin grammar instead of English grammar is likely to have bemused many a pupil who found examples of 'English' which he had never heard or spoken before. Apart from the misconception that English was structured in the same way as Latin, there also arose a second misconception (originating, according to Hoyt 1906, with Quintilian and restated by Melanchthon) that 'grammar is the science of speaking and writing the language with correctness and propriety'. Pupils would be warned of the sin of the split infinitive, the perils of ending a sentence with a preposition, the penalties for using a double

---

[1] Or should I say, *Is it she for whom you are looking?*

negative and so on and so forth. These proscriptions have mixed origins. Some are based on Latin sentence-construction rules, some on myths developed in the eighteenth and nineteenth centuries and some are based on the rules of the most prestigious dialect, that is, Standard English. The proscriptions largely reflect linguistic convention or etiquette rather than language rules. While this is not to imply that some of the conventions should not be introduced to children, focusing so much attention on these rules makes English lessons an event far removed from the child's own language experiences. A text book which asks pupils to correct

I cannot remember who I was with

or which provides a model sentence

Near whom are you staying?

is going to seem very far removed from the language normally used and heard by native speakers.

One does not want to parody traditional grammar text books. They do provide much information, particularly about formal styles of written language, and some of the analytical procedures are similar to those of modern linguistic accounts. However, they are restricted in the areas covered and, often, they lack the coherence and objectivity of modern linguistic description. In striving to set down rules for correct usage (and that usually only for writing), the result was a selective and often distorted account. Crystal (1976) gives an example of such selectivity, noting that great emphasis was often placed on the correct use of *only*: to be placed directly before the word it qualifies. But little, if any, attention was given to other adverbs. Does it matter where adverbs such as *clearly*, *honestly* and *happily* occur? If one contrasts the utterances

Clearly, she cannot see
She cannot see clearly

one is aware of the things that can be said about adverb-placement rules ignored by traditional accounts concerned solely with the correct use of *only*.

Apart from its selectivity, traditional grammar also lacked coherence and consistency. For example, accounts tended to be content with presenting categories such as the 'eight parts of speech' defined by an assortment of criteria. One might meet, in parsing or sentence analysis, a *noun clause as object*, that is, a category defined in grammatical terms, and *adverbial clauses of time, place and manner*, that is, defined according to semantic criteria (i.e. when, where or how something happened). It is difficult to know whether definitions were ever questioned but one wonders what school children made of statements such as 'A sentence is a complete thought' (what is an incomplete thought?) or 'A clause is a group of words expressing a thought but forming part of a sentence' (what is 'a thought' as distinct from a 'complete thought'?) or 'A phrase is a group of words which express a distinct *part* of a thought'.

This lack of conciseness and coherence of many traditional grammar books demonstrates their underlying linguistic weakness: they lacked an underlying theory of language from which principles could be derived. In its place was a number of *ad hoc* rules of language, some valid and some inaccurate, but, overall, lacking in consistency and focusing on only a restricted range of language forms. With such linguistically-based shortcomings, these text books were unlikely to achieve such aims as teaching the child about the objective aspects of language, or even training in logical thought.

Such defects could be overcome. One could prepare text books which are based on linguistically sound principles, and such books have in fact been written. But it is not only the linguistic fallacies that have been criticized. There are also questions to be asked concerning their pedagogical adequacy. Content and method are interrelated. For example, teaching that it is 'correct' to say or write *It is I* is based on a linguistically fallacious rule but it is, at the same time, questionable whether children should be taught such 'rules' at all in a way that prevents them from looking at their own language. The deductive approach of most traditional grammar books will give most children the impression that the English language is something which is found in the classroom, not something they, themselves, bring to the language lesson.

The type of tasks that a child was required to carry out would have little to do with his behaviour when speaking or writing. Exercises might include analysing and labelling sentence parts, conjugating verbs, defining terms or providing rules for the use of punctuation. Some examples (from an early grammar textbook) will give the flavour of such exercises:

> Discuss the origin and grammatical use of the Gerundial Infinitive
> Correct or justify the following:
> > *Who do you speak to?*
> > *I like it better than any*
> > *The people is one; they have all one language.*
> Define a sentence.
> Write down the plural of *gallows, topaz, solo, who, Mary*

These are extreme examples, but more moderate ones can be found in textbooks in use today. For example:

> In the following sentences pick out the adverbial phrases of conditions,

and replace them by adverbial clauses of the same kind with a similar meaning.

    You may go, with one condition
    We shall go for a picnic, weather permitting
    Supposing him lost, what shall we do?
Analyse the following sentences into clauses, and name the kind of sentence
    Happy is the man who findeth wisdom
    Who caught the thief?
    O fat white woman whom nobody loves

The arid nature of such exercises is very apparent. Language seems to be treated as some rather obscure art, examples being far removed from most pupil's verbal experiences, and drills being worked through of value only, it seems, for passing the English examination. The grammar lesson becomes a time for, as Britton (1973) puts it, 'unproductive busywork'.

The pedagogy of such grammar teaching comes under even closer scrutiny if the aims of the lesson are not only teaching about language and the training of children's minds but also the improvement of children's writing and speech. It is this latter aim which seems to have led the continued use of drills in language usage. An assumption of this language-teaching approach is that aptitude at such exercises will lead to improved writing and speech. If a child learns and practices a 'rule' of grammar errors will be eliminated. (Recall the 'components' of the language curriculum proposed in the Newbolt report in which 'training' in standard English was assumed to be the means of 'securing' correct use of English).

The reaction against traditional grammar approaches was largely against their pedagogical efficacy rather than against their linguistic adequacy; their assumptions about learning rather than their assumptions about language structure. The change in approaches to language teaching were part of a shift in the approach to education as a whole. Anyone connected with education will be aware of the changing nature of schools, particularly primary schools, during the 1960s, with the former subject-centred view of education being replaced by a child-centred view. Emphasis was placed on what the child brought to the learning task and how areas of knowledge could be related to that experience. Recognized as one of the most important 'assets' which the child brought to school was language itself. The language abilities of the child were seen as a major factor determining educational success or failure. Naturally, the combination of a child-centred approach and a new significance being given to the child's language led to a greatly changed approach to language teaching. Exercises were rejected in favour of 'creative' and individualized activities which could tap the child's language resources. Teachers began to use real-life contexts, instead of lists of abstract rules, as starting points for language work. Instead of asking children to give the singular form of *the natives are killing the bullocks*, teachers were asking children to talk, question, and write about their own experiences in their own language. Personal reactions to objects and events, feelings and emotions were encouraged with the children expressing themselves in verse, plays, stories and so on. For a while at least, the new 'creative' language approach flourished.

One can see how the pendulum had swung. The aims of both the Newbolt report and the UNESCO report could be said to lie behind a language curriculum of a traditional or creative kind, but the means of studying language, learning to communicate and of promoting social and individual development have been reversed. In the traditional model, the language-to-be-learnt is provided and the child's response is highly controlled; he is only required to demonstrate skill at manipulatting the forms provided. Whereas in the creative approach, the teacher merely supplies a stimulus to the child – from seashells to poetry – and the child is left with the freedom to respond in the form of language of his choosing.

But, as well as seeing how and why this shift in language-teaching approaches occurred, one can also, at least in retrospect, see the disadvantages of a language curriculum committed to self-expression and creativity. While the child is able to bring his own language to the classroom, to express himself in his own style and form, such freedom may actually prevent his language resources being fully exploited. The risk of too permissive an approach is that if the child is left to explore areas of experience without guidance, the direction he takes may be inappropriate, misleading or meaningless. Nisbet (1973; also quoted in Richards, 1978) recounts a classroom scene in which the personal reactions of pupils to a poem showed that they had missed the point of the poem completely. Despite their objections, Nisbet insisted that they examine the significance of the words used in the poem more closely. He comments on his rejection of their 'superficial response'

A pupil left to respond to a poem without guidance, is only too likely to find in the poem what he feels about this subject already, and what he wants to feel. It is our job, when necessary, to guide him towards a response which is a response, in other words represents a direct reaction to the poem which is being studied.

In rejecting the highly structured approach of traditional grammar on the grounds that it failed to relate abstract 'rules' to children's language use, some also rejected that language teaching should be structured at all. As a result, creative-language approaches, while remedying some of the negative aspects of former teaching methods, had the new disadvantage of a lack of language objectives and means of achieving those objectives.

Furthermore, creative approaches run as great, if not greater, risk of selectivity as any traditional approach. Traditional grammar books were based, as noted above, on an inadequate theory of language. But at least there was an overall framework allowing the major areas of language structure to be covered by pupils. The traditional grammar approach has also been severely criticized for its insistence on correct forms, and its formulation of rules which applied only to a restricted type of language, usually formal written language. But it did, at least, attempt to present children with a model, albeit of only one language variety. The creative approach, on the other hand, may provide no models of different varieties appropriate for the tasks presented them. Pupils might be experiencing many exciting new stimuli, but to express their feelings in talk or writing in a way that is effective there is a need for models of language to be presented. To write a poem or a newspaper account of a school trip, guidance is needed about the forms that such writing can take. Where the responsibility seems to lie mainly with the child about which aspects of language to explore, and how to explore them there is an inevitable danger that only certain aspects will be covered. For example, while much attention might be paid to vocabulary development little attention may be paid to sentence structure, and the conventions for writing (spelling, punctuation, text organization etc.) may be completely ignored.

The arguments that developed against the laissez-faire creative approaches emphasized the need to guide the child's 'discovery' of language and to give some indication of what the search should involve. These arguments placed an onus on teachers to know which aspects of language each child should be developing, to know the structure of different language varieties children are attempting to use and to ensure that language objectives are set which will allow systematic coverage of those assessed areas of need. The major problem facing teachers becomes one of knowing what these objectives should be. The Bullock report (DES, 1975) revealed, in its survey of language teaching, the uncertainty in the minds of teachers about what to actually teach:

> Some regarded language improvement as a by-product of the talk, writing and literature which formed the core of their work; and they gave it no specific attention. Others set aside at least one period a week for it, usually working from a course book. A substantial number considered that the express teaching of prescriptive language forms had been discredited, but that nothing had been put in its place. They could no longer subscribe to the weekly period of exercises, but they felt uneasy because they were not giving language any regular attention. It seems to us that this uncertainty is fairly widespread, and that what many teachers now require is a readiness to

develop fresh approaches to the teaching of language. (DES, 1975, para. 11.20)

What should such fresh approaches be like? The Bullock report puts forward its conception of an effective language approach:

> What we are suggesting ... is that children should learn about language by experiencing and experimenting with its use. There will be occasions when the whole class might receive instruction in some aspect of language. More frequently, however, the teacher will operate on the child's language competence at the point of need by individual or group discussion. As a background to all this activity he should have in his own mind a clear picture of how far and in what direction this competence should be extended.

One response to this need for an approach which allows the child to explore language but which controls such exploration along linguistically informed lines, came from the work of M. A. K. Halliday. Halliday's theoretical approach to language analysis (see 1973; 1978) emphasizes the need for treating language as part of the social system. That is, as well as analysing the linguistic structure of *what* is said he also looks at *how*, *when* and *why* it is said. For instance, to take a simple example, the utterance *Dogs are not allowed in the park* can be analysed according to its grammatical and semantic structure. But one can also analyse the linguistic pattern in terms of the situation in which it occurs, its purpose, the attitude of the person saying it and so on.

Halliday's work was developed by Doughty *et al.* (1971) into a set of classroom activities, *Language in Use*, for secondary pupils. These materials were designed to allow pupils to discover the varieties of uses to which language might be put and to explore and experiment with different varieties. Crystal (1976) describes the objectives of this approach:

> In a real sense, the aim is to make the child a polyglot in his own speech and writing, by giving him a command of a *range* of formal patterns of language, the knowledge of when and where to use them, and the ability to put his knowledge into practice. (p. 74)

Gone is the idea that there is one 'correct' model for children to learn, gone, also, is the idea that children will learn about language either by drill or by mere exposure. In their place, there are materials which treat language varieties as equal but different and which are structured to guide the children, systematically, along their paths of discovery. Thus, from both a linguistic and pedagogic viewpoint, these and similar materials seem to overcome the major disadvantages of earlier approaches.

While recognizing the many advantages of this new intitiative, such materials have limitations. The major limitation is that only in the hands of a teacher informed about the language structure of different varieties and able to assess the child's response to the language exploration, will the materials be completely effective. Recalling the quotation from the Bullock report above, the teacher needs to know 'how far and in what direction' language work should be extended at 'the point of need'. The type of knowledge which a teacher needs to have to ensure that pupils benefit from their language explorations is examined by Crystal (1976). Taking, as an example, the problem of assessment, he writes:

> given two children engaging in a 'use' of language, how are we to judge their relative success, or induce the less successful to improve? Apart from any pedagogic problems, the teacher must carry out at least four preliminary tasks:
> (a) identify the difference between the two, i.e. determine which features of linguistic *form* account for their differing performance – for which he needs an awareness of language structure in general, a knowledge of some classificatory terminology, and a sense of the possible qualitative and quantitative variations affecting performance. He has to be able to answer the question 'How different?'
> (b) He must be clear as to the salient linguistic characteristics of a 'good' example of the language use being aimed for – assuming that it has been possible to isolate the function in a meaningful way. What is a 'successful' instance of scientific, or persuasive, or instructional language, for example – and why is it successful?
> (c) Once he has made a diagnosis, he must be aware of the possible linguistic pathway towards achieving this use of language which will affect decisions about teaching policy, e.g. whether he should build up a use of language in some graded, structured way.
> (d) Having decided to implement a particular line of action, he needs to be able to identify progress – which amongst other things involves an ability to identify unexpected or misleading linguistic developments, such as the emergence of a structure which in fact militates against the development of the target use of language (e.g. the use of too many variations in pronoun or tense form in building up a style of scientific English).
> In other words, the teacher must have some formal knowledge of language structure. (pp. 79–80)

This evaluation of the major language-teaching approaches has revealed some of the different types of assumptions about the nature of child learning and about the nature of language underlying various approaches. 'Excrescences' and inappropriate practices mentioned in the Hoyt article above have been identified in traditional grammar books; the replacement of these by 'creative' approaches was shown to provide no proper solution given their lack of control over the child's response and their lack of systematicity. The more recent approaches, exemplified by *Language in Use* materials have been shown to have inherent weaknesses due to the onus they place on teachers to direct and control children's use of language.

From such critiques of approaches one needs now to formulate a set of criteria which need to be fulfilled by future language teaching approaches. What are the necessary conditions which need to be met when teaching children language?

One condition is that the language presented to children should be seen to be related to their own language experience. Presenting examples of utterances which they are never likely to have spoken or written (e.g. *Near whom are you staying?*) divorces language teaching from the child's own knowledge of language and is likely to be seen, at best, as some sort of game and, at worst, as an entirely meaningless and bewildering activity. Further, what the child is asked to *do* with language should be seen to be related to real language activities. Providing synonyms, antonyms or the plural forms of a list of words are not activities which the language user often indulges in. Analysing language may, like any problem-solving task, have its merits and may provide a suitable subject matter for a fifth or sixth form curriculum, but such exercises are unlikely to have much effect on language abilities. Real contexts need to be developed for language development work. Real language activities are ones in which language is used for an identified purpose and for an identified audience. Once purposeful contexts are found, and recognized by pupils as such, then different forms of language can be explored and judged for their appropriateness.

The guiding principles for the designing of resources are that they are related to the child's own language experience and about the language used or needed to be used. The 'inseparability of language and the human situation' (DES, 1975) needs to guide what resources are drawn upon.

Ensuring that materials are relevant is only part of the task. As the evaluation of 'Language in Use' approach demonstrated, to use meaningful materials effectively the teacher needs more than awareness of different language forms. Their use needs to be structured, tailored to individual pupils and developed along clearly defined paths. There are, in other words, prerequisite conditions which the teacher needs to meet. Firstly, there needs to be a set of clearly stated objectives for each individual child. Secondly, these objectives need to be formulated according to a theory of language such that selectivity is avoided. Thirdly, these objectives need to be formulated on the basis of knowledge about child language development such that they are feasible given the child's age and ability. These are hard conditions to meet. Setting language objectives requires considerable knowledge about language and language development on the part of the teacher, and achieving these objectives involves developing classroom work which neither leaves language development to chance nor provides explicit instruction out of context.

How might such a structured language approach proceed, and is it really feasible given the pressures under which most teachers work? It is obviously not possible to outline an entire approach here partly because there is not enough space but more importantly because a structured language approach must be designed according to the needs of specific children, and according to the curricula constraints of the school. But an example of the type of steps that need to be taken for such a structured approach to be realized can be given.

The following piece of writing was written by a seven-year-old child:

> Once upon a time there was a mean old witch (1) and she had a chocolate house (2) and she had a big black cat (3) and one day two children came to her house (4) and they saw her making a spell (5) and because she had a chocolate house chocolate kept dropping in her spell (6) so she threw the spell at the cat (7) and the cat turned green (8) and the cat went mad (9) and where the chocolate kept dropping the witch got covered in chocolate (10) she made a different house (11) and all stuff in her old house was covered in chocolate (12) so she had to make all new stuff (13).

Before setting teaching objectives and deciding on suitable language development activities for this child, one needs to assess what the child has or has not achieved in his writing. (Clearly, just one piece of writing is inadequate for a fair assessment but we shall assume that it is representative of the child's abilities.)

At an impressionistic level one might comment on the lack of sophisticated sentence structure, the lack of punctuation, the over-use of *and* and perhaps the limited vocabulary. There is often a tendency of impressionistic remarks to be negative, to note errors and to fail to note what the child has achieved. A linguistic assessment, on the other hand, will allow evaluation of what the child has or has not achieved at different levels of analysis: at the graphological level (spelling and punctuation); at the grammatical level (word and sentence structure); at the semantic level (vocabulary and expression of meanings), and at text level (sentence connection). Assessment at each level will involve asking two questions: what has the child achieved? And, what could the child have achieved? That is, one compares the observed forms of language with the expected. For example, at the graphological level one might note that the spelling is accurate but there is no use of punctuation marks. Lack of full stops is a common complaint among teachers, but this child certainly uses complete sentences and seems to have marked the beginning of a new sentence with *and*. Turning to the grammatical level, one observes that the child uses a wide range of sentence structures. Using an analysis based on a contemporary grammatical description (Quirk *et al.*, 1972) one finds that most basic sentence types are used, e.g.

She had a big black cat: Subject–Verb–Object
They saw her making a spell: Subject–Verb–Object–Complement

Two children came to her house: Subject–Verb–Adverbial
The cat turned green: Subject–Verb–Complement
She threw the spell at the cat: Subject–Verb–Object–Adverbial

While most sentences are simple there is a wide range of sentence patterns. There are also two complex sentences

(6) because she had a chocolate house chocolate kept dropping in her spell
(10) where the chocolate kept dropping the witch got covered in chocolate

in which one sentence (e.g. *she had a chocolate house*) is embedded in, or subordinated to another (e.g. *chocolate kept dropping in her spell*).

Comparing what the child has written with an adult model of grammar, one can see that most simple sentence patterns are used but that most sentences are active and there are only two attempts to combine sentences other than by the use of *and*.

We need to compare what is used not only with the expected adult forms but also with the expected forms for a child of this age. For a seven-year-old, few complex structures would be expected though it is encouraging to find attempts, as in (6) and (10), to combine sentences. Attempts to vary the grammatical structures often, at first, lead to errors but such errors need to be viewed positively: far better to find errors in sentences where a child is experimenting with new forms than to find no errors and no attempts to elaborate simple sentence patterns.

Looking at the child's vocabulary, one finds a great deal of repetition and little modification in the noun phrase. Where adjectives are used (e.g. big black cat) they seem rather conventional. This may reflect the type of vocabulary and use of repetition to be found in the child's reading books, or perhaps in order to write a story the use of a varied vocabulary was not given high priority.

At the level of text, there is the very noticeable use of *and* to connect sentences, a common occurrence in the speech and writing of children of this age. As noted above, *and* often seems to be used as a kind of 'filler' something which occurs while the child pauses between sentences. There are occurrences of other ways to connect sentences: (and) *one day* (4); *so* (7); *so* (13) and the two instances of subordinated sentences in (6) and (10). Compared with the adult model, the text 'hangs together' in a coherent way but with little exploitation of text-making devices. (See Crystal (1979) for a fuller analysis of children's use of sentence connectives). Compared with the norms for this age group, the child seems to be developing well, beginning as is normal at this age, to try out new ways of connecting sentences.

This is by no means a full analysis but it has tried to demonstrate the types of questions which need to be raised in a linguistic evaluation. To answer questions about what has and what could have been written involves knowing about the structure of adult language and the developmental norms for each age group. And for this knowledge to be more than ad hoc, based on one's intuitions about language and one's observations of pupils in one class, there is an implied need for a linguistic framework. Merely saying 'no punctuation' (often with the implied assertion that the child does not write 'proper sentences') will fail to show how the child has marked the division of the story into sentences; or just commenting 'immature sentence structure' will fail to illustrate the range of sentence patterns employed and the child's early attempts to use subordination in his sentence structure. First impressions may guide one to the areas in need of closer examination but having arrived at those areas one needs to employ more systematic procedures to determine what the child has or has not developed. Furthermore, systematic analysis may reveal aspects not noted in first impressions.

After the assessment comes the setting of objectives. One might decide (and decisions will be based on one's current language activities and one's knowledge of the child's interests) to develop the child's use of complex sentence structures – an area where promising beginnings are already in evidence. From what has been said before, providing exercises which ask children to look at subordinated sentences and analyse them or to ask children to combine sentences using 'relative clauses', 'adverbial phrases of concession' etc. may have little effect on later writing.

One needs to plan activities to meet one's objectives which are related to real uses of language. One such activity might be to ask the child, or a group of children, to continue the story of the mean old witch but to write, at the beginning of the continuation, a summary of the 'story so far' (a format used at the beginning of many comic stories)[2] Such a summary should, with some direction, lead children to work out ways of combining sentences, for instance

> There was a mean old witch who lived in a chocolate house with a big black cat.

A second objective might be to encourage the child to use a more varied vocabulary. A suggestion, here, might be to ask the children to write an advertisement for the chocolate house, or perhaps, the witch's cat, which would allow exploration of different ways of presenting information and ways of describing things. Again, direction would be needed to provide suitable models of language and one would need to ensure that such a task was within the child's experience.

One child's piece of work and a few suggestions for language development work do not make a coherent language curriculum. But the example does indicate how a comprehensive language programme might be designed. Starting with an assessment of the child's work (a full assess-

[2] This suggestion is based on an activity described by M. Riddle.

ment being feasible perhaps once or twice a term) one can formulate objectives directed to the 'points of need'. Plans to meet these objectives can draw on the ideas to be found in published language kits or one's own resources and then adapted so that they relate to the individual child's interests and current work. A structured and coherent language programme is one which builds on a child's strengths and weaknesses, extends language along normal developmental paths leaving no areas of language to chance.

Setting up such a programme is no easy task and may seem to be more than any hard-working teacher can cope with. Initially, perhaps, the workload is heavy but once a programme is worked out, teaching children language should be far more rewarding than former practices, with the children as well as the teacher developing new ways of using language.

A number of different issues have been explored here. A number of different practices have been evaluated, some guiding principles have been put forward for a language-teaching approach and some suggestions given for how a structured approach might be realized. The onus is left with the individual teacher to design his or her own approach for only the teacher can determine how much and in what direction language work is needed for each individual child. To determine what is needed the teacher, it is argued, should possess a background knowledge of language organization and language development: a knowledge to inform and service his or her language-teaching decisions. The *Curriculum 11–16* report (DES, 1977) puts forward this point in its chapter on language:

> [This chapter] will argue the case for 'linguistic education', much of the responsibility for which lies in the school as a community. The argument implies that we shall need teachers of all subjects who have a sure understanding of the ways in which language is used in effective learning, and that English teaching demands a more specialist understanding of language and literature. It implies also that we should develop the skill of all teachers in organizing their work so that appropriate individual opportunity for language use is consistently offered to pupils.

Teaching children language, it is argued, is of central importance, a component of the curriculum which needs to be planned and structured in a principled way. Any approach which is adopted should be examined for its assumptions about language and its assumption about how children learn. Only if such assumptions are examined can one achieve a coherent language teaching curriculum.

References

BOARD OF EDUCATION 1921: *The Teaching of English in England* (The Newbolt report). London: HMSO.

BRITTON, J. 1973: How we got there. In N. Bagnall (ed.), *New Movements in the Study and Teaching of English.* London: Maurice Temple Smith.

CRYSTAL, D. 1976: *Child Language, Learning and Linguistics.* London: Edward Arnold.

— 1979: Language in education – a linguistic perspective. *Supplementary Readings for PE232 Language Development, Block 5.* Milton Keynes: Open University Press.

CURRIE, W. B. 1973: *New Directions in Teaching English Usage.* London: Longman.

DES 1975: *A Language for Life* (The Bullock Report). London: HMSO.

— 1977: *Curriculum 11–16.* London: HMSO.

— 1979: *Aspects of Secondary Education.* London: HMSO.

DOUGHTY, P., PEARCE, J. and THORNTON, G. 1971: *Language in Use.* London: Edward Arnold.

GANNON, P. and CZERNIEWSKA, P. 1980: *Using Linguistics.* London: Edward Arnold.

HALLIDAY, M. A. K. 1973: *Explorations in the Functions of Language.* London: Edward Arnold.

— 1978: *Language as a Social Semiotic.* London: Edward Arnold.

HOYT, F. 1906: The place of grammar in the elementary curriculum. *Teachers College Record* **VII** (5) pp. 1–34.

NISBET, R. 1973: Poetry and permissiveness. *AMA Journal*, November pp. 197–8.

THE OPEN UNIVERSITY, 1979: *PE232 Language Development.* Milton Keynes: Open University Press.

OPITZ, K. (ed.) 1972: *Mother Tongue Practice in Schools.* UNESCO Institute for Education.

QUIRK, R., GREENBAUM, S., LEECH, G. N. and SVARTVIK, J. 1972: *A Grammar of Contemporary English.* London: Longman.

RICHARDS, J. 1978: *Classroom Language – What Sort?* London: Allen & Unwin.

ROSEN, H. 1978: Linguistics and the teaching of a mother tongue. *AILA Bulletin*, Special Issue **21**, pp. 48–76.

9

Language development in and out of school

Sally Twite

We know a great deal more now than we did about the way in which normal children acquire their native language. Research during the last 20 years has posed important questions and has answered some of them, in part at least. Those questions have included: what is the exact nature of a process whereby in the space of a few years a child is able to understand and produce whole stretches of language which he has never heard before in that form? Are certain aspects of language acquired by all children? How important to language development is the child's early interaction with adults? What is the quality of that interaction?

To the first question there is as yet no clear-cut answer. But at least it is clear that the human predisposition to language learning involves more than the ability to attend and to imitate. Answers to the second question show greater agreement: it seems that there is a well defined order in which, for example, grammatical features are acquired and that this order is determined to some extent by the kinds of meanings children need or wish to express.

Recent research has shown very clearly that adult interactions with young children are quite regularly patterned and that the ways in which adults repeat and expand children's utterances appear to be very important to language development.

All this research is widely reported and is probably just as accessible to teachers as to other professionals. The questions mentioned here, for example, are discussed in a number of introductory texts of which the following are only examples: Clark and Clark (1977), Dale (1976), de Villiers and de Villiers (1979). Moreover, nowadays language acquisition is usually studied by teachers in initial training. Later in their careers they may encounter the subject again through in-service courses. Yet, all too often, the approach taken is theoretical and fails to address the important questions in the mind of the teacher – given that the process of language acquisition has a pattern and a regularity that can be observed and demonstrated, what are the implications for those who work with the children who are going through the process? How can theoretical knowledge inform classroom practice?

The answers are not particularly simple. The links are not always direct, but still it may be helpful to choose three areas in which the development of young children's abilities has been well researched, and attempt to show the relevance of research findings to decisions about classroom practice. Useful examples can be taken from the areas of the development of syntax and its relation to children's writing, the development of word meaning in young children and the growth of metalinguistic awareness.

Connecting sentences

Teachers sometimes find it difficult to know how to respond to a page of writing from a six or seven-year-old. Perhaps there is little punctuation; the sentences appear to run into one another. This makes it all the harder to determine what level of syntactic complexity the child's writing has reached, both in terms of sentence construction and connections between sentences. We need to look first at how complex sentences begin to appear in children's speech.

At about the age of three sentences like

I'll show you how to do it

or

I remember where it is

emerge (Brown, 1973; Limber, 1973). These complement constructions can occur with common verbs like 'want', 'hope', 'make', 'like' and 'think', for example. Somewhat later relative constructions appear. In the speech of most children a sentence like

I found the doll *that hurt her leg*

will occur before one like

The house *that Peter built* has fallen down.

(Limber, 1973; Slobin and Welsh, 1973). Relative clauses (italicized above) are tacked on to the end of the sentence, as in the first example, before they are used in mid-sentence, as in the second example.

Other simple means of connecting elements within the sentence also begin to appear at this age. Markers of time like 'when', 'until', 'before' and 'after' are among the first. Children's understanding and use of sentences joined by 'before' and 'after', for example, take time to develop and are perhaps not completely adult-like until about five or six. Clark (1971) asked children to act out the following sentences:

The boy patted the dog before he kicked the rock
After the boy patted the dog he kicked the rock
Before the boy kicked the rock he patted the dog
The boy kicked the rock after he patted the dog

The youngest, aged four, were able to understand the first two, probably because the clauses follow the order of events, but only by 5 or 6 could children understand sentences like the second two, where the order of events is reversed (Johnson, 1975). Of course, the ordering of clauses here is quite arbitrary: in the absence of context there is no reason why the dog should be patted before the rock is kicked, or vice versa. In another study (French and Brown, 1977) children of four understood 'logical' sentences better than arbitrary ones, even when the order of events was reversed.

A sentence like

Before the girl calls the doctor, the dog bites the baby

was easier for them than the arbitrary

After the girl puts the baby to bed, she takes off her hat

This only exemplifies what common sense would suggest: plausibility and relation to context are probably more important factors in understanding sentences than word or clause order. The fact remains, however, that such sentences may be difficult to understand and thus unlikely to be used by four or five-year-olds.

The commonest connecting device of all is, of course, 'and'. It appears in most children's speech at about the age of three and is typically used in narrative, for example:

Henry pushed the swing and it went ever so high and I fell off and I hurt my knee and I cried and he cried and his mummy shouted at us and ...

(Here 'and' is connecting simple sentences. This use of 'and' develops earlier than the coordinating function, as in

They sang and danced all the way down the road)

More sophisticated connecting devices are not often heard in the speech of five-year-olds. For example, sentence adverbs like unfortunately' are quite rare under the age of seven or so (Crystal, 1976). Children of this age do not use the full range of these and other 'comment phrases' either in their everyday conversation or even in the slightly more formal context of classroom talk.

So far we have looked at the kind of connecting devices within and between sentences which children might be using in speech when they enter school. Their first attempts at writing will be unlikely to demonstrate greater complexity. However, once the mechanical skills have been mastered and the purposes of writing understood, the teacher will want to use her knowledge of the acquisition of syntax in the normal child to help her plan for and monitor writing development. One useful example comes from a small-scale project which we undertook at the Open University, in consultation with Professor David Crystal of Reading University. This involved a class of children in one junior school, aged between seven and nine. One of them – by no means the best or the worst writer in the class – produced the following passage when asked to write about a 'narrow escape':

A narrow escape
I was building a camp with my mate and I was walking along not fare from the camp and than I saw smok and I smelt fier and then I herd a crakut and it was fier and it was coming this way so I rushed to my mat and I told him and then I went to the nerrist telyphon and I rang for the fier men and they put it out.

This boy was not untypical of his class: for the same assignment 72 per cent of the connective words used were 'and'. 'Then', 'so', and 'but' also occurred quite frequently. Against a background of the kind of information sketched above, the teacher wanted to encourage a more mature use of connecting devices in writing, given that some of these are beginning to emerge in speech at this age and given that others are most commonly found almost *only* in writing (Halliday and Hasan, 1976).

To this end, we designed activities which would develop the use of connectives expressing attitude (e.g. 'fortunately', 'of course'), time (e.g. 'meanwhile', 'some time later') and logical progression (e.g. 'so', 'on the other hand'). These activities included story-telling round the class using the connectives above and others from a list on the board; comic strips – the children made up picture stories with a suitable linking word above each 'frame'; illustrated stories focusing on contrasting terms like 'fortunately' and 'unfortunately'; cloze passages with connectives omitted, followed by group discussion of the suitability of the words chosen to fill the gaps. The signs of progress were encouraging: the children seemed to be developing a more mature written style with a more varied use of connecting words and phrases and with greater flexibility of word order within the sentence.[1] The particular value of such an approach is that the teacher selects activities which fit into the normal patterns of work in her own classroom and bases her choice upon informed expectations of normal syntactic development for this age group.

---

[1] More details of the project can be found in the Open University television programme 'Grammar Rules' and its accompanying notes: TV3, PE232 'Language Development' Open University, 1979.

Some 'simple' words and their meanings

By the time most children start school they are manipulating a large number of words quite skilfully. Estimates of the average vocabulary for a five-year-old vary greatly. Depending as they do upon so many factors – including not least the answer to the difficult question 'What is a word?' – such numerical estimates may well be considered less than ideally useful. At any rate, the words that children use are common currency between them and their teachers – they understand each other pretty well. Or perhaps they only seem to do so. It is important to realize to what extent adult and child attach the same meaning to the same word.

The potential for mismatch in meaning may be better appreciated if we return briefly to the earlier stages of the development of meaning. A two-year-old may use the word 'ball' to refer to a stone, a radish, a tennis ball and an orange, or the word 'fly' for all small insects and a variety of tiny objects, including the child's own toes. It is quite clear that a meaning gap exists at this stage. The child and the adult meanings overlap only partly, with the child's meaning extended to cover other objects, probably on the basis of roundness and smallness in the first case and smallness only in the second. In the course of a short time the gap closes as the child learns to operate with the adult set of criteria for labelling objects. Much has been observed about the early stages in the development of word meaning and many hypotheses about the process have been advanced (Dale, 1976; Clark and Clark, 1977). Other 'simple' words like 'more' or 'less' may sometimes be understood by three-year-olds and even some four-year-olds as if they both meant 'some' or 'amount' (Donaldson and Balfour, 1968; Palermo, 1974). According to some theorists, features or 'bits of meaning' are slowly added to the child's knowledge of a word. For example, some common kinship terms may not be fully learned until the age of about eight or even later. Children of this age may know that a cousin is an aunt or uncle's child but may not be aware that in order to have a cousin one must be a cousin oneself, i.e. they have not yet acquired the reciprocal aspect of the meaning of this word or others like it (brother, sister, nephew etc.) (Haviland and Clark, 1974).

Whatever the full nature of the acquisition process with these terms and others, there are undoubtedly periods during which children's understanding of quite common words will differ from that of an adult. Consider two other simple terms – 'same' and 'different' – both used quite frequently even to the youngest children. Yet adults may not appreciate fully the complexity of the words they are using. Imagine a collection of coloured shapes in a box with pencils, keys and other paraphernalia. An adult points to a red square and asks the children to point to something which is the same. In this context the adult might mean by 'different' an object differing on at least one visible dimension (e.g. a blue square) or an object sharing all visible dimensions (i.e. another, identical, red square) or an object differing on all visible dimensions (e.g. a key). For 'the same' the adult might mean the very object itself (i.e. the red square she is holding) or an object sharing all visible dimensions (i.e. an identical red square). Note the overlap in meaning between the second instances of both 'same' and 'different'. Children's understanding of the terms was investigated (Donaldson and Wales, 1970; Webb *et al.*, 1974). Under-fives seemed to understand the first two meanings of 'different' and the second meaning of 'same'. The other meanings are apparently acquired later.

Such research results are certainly not definitive. After all, much depends on the children's interpretations of the tasks they were set. The age of understanding will vary considerably according to the child. The words may be understood without difficulty in a different, more meaningful context. The implications for the teacher are, however, very plain: when phrasing instructions or explanations, particularly in topic areas which may be new to her pupils, she should be aware of which 'same' or 'different' she has in mind and aware too that some of her class may not yet have this particular meaning. The same kind of care is due with other apparently simple common terms.

Learning the meaning of a word, then, is a complex matter; it may take months or even years before meaning gaps between adult and child have closed completely. In the light of this we are forced to take a cautious view of the results of vocabulary tests and counts, both formal and informal. A child of eight might use the word 'nephew' without fully understanding it.

Can we say that he 'knows the word'? And what of the many common words which are polysemous, i.e. used in a number of senses? Of the eight definitions given in the Shorter Oxford Dictionary for the adjective 'bright' one is 'shining' and another is 'quick-witted'. Yet many seven-year-olds would not know the second meaning (Asch and Nerlove, 1960). Reading books and adult conversation are full of words used in this extended or figurative sense: 'bright', 'cold', 'hard', 'soft', and 'crooked', to name a few, are adjectives often used to describe people. But under-eights may not understand them in their 'psychological' sense. This is not, of course, to argue that the teacher should avoid such usage. On the contrary. But her awareness of this developmental stage will be important to her in deciding how far her pupils may have understood and whether more questioning and explanation are called for. One of the most significant features of meaning gaps such as we have been discussing is the confidence which each conversational partner has that the other understands and shares his meaning. The problem of new and unknown words is, in this respect, simpler to deal with.

Applying within the classroom a knowledge of the processes of acquisition of word meaning is very much a matter of consistently sensitive monitoring by the teacher rather than of specific classroom activities. Counts of words 'known' by the class or lists of vocabulary to be 'learned' will not generally be worth the trouble needed to devise them.

The growth of metalinguistic awareness

The first two examples have dealt with processes in the acquisition of syntax and of word meaning which are largely inaccessible to the learner himself. The third example will be concerned, in part at least, with the way in which children become aware of language as an object outside themselves, as an entity which they can contemplate and consciously manipulate. This ability, though less obviously vital in the interactions of everyday life, is of great significance in helping the child to develop the skills necessary to accomplish the tasks imposed by school.

Children starting school face new and unfamiliar language demands. Among the hardest for some are the problems and tasks, apparently simple, which depend for the 'correct' solution upon careful attention to the detail of the adult language in which they are presented. Margaret Donaldson (1978) gives an example of an experiment conducted with children between three and five which has much in common with such decontextualized classroom tasks. Two rows of five and four toy cars on two shelves were shown to the children who correctly answered questions about which row contained more cars. Then toy garages were placed over the cars so that the row of five cars was enclosed in a row of six garages, i.e. one garage was empty. Then the children were asked the same questions that they had answered correctly before: 'Are there more cars on this shelf or more cars on that shelf?' Over a third of the children changed their minds, answering this time that the shelf with four cars contained more than the shelf with five. This surprising result points up the different perspectives which children and adults may have upon the same task. The children who changed their responses were making their own sense of the situation. They may have expected that, in changing the disposition of the toys, the adult required a changed response from them; they may have found that the most salient aspect of the new situation was the fullness or emptiness of the garages and so, in their answers, they responded to that. But one thing is clear – for those children the language of the question was not the most important feature. It did not have priority for them and it seems that they were not able to attend to the words used in isolation from the situation as they interpreted it.

Apparently it is particularly difficult for young children to allow linguistic forms to override the other features of a situation. Investigations of children's ability to judge the grammaticality of sentences illustrate this point quite well. When presented with sentences like

John and Jim is a brother

or

I am knowing your sister

where the meaning is clear despite the syntactic deviance, many children under six will accept them as 'good', just as long as the content conforms with the truth values of their worlds. (Gleitman, Gleitman and Shipley, 1972). However, at the same age they may reject perfectly grammatical sentences such as

I am eating dinner

because 'I don't eat dinner any more'. We see that, when children under six or seven are face with decontextualized sentences, their reaction is to try to fit them into the context of their own experience – and to reject them if this proves impossible. A five-year-old, when asked whether the sentence

Anne poured some water into the kettle

was good, rejected it, saying, 'That's wrong. Little girls don't play with kettles'. Under the age of six or seven children seem to find it difficult to disregard what they conceive to be the whole meaning of an utterance in order to focus their attention on individual details within it. There is some parallel here with the difficulty which the children in the Donaldson experiment found in paying attention to the detail of the accompanying language, which for them was much less salient than the other dimensions of the problem: what does the adult expect me to say or do now? Why has she changed these toys around? That is, they brought the task within the confines of their own known world of behaviour and motivation.

It would, of course, be easy to dismiss the evidence of young children's relative inability to deal with language out of context on the grounds that some of the tasks described here are artificial and apparently unproductive. But this would be to ignore the parallel with some of the most crucial learning of the first years of school, which depends on the child's ability to cope with language as an object, out of the contexts where he is accustomed to meeting it, well supported by the meanings of everyday life. This crucial learning includes the beginning stages of reading and writing.

In these early stages five and six-year-olds are required to focus their attention on minute elements of language – the sounds and letters which make up words. They are assumed to know the meanings of 'specialist' terms like 'sound', 'word', 'letter' and perhaps even 'sentence'. Moreover, we expect them to know what reading is and why they are being asked to do it.

If the following description is accurate, then such tasks are more complex than they appear. Luria (1946) was writing about five-year-olds: 'in this period a word may be used but not noticed by the child and it frequently seems like a glass window through which the child looks at the surrounding world without making the word itself an object of his consciousness and without suspecting that it has its own existence.' (p. 61). This 'glass window effect' is substantiated by a number of studies of children's understanding of what a word is. In one of them, an investigation by Papandropoulou and Sinclair (1974), at about age five children described words as 'when I do something' or 'a pencil is a word ... it writes'. For long words they gave examples like 'a train ... there are a lot of carriages'. A difficult word was 'to put away your toys'. In this age group words were invariably confused with objects and actions. Later, between five and seven, the confusion no longer occurred and words became comments on reality, 'what you use to say about something', but at this stage function words, like articles and prepositions, were not admitted as words. When asked for long words this group of children proposed two clauses like 'He goes away and then he gets in to the car.' For a short word the same child (aged nearly six) gave 'he goes away'. This seems a transitional stage in which length, for example, resides partly in what is said and partly in the number of actions or objects being spoken about. Only by seven or eight were all words – not only contentives – accepted as words. Examples of long, short and difficult words were given according to adult criteria. This work and other investigations (Downing and Oliver, 1973, Reid, 1966) make it fairly clear that children enter school and start to learn to read and write with a very different concept of, for example, 'word' than their teachers, as adults, possess. It is after all, part of an adult language-user's more or less accessible knowledge that words are arbitrary symbols, themselves made up of arbitrary symbols (sounds, letters), and that, as well as being autonomous meaningful units, words enter into grammatical relationships within the sentence.

In these respects even children who are to become proficient readers and writers start on the tasks in a certain state of 'cognitive confusion'. This phrase, used by Vernon (1957) to explain some of the problems experienced by backward readers, is perhaps also descriptive of their particular difficulties in segmenting speech. Savin (1972) has observed – and many infants' teachers would support the observation – that children who have completely failed to read by about the age of seven are also insensitive to rhyme and indeed are unable to understand that two words may begin with the same sound – /pet/ and /pæt/, for example, or that /et/ forms part of /pet/. The same children may not, however, find it hard to recognize that /wɪndəʊ/ consists of the elements /wɪn/ and /dəʊ/. Such non-readers are also, apparently, unable to learn a secret language such as Pig Latin, where initial consonants or consonant clusters are transposed, followed by a vowel, to the end of a word (En-whay o-day e-way eave-lay? 'When do we leave?'). And this is an activity usually much enjoyed by young children. Thus it appears that, while young non-readers can segment words into syllables (win-dow), they cannot segment syllables into phonemes, as their reading contemporaries are able to do. This ability calls for a degree of linguistic awareness, a certain understanding of the abstract notion that the sounds, or phonemes, of the language are patterned in a regular way – that is to say, what is needed is an ability to stand back from language and contemplate it as an object.

The question that arises in the classroom is obviously, 'If metalinguistic awareness is as important to the beginning reader as research work suggests, how is it to be developed by the teacher in her pupils?' There are no simple answers. In many respects there is a chicken and egg situation here: good readers become more aware of the patterned aspects of language because their attention is focused upon language as an object – in its written form. Non-readers cannot make progress towards the level of awareness which would help them *because* of their inability to read. However, the teacher's sensitivity to the interactive nature of the process is helpful here: among the first words which a child learns to read are those which he already recognizes as individual words. His understanding of what a word is has helped him to learn to read. Being able to recognize these words in their printed forms may aid him in marking off as separate entities the new and unfamiliar words which he encounters. In this way reading or decoding print has helped to develop his concept of a word.

The teacher's understanding of how metalinguistic awareness develops in children is obviously of the greatest importance when the terminology associated with reading and writing begins to be used in the classroom. To return for a minute to the notion of the 'meaning gap', a teacher who recognizes how the concept of a 'word' develops is more likely to be consistent and clear in her use of terms like 'word', 'sound', 'letter', if she has appropriate expectations of how different pupils' understanding may be from her own. Only if he knows he has misunderstood will the child ask for clarification – and frequently not even then. The initiative is thus clearly with the teacher.

Introducing classroom activities designed to raise awareness of language as an object may be another significant contribution from the teacher – who ought not to be too much deterred by the chicken and egg argument as there is no reason why both kinds of development (skill in reading and an awareness of the nature of language) may not be mutually enhancing. For example, investigating puns, jokes, riddles in class is intrinsically enjoyable for most children, not least because they themselves can contribute to the content of the lesson. They are helped in this way to analyse and manipulate language in a 'painless' way. In a study of the comprehension of verbal riddles with children aged from five to nine Fowles and Glanz (1977) noted that the more proficient readers in their group were better at re-telling and explaining the jokes. With Downing (1971) these researchers agree that this enjoyable, yet analytical, approach to language is likely to pay dividends in terms of reading performance. Wider claims for the benefits of investigating the ambiguity which underlies most verbal humour include the potential for fostering flexibility in children's thinking and in their ability to categorize.

Finally, one of the most important implications of this discussion of metalinguistic awareness is the benefit in terms of learning which will accrue to the child who understands the purposes and, to a great extent, the structure of the task he is engaged upon. Some time ago Reid (1966) showed that a disturbing proportion of children, after a few months at school, were still unaware of the purposes of reading and were quite confused about the nature of the activity and what it involved. Some, for example, did not know whether one read the pictures or the 'numbers' or 'names' in a book. Children unprepared in this way for school learning, indeed all children, must surely gain from being made aware of the goals which their teachers have in mind. 'What this means in the formal educational setting is far more emphasis on making clear the purpose of every exercise, every lesson plan, every unit, every term, ... surely the participation of the learner in setting goals is one of the few ways of making clear where the learner is trying to get.' (Bruner, 1971 p. 113). Not, of course, that this is easy. To reveal to the beginning reader or writer every complexity of the English spelling system would be difficult, if not impossible and unproductive. Yet, to introduce early a series of 'rules' which later prove to be false may be equally confusing and unhelpful. In her valuable book, *Children's Minds*, Margaret Donaldson writes, 'There is no reason to suppose that children of five cannot understand a system that contains options ... if the system they are dealing with does involve options, we should tell them so. They will then understand the *sort of thing* thing they have to learn.' (p. 105). Children of school age already know a great deal about how to use language, but their teachers have a vital part to play in helping them to understand the *sort of thing* that language is.

References

ASCH, S. E. and NERLOVE, H. 1960: The development of double function terms in children: an exploratory investigation. In B. Kaplan and

S. Werner (eds.), *Perspectives in Psychological Theory: Essays in Honour of Heinz Werner*. New York: International University Press.

BROWN, R. 1973: *A First Language: the Early Stages*. Harmondsworth: Penguin.

BRUNER, J. S. 1971: *The Relevance of Education*. London: Allen & Unwin.

CLARK, E. V. 1971: On the child's acquisition of the meaning of *before* and *after*. *Journal of Verbal Learning and Verbal Behaviour* **10**, 266–75.

CLARK, H. H. and CLARK, E. V. 1977: *Psychology and Language*. New York: Harcourt Brace Jovanovich.

CRYSTAL, D. 1976: *Child Language, Learning and Linguistics*. London: Edward Arnold.

DALE, P. S. 1976 (2nd ed.): *Language Development: Structure and Function*. New York: Holt, Rinehart & Winston.

DE VILLIERS, P. A. and DE VILLIERS, J. G. 1979: *Early Language*. London: Fontana Open Books.

DONALDSON, M. 1978: *Children's Minds*. London: Fontana Open Books.

DONALDSON, M. and BALFOUR, G. 1968: Less is more: a study of language comprehension in children. *British Journal of Psychology* **59**, 461–72.

DONALDSON, M. and WALES, R. J. 1970: On the acquistion of some relational terms. In J. R. Hayes (ed.), *Cognition and the Development of Language*. New York: John Wiley.

DOWNING, J. 1971: The development of linguistic concepts in children's thinking. *Research in the Teaching of English* **4**, 5–19.

DOWNING J. and OLIVER, P. 1973: The child's concept of a word. *Reading Research Quarterly* **9**, 568–82.

FOWLES, B. and GLANZ, M. E. 1977: Competence and talent in verbal riddle comprehension. *Journal of Child Language* **4**, 433–52.

FRENCH, L. A. and BROWN, A. L. 1977: Comprehension of *before* and *after* in logical and arbitrary sequences. *Journal of Child Language* **4**, 247–56.

GLEITMAN, L. R., GLEITMAN, H. and SHIPLEY, E. 1972: The emergence of the child as grammarian. *Cognition* **1**, 137–64.

HALLIDAY, M. A. K. and HASAN, R. 1976: *Cohesion in English*. London: Longman.

HAVILAND, S. E. and CLARK, E. V. 1974: 'This man's father is my father's son': a study of English kin terms. *Journal of Child Language* **1**, 23–47.

JOHNSON, H. L. 1975: The meaning of before and after for preschool children. *Journal of Experimental Child Psychology* **19**, 88–99.

LIMBER, J. 1973: The genesis of complex sentences. In T. E. Moore (ed.),

Cognitive Development and the Acquisition of Language. New York: Academic Press.

LURIA, A. R. 1946. On the pathology of grammatical operations. *Proceedings of the Academy of Educational Sciences of the RSFSR Vol. 3.*

PALERMO, D. S. 1973: More about *less*: a study of language comprehension. *Journal of Verbal Learning and Verbal Behaviour* **12**, 211–21.

PAPANDROPOULOU, I. and SINCLAIR, H. 1974: What is a word? *Human Development* **17**, 241–58.

REID, J. F. 1966: Learning to think about reading. *Educational Research* **9**, 56–62.

SAVIN, H. B. 1972: What the child knows about speech when he starts to learn to read. In J. Kavanaugh and I. Mattingly (eds.), *Language by Ear and Eye.* Cambridge, Mass.: MIT Press.

SLOBIN, D. I. and WELSH, C. A. 1973: Elicited imitation as a research tool in developmental psycholinguistics. In C. A. Ferguson and D. I. Slobin (eds.), *Studies of Child Language Development.* New York: Holt, Rinehart & Winston.

VERNON, M. D. 1957: *Backwardness in Reading.* London: Cambridge University Press.

WEBB, R. A., OLIVERI, M. E. and O'KEEFE, L. 1974: Investigations of the meaning of *different* in the language of young children. *Child Development* **45**, 984–91.

10

Children's reading and social values

Mary Hoffman

> The advance of children's literature from its dismal pre-war condition is ...
> as a response to curious and wonderful convulsions in the literary, moral
> and social landscapes, (Blishen, 1975, p. 9)

Of recent years, the content of children's reading, in and out of
school, has caused much concern, first among teachers, parents and
librarians and later among publishers and critics; it has now even
reached children's writers themselves, even if only as a subject for
controversy, disagreement and alarmist threats of a New Censorship.

And yet some of the best writers for children, with that streak of
anarchy which characterizes the creative process, were among the first
to reject the literary *status quo* of the inter-war years and establish a
more vigorous ethos. Geoffrey Trease's (1975) imaginary 'do's' and
'don'ts' for British authors of the 1920s and 1930s, include 'A "loyal
native" is a man, dark of skin and doglike in devotion, who helps the
British to govern his country. A "treacherous native" is one who does
not. Similarly, in history, the common people sub-divide into simple
peasants, faithful retainers and howling mobs ... Girls *could* be
introduced as characters into the boys' adventure story, but only as
second-class citizens.' (p. 14). In other words, race, class and sex were
not only areas of inequitable treatment in the run-of-the-mill children's
story, they were also presented within a framework of social values
which had already begun to disintegrate. This is a characteristic to
which I shall return.

The rise of children's books as a subject for serious criticism

Another aspect of children's literature earlier this century, deplored by
Trease and many others, was that it was accorded little or no literary
status and was not subjected to any sustained criticism. Which was the
result of which is not an answerable question. Both have now changed,

at least within a small circle of readers, writers and reviewers (who are often the same people). Many journals about children's literature are now available, the TES and TLS publish four Children's Book 'Extras' a year and many national daily newspapers boast a Children's Books Editor. For the last ten years the National Book League has run a popular annual touring exhibition of *Children's Books of the Year* and has for many years stimulated and encouraged activities within a national programme for Children's Book Week.

So, on the literary and critical front, children's books have – if not come of age – at least been allowed to come down from the nursery, and be inspected by the grown-ups. Controversies there are, particularly wherever one set of practitioners e.g. teachers, comes up against another set, e.g. writers. Critics tend to be either those who evaluate books according to literary criteria or those whose prime concern is socio-cultural content. But there is now an indisputable children's book world, in which serious people take seriously what children read.

Children's voluntary reading

But what about the children themselves? What *do* they read from choice and what relation does it have to the self-congratulatory or self-scrutinizing world of these serious people? Whitehead *et al.* (1977) in their final report on the schools council research project into Children's Reading Habits, 10–15, questioned a very large ($N = 7,839$) representative sample of school children about their recent voluntary reading of books and periodicals. One of the most striking of their findings, across three age groups, is the number of children who claimed to have read *no books at all* in the preceding four weeks. This ranged from 9.4 per cent of the 10+ girls in the sample to 40 per cent of the 14+ boys. The average number of books read over four weeks by all ages, boys and girls, was 2.39.

Because of the unprecedented scope of the Whitehead research, it is worth looking further at its results, in terms of what kinds of reading constitute that just over half a book per week. Seventy seven per cent of all book reading was of narrative material (fiction and non-fiction). The researchers also sub-classified narrative books, subjectively and by consensus, into 'juvenile' and 'adult', 'quality' and 'non-quality'. Using these definitions, they report that over the whole sample there was twice as much non-quality juvenile narrative being read (33.4 per cent) as quality juvenile narrative (17 per cent). The most widely read book at age 10+ was *Black Beauty*, and at 12+ was *Little Women*. At 14+ there was an incongruous tie for top place between *Little Women* and *Skinhead*. It must be remembered that these most widely read books represent tiny percentages of the age group, ranging from the 4.5 per cent of ten-year-olds who read *Black Beauty* to the 1.7 per cent of fourteen-year-olds who read Louisa Alcott and Richard Allen. *Little Women*, it should be noted, which was the fourth most-read book in the 10+ category, as well as heading the other two lists, was read by fewer than ten boys in each age group.

The authors comment on 'the overwhelmingly nineteenth-century flavour' (Whitehead op. cit. p. 133) of the 10+ list and describe the 12+ nominations as 'similarly redolent of the past'. This is a point I shall return to later. The children in the sample were also asked to name their favourite writers and here there is a further surprise. Enid Blyton, firmly categorized by the team as a writer of 'non-quality juvenile narrative', heads all lists. She was chosen by a remarkable 20 per cent of the whole sample (with no less than half of the 10+ girls naming her), although Louisa May Alcott, the author of the ubiquitous *Little Women* was given a derisory 43 mentions by nearly 8,000 children.

It is important to remember that the Whitehead research, although published in 1977, was based on data collected in March 1971. It also tells us nothing about the reading of the under-tens, which was not within its brief. So there are dangers in extrapolating to the reading of present day children; a decade is a long time in education. In the context of the discussion, however, the three main points to remember about what 10–15 year-olds were reading ten years ago are:

it was very little and a quarter of the children read nothing at all
it was mainly narrative and, at the lower ages, mainly nineteenth century
it was mainly 'non-quality'.

These aspects, together with the tremendous range of books mentioned (7,839 children yielded 7,557 titles) form the background to the picture of the content of children's voluntary reading which I want to consider here. Though the particular titles will have changed over the last ten years, it is perhaps less likely that a new overall trend will have emerged. I shall also consider the content of children's compulsory reading in school. Because of the nature of the social values inherent in the material I shall treat reading in and out of school together, in relation to different areas of social importance.

Reading and social values

I'm here using the term 'social value' to refer to any belief held by an individual which affects his or her actions in relation to others. Cumulatively, within a society, those individual beliefs also make up the social values of the community to which the individuals belong. In some cases it is the sharing of these social values, as much as geography or income, which constitutes a recognizable community. Any writer, both as an individual and as a member of a community, holds social values and is bound to demonstrate them in what he or she writes, whether fiction or non-fiction. Only such materials as tube maps may be outside that scheme. It is also to be hoped that more idiosyncratic values and opinions will also find their way into the writing of any individual. No one in the children's book world is advocating, even if it were possible, either the blankness of writing which would share the value-free nature of the tube map or the blandness which stems from writing, without any personal involvement, within a framework of received social values.

Children's books and class

The concern in the UK with the content of children's books began with an uneasiness about the limited treatment of social class. Trease (op. cit.) and other historical novelists, such as Rosemary Sutcliffe, were concerned to rid historical fiction of its 'gadzookery' and engage more closely with social and political realities. *Bows Against the Barons* and *Comrades for the Charter* (both 1934) were Trease's unglamorous but invigorating treatments of the Robin Hood story and the conditions out of which the chartist movement grew, starting a line of children's fiction that continued with such books as Frederick Grice's *Bonny Pit Laddie* (1960) and Susan Price's *Twopence a Tub* (1974).

Reading schemes and class

By the mid 1960s there was a growing feeling of dissatisfaction with the picture of life shown in the primers through which most small children were being taught to read. The two-parent, two-child, one-dog and at least one-car family living in a suburban house with a well tended garden has become a standard target for criticism now, because of its remoteness from the more complex and shifting family and economic patterns of most British children. Yet, until the advent of *Nippers* (1968) and *Breakthrough to Literacy* (1970), the Janet and John ambience had held the stage for over 20 years. The objections to that ambience are manifold and more complicated than its simple dismissal as 'middle-class' can reveal.

Firstly, the presentation of social values in reading schemes is seen as particularly important because this is the material through which the majority of children have been, and still are, introduced to reading as an activity. This argument assumes both that attitudes are formed or at least affected by what we read and that the first books encountered are likely to be particularly influential. The objections to reading primers are thus poised on an axis between what attitudes it is considered harmful or life-enhancing to convey and what is motivating for children to read in their first encounters with print. These objections, although linked, are different. One is critic-centred; the other child-centred. Taken together they imply that early reading materials should be subjected to a closer scrutiny than any others, as indeed they have been. Later, I shall look at them from the point of their implicit racial and sex-role attitudes.

But to continue with class. There is a further question as to whether that suburban idyll of *Janet and John*, *Ladybird Keywords* and the like, reflects a recognizable social milieu for *any* reader. It is rather, in an admittedly limited and unimaginative form, a romantic idealization of a particular way of life, with all unpleasantness smoothed away. The dog has no teeth, the siblings no rivalry, the house has no connection with main drainage. Perhaps this is not so important as the cruder surface props of dress, decor and diet which may enable children of similar surroundings to feel 'That's me!' as Berg (1972) claims 'every middle-class child has done practically since babyhood'. I doubt it, since even in their revised editions Ladybird families do not seem part of the last quarter of the twentieth century when, for example, 'middle-class' mothers are as likely to work outside the home as anyone else.

Linked with this second objection is a third, based on language and literary values. The controlled vocabulary and syntax of this kind of primer leads to the often-parodied type of 'look, look John, see the little red car' inanity which bears no relation to the language experience of any child.

These three objections are often confused. Often when the social values of such reading schemes are criticized, whether on grounds of attitudes to class, race, or sex-roles, others will reply that these criticisms are irrelevant because of the low literary quality of the books overall. This of course is to ignore the fact of the enormous number of children who have cut their literary teeth on them. *Janet and John* was in use in 81 per cent of primary schools in the Home Counties and Midlands in 1968 according to Goodacre (1969). Grundin (1980) questioned a random sample of 631 headteachers of infant schools over Great Britain in 1978 and found that 27.7 per cent still use *Ladybird* as the principal scheme and a further 26.6 per cent use it regularly to supplement the main scheme.

When Leila Berg wrote the first *Nippers* books in the late 1960s, they were disliked by many teachers because their social milieu was intentionally working class. Typical of the many abusive reactions were 'I feel the subject matter is very poor and low-class, and in several cases ungrammatical. Perhaps they would be suitable for children in slum schools or from deprived backgrounds, but even so they tend to show a side of life from which we are trying to lead the children away.' (quoted in Dixon, 1977 p. 88). It is necessary to remind the reader here that the subject matter was not drugs or abortion but a family having a take-away supper of fish and chips. *The Nippers* and *Little Nippers*, several of which are now available as trade books as well as in schools, have sold millions of copies and have brought a new vitality to the world of reading primers but they have in their turn been criticized for creating a new set of social sterotypes, this time working-class ones.

Fiction and class

Similarly, some works of children's fiction, such as *The Family from One End Street*, and *Magnolia Buildings* which were greeted as new and revolutionary for being about families where Dad was a dustman or railway man, now reveal a condescending tone and a dated and inaccurate view of working-class language – plenty of 'cor!' with or without 'blimey!', and everything 'flippin'' and 'bloomin''.

Textbooks and class

The issue of class in education has been dealt with extensively by other authors in this collection, from the point of view of cultural discontinuity. Before moving on to the treatment of race in children's reading materials, I want to add one example of the ways in which social attitudes can be accepted wholesale as part of the learning package. When collecting case-study material for part of the Open University's *Language Development* course (Hoffman and Torbe, 1979) my colleagues and I visited an ILEA primary school where children in their last year were having a social history lesson. Their textbook (Hoare, 1975), on industry and communications 1896–1913, defines 'mass society' as 'a society in which differences between social classes have largely disappeared and people's needs and tastes are taken to be alike'. (op cit. p. 16). In the discussion which followed (Hoffman and Maybin, 1979) although the children did not all understand the concept of class with equal sophistication, there was a general agreement with the teacher's summing up 'you think that the class system is still with us?' When it came to writing about their work, however, several of the children said:

'Mass society was when everything became fair.'
'The social class were disappearing, clothes and needs were becoming the same in which some ways was not so good.'
'Mass society means when the differences between the social class has disappeared.'
'Round 1900 the differences between the working class and the middle class and the upper class diminished.'

I have no way of knowing what the children learned from the combination of textbook, discussion and writing, not to mention the attentions of a small team of University language-collectors. They do seem to have gathered the notion that when you reproduce, for assessment, something about a lesson, you may return to the certainties of the printed book as a more reliable guide than the ambiguity and hesitations of your own exploratory talk.

Children's books and race

Concern about attitudes to race in children's reading, both in and out of school, has also grown over the last decade. It has developed out of the wider movement against racial prejudice in education generally. Teachers Against Racism (TAR) was formed in 1971 and later became subsumed under the *National Association for Multiracial Education* (NAME). The Commission for Racial Equality has education officers, including one with a special brief for looking at children's books. In 1979 a new quarterly magazine *Dragon's Teeth* was launched by the National Committee on Racism in Children's Books, one of whose aims is to 'campaign against racial bias in children's books'.

Fiction and race

Many writers have given detailed criticisms of the racial bias in specific children's titles. (See Milner, 1975; Children's Rights Workshop, 1975; Zimet, 1976; Dixon, 1977). The most common targets in fiction have been the 'Biggles' books of W. E. Johns, several titles by Enid Blyton, particularly *The Three Golliwogs* (re-issued 1973) and *The Little Black Doll* (1937), several titles in Hugh Lofting's Dr Dolittle series, particularly *The Story of Dr Dolittle* (1920) and Helen Bannerman's *The Story of Little Black Sambo* (1899). This list at first appears an assembly of rather elderly Aunt Sallies. But we should look again at Whitehead's (1977) survey results before dismissing these books as rendered harmless by age or neglect. (No one, now, I think would make the other possible defence that their degree of artistic achievement mitigates their racist bias.)

Blyton was declared 'most popular writer' by 20 per cent of Whitehead's sample. She is a writer whose popularity is linked with her prolific output; when one title has been enjoyed, there is always another for the reader to move on to. The titles particularly singled out for criticism, which blatantly equate blackness with wickedness, ugliness and inferiority, are as likely to be read as other less racially offensive of her stories, simply because they carry her name. *Five Fall into Adventure* (1950, re-issued 1968), in which a girl is frightened by a 'dreadful face' at the window – 'It looked very dark – perhaps it was a black man's face!' (p. 30) was in fact mentioned by more than ten children as having been read in the previous four weeks, as one of 19 *Famous Five* titles thus listed.

Three *Biggles* titles were listed by more than ten children, and

W. E. Johns was named favourite writer by 96 children (all boys); 241 of his books were read over the four-week period. The *Dr Dolittle* books were also listed among the more popular, although Hugh Lofting himself received no mentions.

As for *The Story of Little Black Sambo* in spite of its age Dixon (1977) mentions its successful (over $\frac{1}{4}$ million) sales and the controversy that arose when Bridget Harris of TAR outlined its racist content in *The Times* newspaper in 1972. Currently, there is a 'revised and updated' pamphlet *Children and Books* available from the National Confederation of Parent-Teacher Associations, which lists *Little Black Sambo* as 'a lovely book for babies' (reported in Children's Book Bulletin No. 3, Spring 1980 p. 13–14). The term 'sambo', like 'Golliwog', 'Wog', and 'Nigger', has been used as a term of racialist abuse for a long time in this country, (Blyton's *'Three Golliwogs'* were originally named, Golly, Woggie and Nigger) an uncomfortable reality surpressed not only by those who felt that Bannerman's book 'did them no harm' but also by Robertson's Foods Ltd., the jam manufacturers, who are celebrating their Golliwog symbol's fiftieth anniversary at the time of writing (1980). Their marketing director refers to 'Golly' (sic) as 'a warm and sympathetic symbol' but Murray (1980) affirms 'black people have said that Golly is offensive to them as members of a racial group'. Yet, in 1979, a brand new reincarnation of this racist symbol surfaced in an expensive illustrated children's book *Here Comes Golly!* by Giles Brandreth.

Another book, mentioned in the Whitehead research is *Skinhead* by Richard Allen. Remember that it was jointly most popular book for the 14+ age group with *Little Women*. Attitudes held in this book and its sequels have been analysed by Salter (1972). Joe Hawkins, hero of *Skinhead* is an overt racist: '"Spades" or "wogs" don't count. They were imposters on the face of a London which should always be white...'. Salter convincingly argues that Allen is also 'Peter Cave', author of *Mama*, a book in which a 14-year-old Pakistani boy is scalped by Hell's Angels after mama has said 'Turn the little bastard into curry if you want to.'

Some higher-quality children's books which have also been criticized for racial stereotyping are *Sounder* and *The Cay* (both 1969) and *Charlie and the Chocolate Factory* (1964). The two former were award-winning American books about blacks and the objections to their content and treatment of race, brought in the new perspective of white writers being unqualified to write about the black experience. 'Authenticity in this case hinges upon life experience' (Schwartz, 1970). The objections to the original (1964) edition of *Charlie and the Chocolate Factory*, in which Willy Wonka's nauseous and sometimes dangerous confections were made and tested by dispensible black pygmies from Africa resulted in editorial changes to the 1973 version. However, although the little workers are now white, they are still called Oompa-Loompas and sing a song containing the lines

'... and cannibals crowding 'round the pot,
stirring away at something hot.'

The belief in the cannibalism of 'primitive', particularly Black, civilizations is a long-established calumny, which has been described as 'a subtle form of racism' (Arens, 1979). Yet even in a recent maths textbook *O and B Maths Bank 2*, there appear 'two pairs of cannibals, each with white men in their pots'. (Children's Book Bulletin, No. 4 1980 p. 11).

As with the class argument above, there is now a backlash of adverse criticism against books which were initially positively received. *The Trouble with Donovan Croft* (1974) is one such example. Donovan Croft is a West Indian boy who has been temporarily fostered by a white family while his mother has gone to Jamaica to look after a sick relative. The 'trouble' with him is that he doesn't understand that the separation is temporary – no one seems to have explained it to him – and as a result, he withdraws into himself and refuses to speak. This book won the Other Award in 1976 instituted by the Children's Rights Workshop to commend non-biased books of literary merit. Now, however, a practising teacher writes 'under no circumstances should the book be used as a token West Indian story.... Donovan and his father come across very much as English with black skin.' (Griffin, 1980). The criteria for assessing the treatment of race in children's fiction are becoming stricter and it is difficult to find a single book on one of the many recommended 'multi-ethnic' or 'multi-cultural' reading lists which has not also been criticized in some more radical forum.

Reading schemes and race

As far as reading schemes are concerned, for a long time they were racially prejudiced simply through omission, in that they contained no non-white characters at all. In the United States, multi-ethnic basal readers were not produced until the latter half of the 1960s (Zimet, 1976, p. 61). The *Nippers* and *Breakthrough* series mentioned above, which began to be published in the UK at about this time, do contain some blacks and the *Sparks* (1972) scheme is intentionally multi-racial. Nelson also publish a scheme called *New West Indian Readers*, and the *Terraced House Books*, *All Sorts*, *Dominoes* and *Ladybird Sunstart* books all feature at least some titles with multi-racial settings. If anything in contemporary publishing could be described as a boom industry, it would be the production of more multi-cultural early reading books. So far, however, there has been no sustained analysis of what the actual content of these apparently more culturally diverse materials convey about social values in relation to race. The newer schemes are not in use in many schools. 1.9 per cent use *Sparks* as the main scheme and 3.2 per cent use *Dominoes* (Grundin, 1980). With the current limitations on spending, it is likely that the old uni-racial schemes will continue to be widely used.

Textbooks and race

Another area of school reading which has received more attention from the point of view of social values and race is the ethno-centrism, specifically the eurocentrism of textbooks used in geography and history. Preiswork and Perrot (1978), in their analysis of 30 history textbooks in common use in western schools found that 'a critical approach to the European system of values is non-existent'. When it comes to taking 'O' level exams, the content of the syllabus may reveal an overwhelming bias towards the empire-building and colonizing role of the British, with little attention to the effects of this role on the countries they colonized. Inglis (1979) found little evidence that exam syllabuses and papers were at all concerned with 'the reaction of the population to, and their attempts to resist, the imperial power'. He concludes (p. 17) that this bias 'might be understandable if the papers were set for Victorian children, in the heyday of our Empire, but not in the last quarter of the twentieth century when the empire has ceased to exist and a less one-sided picture would be more appropriate'. As Prestwood (1980) asks, 'How do American Indians or African children feel when reading that a European "discovered" their country?'

Leach (1973) claims 'in the name of geography, in schools, colleges, and universities, reactionary and prejudiced attitudes, and a biased – or even wrong – selection of facts, are being presented.... primary school texts are only as good as the biases acquired in the colleges of education.' Hicks (1980) in a study of teachers in Greater Manchester and Cumbria, analysed the content of a 'top 20' of geography textbooks dealing with the third world. The most popular, used by 44 per cent of the sample, was significantly entitled *World Problems*. Hicks's analysis looked at such images as development, underdevelopment, colonialism and minorities. Typical of the comments he found were those in Ferris and Toyne's book (also called *World Problems*): 'Oppressed peoples may often be far better off than those who pityingly describe them as such.' Hicks summarizes the images he found as 'totally ethnocentric and often racist', and urges geographers, as does Leach (op. cit.) to write new textbooks within a raised awareness of possible ethnocentric bias.

Cultural bias may be present in a whole range of assumptions about how school subjects are taught and assessed, as the 'discontinuity' argument discussed elsewhere in this book has shown. Taylor (1980) in marking English language 'O' level exams, discovered that the content of topics set for essays would discriminate against a child without an English background. The four essay topics on the paper he marked were based on fox-hunting, a traffic jam, a blizzard and a record-club's advertisement. As Taylor points out, 'an essay cannot be written in a vacuum, there must be a subject and a subject of which the candidate is previously aware. This implies a shared background of experience among the candidates, from which titles may be drawn and in our multi-cultural society this background is less solid and more varied than it has been previously.'

Clearly the arguments about race and children's reading are complex. What most of the researchers in this area would agree is that the issues, where presented to children at all, take no account of that complexity. Children's own views about race have been documented by Milner (1975), Zimet (1976) and Jeffcoate (1977 and 1979) among others. It has been demonstrated (Litcher and Johnson, 1967; Fisher, 1965) that reading stories which show minority characters in a favourable light, particularly when combined with discussion, does effect a significantly positive shift in attitudes of the dominant group. Even without this evidence, although it is not yet considerable and awaits replication on this side of the Atlantic, teachers' awareness of the racial bias in much classroom material has now gathered sufficient impetus for the move-ment forward to continue.

Children's books and sex-roles

Stereotyping, the simplified assignment of characters to a category to the point where distortion occurs, has received a great deal of attention in relation to sex-roles. The 'traditional' assignment of sex-roles in the UK, in which men work and provide for their families and women do not work outside the home but service their husbands' and families' needs, is often symbolized in children's books by the apron, on the one hand, and the pipe and newspaper on the other. In the case of children, the traditional image is put across, whether consciously or unconsciously, through the active and aggressive behaviour of boys and the passive and quiescent behaviour of girls. My contention is not that such traditional roles are wrong, for any individual child or adult, but that the range of behaviour of both sexes is much more varied and interesting than the images conveyed in children's reading.

Reading schemes

Unlike racism, sexism (a word created analogically to mean adverse discrimination on the grounds of gender) has been well studied in relation to reading schemes. One of the earliest American sources

(Women on Words and Images, 1972) put the case against the reading-primer view of sex-roles forcefully and polemically: 'The authors of this study assume that there are ways in which we can make better use of the talents and energies of our female population beyond directing them into the kitchen and the obstetrics ward. In the coming years there must be a drive in all educational fields to improve motivational incentives for this underrated, under-encouraged, 50 per cent of the population. Grade-school readers are a top priority area for change, since they influence children at their most vulnerable and malleable stage of development.' (Introduction p. 3–4). At the same time, in this country, Cannon (1972) was concluding that *Ladybird Keywords* dealt with 'precisely the difference between boys' and girls' roles and mothers' and fathers' roles'. Rathbone (1970) had already found that even the newer reading schemes continued to present stereotyped sex-roles. *'Things I can do'* (Breakthrough) depicts a variety of children's activities. The text reads: 'I can be good'. To illustrate goodness a little girl is shown sweeping the floor. 'I can be bad' is illustrated by two boys having a fight. Looking on is a prim little girl in a pink dress.

Lobban (1974) coded the content of six British reading schemes published between 1958 and 1970 and updated her study (1975) to include two more published in the early 1970s. She concluded: 'virtually none of the readers presented non sex-typed models, activities or goals to suggest new non-stereotyped behaviours to the children ... children need preparation for present day and future reality but these reading schemes prepare them for a reality of 20 years ago.' (Lobban, 1975, p. 209). This echoes, as do so many studies in social values in reading materials, Trease's (1975) description of the outdated frameworks presented in children's fiction of the 20s and 30s.

Schoolbooks and sex-roles

Other literature encountered in school conveys the same message. Austerfield and Turner (1972) speculate that the relatively low number of girls taking science subjects at GCE 'O' level and 'A' level, is at least partly accounted for by the presentation of sex roles in junior science textbooks. Adult males are portrayed in a wide range of occupations and are shown as sources of information. Women are confined to their nurturant roles and take no interest in explanations or activities in these books. The experiments are likewise conducted by boys while girls look on. Stroking kittens or blowing bubbles are the nearest the girls get to carrying out any activities of their own. Davey (1979) who carried out a survey of the past and present reading habits of women engineers, found that a third of her two control groups (non-technicians) considered that science-linked categories of books were intended for boys only and only a very small number of these girls still read such books.

Over half the girl technicians, however, did read them, even though 13 per cent of them agreed about their intended male audience. In other words, the girls in Davey's survey who read more science-based literature, about how things work and how to do things, and who took up careers in engineering did so in the belief that they were acting atypically for their sex and crossing recognized gender-boundaries.

American maths textbooks have been analysed by Federbruch (1976) who found that boys were frequently shown in illustrations helping the girls to understand mathematical problems, whose range for females did not extend further than the challenge of adding up a shopping bill. 'The expressions on girls' and women's faces are sometimes the model of bewilderment as they struggle to find a way to put order into a seemingly chaotic or even simple numerical situation.' (p. 180).

My own survey of sex-eduation books (Hoffman, 1975) revealed sexist views of female sexuality and a distorted view of marriage in which girls would have to unlearn the modesty and passivity into which they had been socialized, in order to satisfy their husband's sexual requirements . . . 'for a full and happy married life, [a girl] must learn to respond in the bedroom while she maintains a ladylike appearance the rest of the time.' (Pomeroy, 1969).

History textbooks, as with race, may present a partial view of the role of women. 'History has been selected by males and women have been left out. Men have defined what is important in their terms and so they have looked at past civilizations and seen only wars and male politics and antics.' (Spender, 1979). A quick scan through most school history textbooks will confirm the impression that women, with a few notable exceptions such as the wives of Henry VI, Queens Elizabeth, Anne and Victoria, did not exist in this country until the Suffragettes [sic] at the beginning of this century. How the suffragists are treated is also a matter where the historians own social values are clearly demonstrated. For an excellent comparative exercise on the treatment of Emily Davison's death at the Derby in 1913, using primary and secondary sources, see The Schools Councils History 13–16 Project, Book 4, *Problems of Evidence* (1976).

Those women who lived before 1900 and were not of royal or aristocratic birth, or were not public practitioners of the private servicing and nurturant role, such as Florence Nightingale and Elizabeth Fry, go unrecorded. As Virginia Woolf had already noticed 50 years ago, 'The history of England is the history of the male line, not of the female . . . of our mothers, our grandmothers, our great grandmothers what remains? Nothing but a tradition. One was beautiful, one was red haired, one was kissed by a Queen. We know nothing of them except their names, and the dates of their marriages, and the number of children they bore.' (Woolf, 1929). History, as we know it, 'is about chaps'.

This dismissal or omission of women overlaps with another social value, of course. Because the 'chaps' that history is about are the kings and kingmakers, the makers and breakers of treaties, the warmongers and the 'discoverers' of non-European countries. If women are absent so are most men of the largest social class; after the villeins of medieval history, they are nameless cannon-fodder or workhands until the industrial revolution when they re-emerge as machine-breakers and chartists. Yet when ordinary men and women *can* be rediscovered and exhumed from documents of the past, as by LaDurie (1978), their lives are found fascinating and their chronicle becomes a best seller.

Fiction and sex roles

Children's fiction, in the picture books of the early years, has largely reflected the same stereotyped sex-roles as portrayed in the reading scheme. Girls are in the minority as characters, particularly main characters. Brennan (1973) examined over 200 picture books and found only 46 heroines. Moon (1974), who analysed 200 fiction books from pre-reading texts to books with readability levels of 8.5, found 115 stories with male central characters and only 27 with female central characters. Twice as many men as women were present in the books. Weitzman *et al.* (1974) read 'several hundred picture books' before concentrating on an analysis of 18 winners and runners-up for the Caldecott Medal given by the American Library Association for the most distinguished picture book of the year. (The UK equivalent is the Library Association's Kate Greenaway Award), and concluded 'through picture books, girls are taught to have low aspirations because there are so few opportunities portrayed as available to them. The world of picture books never tells little girls that as women they might find fulfillment outside their homes or through intellectual pursuits.... The simplified and stereotyped images in these books present such a narrow view of reality that they must violate the child's own knowledge of a rich and complex world.' (pp. 25 and 27–8).

For a description of the sex-roles in older fiction see Dixon (1977). He devotes much space to Louisa M. Alcott's books which he takes as being deliberately about the learning of appropriate sex-roles by boys and girls, particularly girls. (cf. Cannon's comment on reading schemes above). Dixon describes four themes which recur 'physical movement and deportment; speech; role-enforcement and dress and, lastly ... the reward for conformity, the gilt on the cage.' (Vol. 1. p. 10). It is interesting to see that Dixon also indicts Alcott as a deliberate propagandist. 'There are too many sly digs at feminism, scattered throughout the books, for us to excuse Alcott of unawareness.' (p. 11). *Little Women*, you will remember, was listed among the five most widely read books for each of Whiteheads *et al.*'s (1977) three age groups. These researchers themselves refer to the 'moral wholesomeness' of *Little*

Women and say 'we can be glad that it continues to retain a justified popularity'. I find Whitehead *et al.*'s *own* social values easier to endorse when they turn to *Skinhead*, which I have already discussed in relation to race. Girls and women are treated solely as sex-objects in this book. One quotation, from a rape scene, will suffice to illustrate the social values as far as relations between the sexes are concerned: '"Me next mate", [Tony] yelled, watching Billy penetrate the half-stupefied girl hippie. Her jeans lay on the beach, her thighs pimpled with cold, her buttocks bruised by the relentless rocks...' (quoted in Whitehead op. cit. p. 247).

Skinhead was classified by the Schools Council team as 'non-quality adult narrative' but John Christopher is listed by them as a 'quality' adult writer. Christopher however is the author of a book, *Dom and Va* (1973), whose social values in relation to sex and violence are hardly more enlightened or compassionate than Richard Allen's. Dom and Va are both from African races of 500,000 years ago. Dom's race is of nomadic fighters and hunters, Va's of tool-using, cattle-raising settlers. Va's settlement is raided by Dom's people, who kill all the men and non-nubile women and capture the others. Dom quarrels with his father over which of them should be given Va as a prize and eventually forces her to run away with him to lead an isolated life in the wild. Va loathes her captor and the rest of the book deals with their relationship. Here is how aspects of that relationship are described. 'Then in the moonlight, he beat her, as all his life he had seen hunters beat women who had dared disobey a man's command.... She must learn, as all women must, that a man was her master, and that he, Dom, was that man.' (p. 93). And later, 'That night, his hunger satisfied and feeling secure at last from pursuit, he used her body for his pleasure. It was painful for her but no more than that. She could not hate him more than she did already.' (p. 106). As a result of that union, Va bears a child, whom she loves and she eventually accepts her practical need for Dom's strength to protect her and her child from the rape and pillage of other marauding males. In an Epilogue, John Christopher makes his propagandist purpose clear: 'They had other children, girls as well as boys.... From Dom the boys learned to use clubs, to defend their home from attackers. From Va the children learned to love beauty and all beautiful things.... But this is the story of Dom and Va. In the dawn of human history, he was our father. She was our mother.' (p. 141).

The closeness of the names to Adam and Eve indicates that we are intended to see the two protagonists in a symbolic and allegorical role. As I have said elsewhere (Hoffman, 1974) 'After the first section of the book, the boy and girl are no longer themselves, but representatives of the two cultures and we are invited to see these cultures as "male" and "female". Both contribute to knowledge of the world but each is a sex stereotype.... Tenderness is equated with weakness and Va's only reason for relenting in her understandable hatred of Dom is that she needs him to protect her child. It is a view of the sexes quite as insulting to men as it is to women' (p. 4). Yet this book was selected by John Rowe Townsend as one of the best to be published in the 25 years preceding the 1977 jubilee. It is clearly a case where a critic considers the literary qualities of a writer to outweigh any objections to his presentation of social values.

Comics

It is necessary to make a special mention, albeit a brief one, of comics in relation to social values. All reviews of this topic mention Orwell's (1940) essay on Boys' Weeklies and often refer to it as 'seminal'. It is perhaps this phrase which has earned it its place in the literature: '[Children are] absorbing a set of beliefs that would be regarded as hopelessly out of date in the Central Office of the Conservative Party.' In other words if children's reading in general shows a framework of social values which has begun to disintegrate or no longer exists, then children's comics are at the very furthest extreme of this distant approximation to contemporary culture. And it is the very worst aspects of departed systems that comics perpetrate. Cannon (1972) believed that comics for young girls 'articulate the conflict between the masculine independence a girl may have a child, and the increasing pressures to be feminine as adolescence looms nearer.' This conflict is usually presented in the context of 'posh' boarding schools – a very remote ethos for most comic-readers.

Johnson (1966) found that boys' comics were still teaching xenophobia towards Britain's world war II enemies and nicknames like Kraut, Hun, Nip and Jap were being kept alive for a generation of children whose own parents were themselves children during the last war. Walt Disney's comics, which form 10 per cent of the net annual profits of the Walt Disney organization (Tisdall, 1977) have been used to convey anti-Allende or anti-Vietcong messages. According to Tisdall in Chile in 1971 Donald Duck cried 'Restore the King!' in a special campaign, through the comics, to undermine Allende's government. It should go without saying that, although the kinds of propaganda here are anti-Marxist or anti-Soviet, the objections are to the use of comics for *any* kind of political propaganda.

The attitudes to social class in children's comics are very musty – everyone is familiar with Lord Snooty and his chums – but have recently received a new twist with the story of 'The House that Jackie Bought' in the weekly comic *Tracy*. As outlined by Edwards (1980), Jackie is the daughter of a family harrassed by their neighbours because they have bought their own council house. Called 'Miss Toffee-Nose' and

'Miss Snobby Snout' by the other people on the estate, Jackie is subjected to a campaign of threats and physical violence. Clearly there is some form of propaganda going on here but whether it is intended to discourage or encourage the purchase of council houses it would take a subtle sociologist to decipher!

This content, which may seem laughable rather than amusing, matters when viewed in the context of the heavy comic reading of children. Whitehead *et al.* (op. cit.) discovered that an average of 2.3 comics were regularly read by the children in their sample. 76.4 per cent of periodical reading by boys at 10+, for example, was of comics and 86.2 per cent of girls' periodical reading at 10+. So a large number of these vehicles for propaganda and outworn social values are being read by children every week.

Censorship

It is impossible to talk about social values in children's reading for long without someone saying 'what about free speech?' or 'surely you aren't advocating censorship?' Shackford (1970) discussing *The Story of Dr Doolittle*, which has been criticized as racist (see above) asks 'Is it not possible to develop in children a critical judgement that will make it unnecessary to remove from the shelves such problematical classics?' (p. 163). In this country, King (1980) a children's writer, says 'There are people setting up a whole range of taboos on the subject of *race*.... [this philosophy] is being used to persuade librarians not to buy [certain books], to persuade teachers not to use them, and to frighten writers off writing them.'

In the ten years or so that I have been involved with groups studying the socio-cultural content of children's books and seeking to present those views at conferences, seminars and meetings, I have never come across a list of proscribed books. On the contrary, as the next section will show, lists of *recommended* books have proliferated. The editors of Children's Book Bulletin give a lucid definition of real censorship involving the seizure or banning of printed works and distinguish it from the practice of what King characterizes as New Prudery and they themselves call 'new criticism': 'The first seeks to control and *restrict* what is available. The second, by pointing out omissions and distortions and posing alternatives seeks to *increase* the range of options available to children in their literature' (Stones and Mann, 1980).

Alternative approaches to children's books

If you don't ban books whose social values are dissonant with your own, what do you do? Shackford (op. cit.) in her plea against censorship advocates a method of dialogue and moral reasoning based on the techniques of Biskin *et al.* (1976) and Biskin and Hoskisson (1977). What she offers is a projected lesson-plan with a fifth or sixth grade class (10–11 year olds) on a passage from the *Voyages of Dr Dolittle* (p. 280), based on questions. Unfortunately for her argument, Shackford's own sense of justice and egalitarianism, which has gagged at the notion of censorship, finds it very hard to swallow the gobbets of *The Voyages of Dr Dolittle*, with their insistence on Black Bumpo's cannibalism, polygamy, buffoonery and ignorance, when she quotes. She is forced to take refuge in the consultation of 'recent encyclopaedia articles'. Although Shackford's article contains some helpful ideas and shrewd points, I find it utterly fantastic to suggest that one would first read a racist author for his literary merit and then get out an encyclopaedia to correct his facts. I think the claims of Hugh Lofting are not sufficiently substantial to sustain the weight of such activities.

However, the provision of many alternative books does seem a good idea and there are now many lists of recommended non-sexist books and books for the multi-cultural society. (See bibliography.) Many publishing houses now provide their own lists and it is worth writing to ask for them. Some publishers have also produced guidelines for writers and editors. Scott Foresman and McGraw Hill did this in the States in relation to sexist language and images, in the early 1970s and provoked much adverse criticism over here. However, *Women in the Publishing Industry Group* in the UK drew up their own Non-Sexist Code of Practice for Book Publishing in 1976 and the EPC currently have a working party on sexism in children's books. There are also checklists and guidelines for assessing the racist or sexist content of books, produced by Centre for Urban Educational Studies, Equal Opportunities Commission, NUT, NUS and others.

Reading and social values in the context of language, school and community

Recently there has been a call for researchers and other educators to provide data that the reading of sex-biased material has any effect on the reader (Tibbetts, 1978). This is a much larger question in relation to the power and influence of reading on human belief and behaviour as a whole. Kimmel (1970) says 'it has begun to seem as if the belief that a child's attitudes can be affected by his reading is considered almost as an act of faith among teachers, librarians, parents and publishers.' These authors find the kind of evidence cited in, e.g. Zimet (1976) insufficient, though Tibbetts herself does not refer to that evidence. She also has to admit that her argument implies: 'By the same token, no one can demonstrate that sexist reading material is *not* damaging.' (p. 168).

As a writer on this topic, and a literature graduate I cannot, nor would wish to, claim impartiality on this issue. I believe that great literature and badly written rubbish can both change people's lives. To go further, I think that the written word is the most powerful moulder of beliefs and values that many of us encounter, often outweighing even personal experience. The confident and tough schoolgirl who once bellowed at me in a classroom 'When I go out with my bloke, I want to be treated *fragile!*', the small daughter of a friend who, asked to draw a doctor at school, drew a man, though the only two doctors she had ever encountered were both women, have both acquired sex-role images from outside their own nature and experience and I believe books to have played a part in that acquisition. I do not, of course, offer that belief to Tibbetts or anyone else as 'evidence'.

The social values conveyed in children's reading are a part of the social values inherent in wider language use. One of the worse epithets you can use to anyone involves women's sexual anatomy. 'Effeminate' used of a man and 'mannish' of a woman are derogatory terms, with childhood equivalents in 'sissy' and 'tomboy'. Women and men are even supposed to use language differently (see e.g. Lakoff, 1975). Blackness and whiteness have a long history of polarized usage in association with moral qualities. Class-based words such as 'peasant' are used derogatively by some; in the same way some others now use 'middle-class', even 'very middle-class' as a boo-word. 'Spastic' and 'brain damaged' are used colloquially to mean 'feeble' or 'disoriented'. 'It's a bit Irish', 'French leave', 'to Welsh on an agreement' – the English language is peppered with assumptions about groups of people. A language preserves in a fossilized form the social values of those who speak it.

The social values conveyed in school reading materials will be seen against a background of the social values held within the school itself. Reading does not take place within a vacuum, any more than writing does. Children read 'we dress up as doctors and nurses' (Breakthrough *Dressing Up*) and see an illustration of two girls dressing up as nurses only. They see female teachers doing dinner duty and performing all sorts of nurturant extra-curricular tasks. They see that Headteachers in mixed secondary schools are usually male and deputies female. They see themselves sexually segregated for activities, on the register and in the dinner queue. The boys hear themselves asked to lift and move heavy furniture; the girls hear requests for help with watering plants or cleaning up after cookery. The boys are punished and rewarded in different ways from girls and have different standards of work-presentation and behaviour accepted. The girls are comforted when they are hurt, the boys encouraged to grin and bear it.

All those things happen in some schools; some happen in all schools. An equivalent background could be constructed to social values connected with race and class. The social values in reading materials will converge with or diverge from the background model and teachers should examine this divergence or convergence. The book within the language, the language within the school, the school within the community, each goes to make up a larger whole of values to which the developing child is exposed. The values of the larger society, as conveyed through the mass media, are reflected in the social and moral climate of the school, its language and its reading. The values expressed by the writer can be part of a movement to change that climate and that society.

In all the areas of children's reading examined in this chapter but particularly fiction, we have seen the same pattern emerging. First there develops a restlessness with the monotony of the social values expressed in a given area, usually characterized by the initial omission of a particular group of people – the working class, Blacks, interesting girls. Then in the next phase, a few pioneering books attempt to change the ethos and in their wake, many titles appear which do at least feature those missing persons. Next there is a backlash of more sophisticated criticism which objects to a new kind of stereotype being developed. The fourth phase, in which the social values expressed again no longer constitute the content of a book but are part of its treatment, is yet to come.

References

ARENS, W. 1979: Eating people isn't right *New Scientist*, 20 September. (See also Arens, W. *The Man-Eating Myth*, Oxford: OUP 1979).

AUSTERFIELD, V. and TURNER, J. 1972: What are little girls made of? *Spare Rib*, 3 September.

BERG, L. 1972: Language of *Nippers*. (letter) *Times Educational Supplement*, 15 December.

BISKIN, D. *et al.* 1976: Prediction, reflection and comprehension. *The Elementary School Journal* 77, 131–9.

BISKIN, D. and HOSKISSON, K. 1977: An experimental test of the effects of structured discussions of moral dilemmas found in children's literature on moral reasoning. *The Elementary School Journal* 77, 407–15.

BLISHEN, E. (ed.) 1975: *The Thorny Paradise: Writers on Writing for Children*. Harmondsworth: Kestrel.

BRENNAN, D. 1973: Sugar and Spice and all things... *Shrew* 5, 4 October.

CANNON, C. 1972a: Female from Birth. *Times Educational Supplement*, 14 January.

— 1972b: The Crazy Comic Conflict, *Spare Rib* 5, November, pp. 36–7.

CHILDREN'S RIGHTS WORKSHOP (eds.) 1975: *Racist and Sexist Images in Children's Books*. London: Writers and Readers Publishing Cooperative.

— 1976: *Sexism in Children's Books*. London: Writers and Readers Publishing Cooperative.

DAVEY, A. 1979: *Ballet Shoes or Building Sites?* Birmingham: Birmingham Library School Cooperative.

DIXON, B. 1977: *Catching Them Young* (2 vols.). London: Pluto Press.

EDWARDS, R. 1980: The trials of Miss Snobby Snout. *New Statesman*, 11 July.

FEDERBRUSH, M. 1976: The sex problems of school maths books. In Stacey, J. *et al.*, *And Jill Came Tumbling After: Sexism in American Education*. New York: Dell.

FISHER, F. L. 1965: The influences of reading and discussion on the attitudes of fifth graders towards American Indians. Unpublished doctoral dissertation, University of California, Berkeley.

GOODACRE, E. 1969: Published Reading schemes. *Educational Research* **12** (1), pp. 30–35.

GRIFFIN, C. 1980: Worthy intentions; but whose image? *The English Magazine* **3**, Spring, pp. 17–18.

GRUNDIN, H. 1980: Reading schemes in the Infant School. *Reading* **14** (1), pp. 5–13.

HICKS, D. 1980: Images of the world: what do geography textbooks actually teach about development? Paper at the Conference on Development Education, London University Institute of Education, April.

HOFFMAN, M. 1974: An introduction to sexism in children's books. *CISSY talks to Publishers*, mimeograph.

— 1975: Assumptions in sex education books. *Educational Review* **27** (3), pp. 211–20.

HOFFMAN, M. and MAYBIN, J. 1979: Primary and secondary case studies. Supplementary material to Hoffman and Torbe (1979).

HOFFMAN, M. and TORBE, M. 1979: The language curriculum. Block 6 of *Language Development* (*PE232*). Milton Keynes: Open University Press.

INGLIS, W. F. J. 1979: A content analysis of 'O' level papers on imperial and commonwealth history set by two GCE Examination Boards. *Educational Review* **31** (1), pp. 11–17.

JEFFCOATE, R. 1977: Children's racial ideas and feelings. *English in Education*, Spring.

— 1979: *Positive Image: Towards a Multi-Racial Curriculum*. London: Writers and Readers Publishing Cooperative/Chameleon Press.

JOHNSON, N. B. 1966: What do children learn from war comics? *New Society*, 7 July.

KIMMEL, E. A. 1970: Can children's books change children's values? *Educational Leadership* **28** (2), pp. 133–61.

KING, C. 1980: 'Blatantly racist children's books'. *The Author* **xci** (2), Summer, pp. 90–92.

LEACH, B. 1973: The social geographer and black people: can geography contribute to race relations? *Race* **15** (2), October, pp. 230–41.

LITCHER, J. and JOHNSON, D. W. 1969: Changes in attitudes towards Negroes of white elementary school students after use of multi-ethnic readers. *Journal of Educational Psychology* **60**, pp. 148–52.

LADURIE, E. LE ROY 1978: *Montaillou*, Paris: Editions Gallimard. (Also Harmondsworth, Penguin 1980).

LAKOFF, R. 1975: *Language and Women's Place*. New York: Harper & Row.

LOBBAN, G. 1974: Presentation of sex-roles in reading schemes. *Forum for the Discussion of New Trends in Education* **16** (2), Spring, pp. 57–60 (Reprinted in Children's Rights Workshop (1976)).

— 1975: Sex-roles in Reading Schemes. *Educational Review* **27** (3), June, pp. 202–9.

MILNER, D. 1975: *Children and Race*. Harmondsworth: Penguin.

MOON, C. 1974: Sex-role stereotyping in books for young readers. Unpublished Dip.Ed. Thesis, University of Bristol Library.

MURRAY, E. 1980: What's wrong with golly? *Dragon's Teeth* **2** (2).

ORWELL, G. 1940: Boy's Weeklies. In *Inside The Whale & Other Essays*. London: Secker & Warburg (also Penguin 1969).

PREISWERK, R. and PERROT, D. 1978: *Ethnocentricism and history: Africa, Asia, and Indian America in western text books*. New York: NOK Publishers International.

PRESTWOOD, A. 1980: Racism rating: test your textbooks. *Dragon's Teeth* **2** (1).

RATHBONE, F. 1970: 'Girls are always afraid', said Bill. unpublished paper. An abbreviated version appears in *Shrew* **5** (4).

SALTER, D. 1972: The hard core of children's fiction. *Children's Literature in Education* **8**, pp. 39–55.

SCHWARTZ, A. V. 1970: *Sounder*: a black or a white tale? *Interracial Books for Children* **3** (1) (reprinted in Children's Rights Workshop (1975)).

SHACKFORD, J. W. 1970: Dealing with Dr Dolittle: A new approach to the '-isms.' *Language Arts* **55**, pp. 180–7.

SPENDER, D. 1979: Education or indoctrination? Paper for the Working Party on Sexism of the National Association for Teachers of English.

STONES, R. and MANN, A. 1980: Censorship or selection? *Children's Books Bulletin* **3**, Spring.

TAYLOR, R. 1980: It's not what you say it's the way that you say it ... cultural bias in Ordinary level English Language examinations. *New Approaches in Multi-Cultural Education* **8** (2), pp. 5–6.

TIBBETTS, S. L. 1978: Wanted: data to prove that sexist reading material has an impact on the reader. *The Reading Teacher* **32** (2), pp. 165–9.

TISDALL, C. 1977: Imperialist mousepiece. *Guardian* 25 January.

TREASE, G. 1975: The revolution in children's literature. in Blishen (1975).

WEITZMAN, L. *et al.* 1972: Sex-role socialisation in picture books for pre-school children. (reprinted in Children's Rights Workshop (1976) q.v.).

WHITEHEAD, F. *et al.* 1977: *Children and their books.* London: Macmillan Education for the Schools Council.

WOMEN ON WORDS AND IMAGES 1972: *Dick and Jane as Victims.* Princeton, NJ: National Organization of Women.

WOOLF, V. 1929: Women and Fiction. *The Forum*, March; reprinted in Woolf, L. (ed.) (1972) *Virginia Woolf; Collected Essays, Vol. III.* London: Chatto & Windus.

ZIMET, S. G. 1976: *Print and Prejudice.* London: Hodder & Stoughton.

Children's books and textbooks mentioned in this chapter

All Sorts Readers, J. Marshall. London: Warne (1969)

Black Beauty, A. Sewell. London: Jarrold & Sons (1877)

Boot Boys, Richard Allen. London: NEL (1972)

Bonny Pit Laddie, Frederick Grice. Oxford: OUP (1960)

Bows Against the Barons, Geoffrey Trease. (1934) (Reissued Leicester: Hodder & Stoughton Children's Books)

Breakthrough to Literacy, D. Mackay *et al.* Harlow: Longman (1970)

Charlie and the Chocolate Factory, R. Dahl. New York: Knopf (1964) (also revised edition Puffin 1973)

Comrades for the Charter, Geoffrey Trease. (1934) (Reissued Leicester, Hodder & Stoughton Children's Books)

Dom and Va, J. Christopher. London: Hamish Hamilton (1973)

Dominoes, D. Glynn. Edinburgh: Oliver & Boyd (1972)

Five Fall into Adventure, E. Blyton. Leicester: Brockhampton (1950) (reissued 1968)

Girls and Sex, W. B. Pomeroy. Delacorte Press (1969) (also Penguin)

Here Comes Golly!, G. Brandreth. London: Pelham Books (1979)

Janet and John, M. O'Donnell and R. Munro. Welwyn: Nisbet (1949)

Ladybird Key Words, W. Murray. Loughborough: Ladybird (1963)

Ladybird Sunstart, W. Murray. Loughborough: Ladybird (1974)

Little Black Sambo, H. Bannerman. London: Chatto & Windus (1899)

Little Women, L. M. Alcott. Boston: Robert Bros (1868)

Magnolia Buildings, E. Stucley. London: Bodley Head (1960)

Mama, P. Cave. London: NEL (1971)

New West Indian Readers, C. Borely *et al.* London: Nelson (1969)

Nippers, L. Berg *et al.* London: Macmillan (1968)

O and B Maths Bank 2, K. J. Dallison and J. P. Rigby. Edinburgh: Oliver and Boyd (1978)

Schools Council History 13–16 Project (Book 4 *Problems of Evidence*), A. Boddington *et al.* Edinburgh: Holmes McDougall (1976)

Skinhead, R. Allen. London: NEL (1970)
Sounder, W. H. Armstrong. New York: Harper & Row (1969)
Sparks, R. M. Fisher *et al.* Glasgow: Blackie (1972)
Suedehead, R. Allen. London: NEL (1971)
Terraced House Books, P. Heaslip. London: Methuen (1979)
The Cay, T. Taylor. New York: Doubleday (1969)
The Family from One End Street, E. Garnett. London: Frederick Muller (1937)
The Little Black Doll, E. Blyton (1937). Manchester: World Distributors (reissued 1965)
The Story of Dr Dolittle, H. Lofting. London: Cape (1920)
The Voyages of Dr Dolittle, H. Lofting. London: Cape (1922)
The Three Golliwogs, E. Blyton. London: Pan (reissued 1973)
The Trouble with Donovan Croft, B. Ashley. Oxford: OUP (1974) (also Puffin, 1977)
Turn of the Century, R. Hoare. London: Macdonald Education (1975)
Twopence a Tub, S. Price. London: Faber (1974)
World Problems, B. Ferris and P. Toyne. Amersham: Hulton (1970)
World Problems, M. Long and B. S. Roberson. London: Hodder & Stoughton (1969/1977)

Further reading

Print and Prejudice, S. G. Zimet. London: Hodder & Stoughton, 1976.
Catching Them Young, B. Dixon (2 vols). London: Pluto Press, 1977.
Children's Books and Class Society, R. Leeson. London: Writers and Readers Publishing Cooperative, 1977.
Children and Race, D. Milner. Harmondsworth: Penguin, 1975.
Racist Textbooks, Chris Proctor. London: NUS Publications, 1975.
Children's Books Bulletin, 3 issues a year (£1.80 including postage), CRW.
Dragon's Teeth, 4 issues a year (£1.50 including postage), NCRCB.

Guidelines, checklists, lists

Ending Sex-Stereotyping in Schools, V. Hannon. Manchester: Equal Opportunities Commission (1980)
Assessing Children's Books for a Multi-Ethnic Society, C. Jones and G. Klein. London: ILEA (1980)
Non-Sexist Picture Books, CISSY. London: Campaign to Impede Sex Stereotyping the Young (1979)
Spare Rib List of Non-Sexist Children's Books, R. Stones and A. Mann. London: Spare Rib (1979)
Books for under-fives in a multi-cultural society, M. Taylor and K. Hurwitz. London: Islington Libraries (1979).
'A selection of West Indian Writing, mainly for secondary schools', J. Goody and Hugh Knight. *English in Education*, Spring 1977.

Organizations

Equal Opportunities Commission (EOC)
Overseas House
Quay Street
Manchester
M3 3HN

Centre for Urban Educational Studies (CUES)
34 Aberdeen Park
London
N5 2BL

Children's Rights Workshop (CRW)
4 Aldebert Terrace
London
SW8 1BH

Commission for Racial Equality (CRE)
Elliot House
Allington Street
London
SW1

National Association for Multi-Racial Education (NAME)
c/o Ms Madeleine Blakeley
23 Doles Lane
Findern
Derby
DE6 6AX

National Committee on Racism in Children's Books (NCRCB)
Ravi Jain (treasurer)
NCRCB
46 High Street
Southall
Middlesex
NB1 3DB

11

Black English and dialect-fair instruction

Robert Berdan

We affirm the students' right to their own patterns and varieties of language
– the dialects of their nurture or whatever dialects in which they find their
own identity and style. Language scholars long ago denied that the myth
of a standard American dialect has any validity. The claim that any one
dialect is unacceptable amounts to an attempt of one social group to exert
its dominance over another. Such a claim leads to false advice for speakers
and writers, and immoral advice for humans. A nation proud of its diverse
heritage and its cultural and racial variety will preserve its heritage of dialects.
We affirm strongly that teachers must have the experiences and training
that will enable them to respect diversity and uphold the right of students
to their own language. (Conference on College Composition and Communication, 1972)

No State shall deny equal educational opportunity to an individual on
account of his or her race, color, sex, or national origin, by ... failure by
an educational agency to take appropriate action to overcome language
barriers that impede equal participation by its students in its instructional
programs. (20 United States Code 1703(f))

A widely noticed and commented on aspect of black culture, Black
English is frequently caught in conflicts between cultures. Nowhere is
this conflict more apparent than in the educational process. Facility
in reading, writing and speaking standard English has traditionally
been seen as an integral part of the educational process, perhaps even
the hallmark of true education. Comparable skills employing Black
English have enjoyed no such status. In fact, for some educators the
existence of such skills in Black English is inconceivable, a contradiction
of terms. At one level the conflict is between maintaining the cultural
heritage of the black community, and maximizing individual mobility
in the context of a larger society. At another level the conflict involves
the ethnocentric tendencies of educational systems. Basic literacy skills
need to be taught and learned. This is readily accomplished within the
context of contemporary social dialects, including Black English. Time
and again, however, these skills have been seen only as essential

attributes of standard English. In an overwhelming number of cases the children caught in these conflicts have not succeeded at any level. Their most natural means of communication has been demeaned, yet they have not acquired any truly functional substitute.

Black English is the label used here for the language of much of Black America. Black English is a broad, general term applied to a range of dialects differentiated in part by the geographical and sociological characteristics of their speakers. Historically the development of contemporary Black English has mirrored the cultural heritage and cultural changes of a population dislocated from the West Coast of Africa. Through time Black English, like all languages, has changed. Most of its linguistic characteristics Black English now shares with other contemporary dialects of English; some aspects appear to be unique.

Standard English is perhaps best viewed, not as a real dialect or language, but as an abstraction, an idealization. It is a set of codified rules, and there is no universal agreement on exactly what the rules of standard English are. There is, however, consensus on many of its characteristics, and there is general consensus that those characteristics differentiate it from Black English. It may well be that no one, or at least very few people, actually conform to all the rules of Standard English in their speech. In written English, conformity is much greater. Nonetheless Standard English is perceived to be a reality by many educators, and its acquisition is assumed to be the proper goal of much of formal education.

There is an integral relationship between spoken dialect and acquisition of basic literacy skills. The problems which Black English speaking children confront arise not from their dialect *per se*, but from the mismatch between their dialect and the educational materials and teaching procedures with which they must cope. Within this situation, the essence of the notion of dialect-fair education is that the dialect a child speaks on entering the educational system, or on entering any level of that system, must not in any way restrict access to a quality education. In the case that access to quality education has been restricted because of home dialect, however, contemporary dialect-fair education must go beyond equal access. It must act affirmatively to counter the cumulative effects of earlier restricted access.

What is being considered here is not *dialect-free* instruction. That is an impossibility and would in any event have no particular desirability. All instruction employs some dialect as a medium of communication; all language-arts instruction employs some dialect as a content area. That situation need not change. The goal is dialect-fair education, education that does not penalize a student on the basis of entry dialect.

Dialect-fair education is crucially dependent on two principles. First, instruction in academic skills, particularly basic literacy skills, can be completely independent of a student's facility with Standard English. In order to make that feasible within contemporary American education the second part of dialect-fair education must be that instruction in Standard English be available to all students, but only at the option of students and their families. Without these two considerations dialect-fair education cannot be implemented for speakers of Black English. Attainment of dialect-fair education ought not to pose any particular problem. Nonetheless there are a number of ways in which access to quality education has been restricted because of dialect.

Five ways Black English has restricted access to quality education

1. The Black English speaker is forced out of classroom participation. This restriction develops slowly and subtly. It is imposed by the well-meaning teacher who uses all classroom interaction as an opportunity for dialect intervention. For example, when a Black English speaking child inquires, 'What do this word mean?' the teacher may respond by saying, 'What *does*, what *does* this word mean. Now ask your question again.' Usually it seems that the intent of the teachers is to provide the child with a Standard English model and to encourage its use in the classroom. The child, however, has another alternative: withdraw from active participation in the classroom, and in particular avoid any speaking that might draw criticism, implicit or explicit. Children learn this much less painful strategy very quickly, and many eager, inquisitive first-graders become sullen withdrawn third-graders.

Sometimes teachers respond to the manner in which questions are asked, rather than to their content, as a way of sidestepping content. Lawyers frequently find this a useful courtroom ploy. Challenging the form of a question has the double effect of unnerving the asker and of distracting attention from what could be an inconvenient answer. In the classroom the result is the same, and tends to establish an adversary relationship between teacher and student. The effect is not lost on children who speak Black English.

Sometimes it appears that teachers attend to the form rather than the content of questions as a way to buy time when dialect differences delay comprehension. Often teachers, like others who are not themselves speakers of Black English, find that they do in fact understand their black students; it just takes a bit longer. Challenging the Black English form of a student's comment becomes an automatic, though perhaps unconscious, cover for the momentary delay in comprehension.

Whatever the intent of the teacher, students find this both threatening and embarrassing. The result of this approach to dialect intervention is that many Black English speaking children feel themselves forced out of active participation in their own education. There is no way in which children who are passive observers of their own education can compete with children who have been active participants in their own educational process.

2. Instruction in basic literacy skills is interrupted or displaced by dialect interventions. The strategies used for coping with Black English in classroom conversations are also used during instruction in basic literacy skills, but more frequently and more deliberately. Nowhere are these interruptions more concentrated than in early reading instruction, particularly during oral reading. Rarely if ever is new information being conveyed to the teacher when children read aloud. The teacher's attention focuses primarily on the form of what is being read. All too often successful reading is assumed to mean the use of Standard English pronunciation and grammar. This assumption is often expressed by the demand that children 'read what they see'. The result is that a child's oral reading is often interrupted by a demand for a Standard English equivalency for some Black English word used. Many children find that they must submit to these episodes every time they read aloud. These interruptions are often viewed by the teacher as being part of reading instruction. They are, however, dialect interventions which have nothing to do with basic reading skills. Their effect on the continuity of reading instruction is deadening. Children learn to cope by reading slower so that they will encounter fewer possible interruptions, by reading at a barely audible level so that teachers cannot determine exactly was was said, or by simply refusing to read at all. The overall effect is to reduce the total time spend on *bona fide* reading instruction for Black English speakers. Thus children who may in fact need the most instruction tend to get the least. This is another direct way in which dialect restricts access to quality education.

3. Access to instruction is delayed. In the late 1960s it was commonly advocated that Black English speaking children should not begin reading instruction until they had developed some facility with the Standard English presupposed by the instructional programme. Advocacy of this position is perhaps less common now, but is still to be found. Carried to its logical extreme this would suggest that literacy skill would never be taught to children who could not or would not first learn Standard English. It is doubtful that any school system has actually adopted such an extreme position, but in many school systems the beginning of reading instruction for Black English speaking students is routinely delayed weeks or even months. If children in these programmes are not channelled into reading programmes which work affirmatively to overcome this delay, the effect of this restriction, combined with those mentioned previously, is a cumulative loss in reading instruction time.

4. Restricted access to quality education can also result from the use of educational materials and procedures which are inappropriate for speakers of Black English. Most of the grammar instruction throughout schooling concentrates on the areas in which most other social dialects differ from Standard English: e.g., the form of pronouns in compound subjects ('*She and I* looked around' rather than '*Me and her* looked around'). Questions relevant to Black English characteristics are never broached, e.g., the role of accent or stress in determining whether sentences are active or passive ('Martha been paid the rent' can mean that Martha paid the rent if *been* is heavily stressed; otherwise it means that someone paid the rent to Martha.) In general the divergences from Standard English that are unique to Black English do not form part of the curriculum: nonetheless compositions in Standard English are demanded from Black English speaking students just as they are from other students for whom instruction has been provided.

In most phonics-based reading programmes 'silent' consonants are introduced rather late in the sequence (e.g., the *b* in *lamb* and *comb*), often not at all in the first year. When words with these special problems are introduced they are accompanied by special instruction for this rather difficult concept. Black English speaking children are often confronted very early in reading instruction with what are for them silent letters: the *d* of *and* may be taught the first week of instruction. Not only do black children confront these problems early in reading, they receive no special instruction, or perhaps only unintelligible instruction about the sound value of the letter *d* in a context in which they do not hear it. Examples of such inappropriateness of instructional materials are numerous. The net effect of many such mismatches between children and instructional material is that the quality of instruction is lowered and dialect-fair education is not achieved.

5. The negative effects of restricted access are allowed to accumulate. Schools have in the past coped with children who do not achieve by labelling them and tracking them through classes which substitute for normal academic instruction. Rather than being placed in programmes which overcome the effects of past instructional inadequacies, Black English-speaking children find themselves shunted into programmes where they are simply allowed to mark time, while their contemporaries advance through the regular academic sequence. In its most extreme form this once resulted in black children being placed in classes for mentally retarded or educationally handicapped children. More frequently they are simply tracked into sections of classes which compound their past failure to achieve by offering reduced expectations for current achievement. Many children opt out of the entire educational system as early as the law allows, some even earlier.

The cumulative effect is apparent when one examines the achievement scores across grade levels for virtually any large school system in the United States. In the schools with concentrated populations of Black English speakers the disparity in achievement with other children increases for each year of schooling. Whatever difficulties related to dialect Black English speaking children may have when they begin their schooling, their problems get worse, not better, as they get older.

There is yet another way in which access to quality instruction is restricted for Black English speakers. Many measures of achievement, particularly in language arts, contain dialect-specific biases. As a result, not only is *bona fide* achievement made more difficult for Black English speakers, they also have greater difficulty demonstrating their achievement. Consequently they are frequently denied educational opportunities from which they could profit greatly. With the advent of competency testing as a prerequisite to graduation, many Black English speaking students will also be without diplomas, not because they learned less than their peers, but because they did not enter school with the same dialect knowledge that others had.

In these examples of restricted access to quality education teachers have been repeatedly cast in the centre of the problem. There is a very real sense in which this is manifestly unfair. Teachers are simply the most visible aspect of an educational establishment which also includes school boards and administrators, and schools of education and educational products developers and publishers. Teachers bring to the classroom not only the methods and procedures of their training, but also the beliefs and values of the culture around them. The attitudes and practices which restrict access to quality education for speakers of Black English are deeply embedded in all of formal education and the culture it reflects.

Principles underlying dialect-fair education

In a sense, the principles underlying successful dialect-fair education might be stated simply as avoidance of the restrictions on access to quality education that have been outlined above. Truly dialect-fair education does indeed presuppose avoiding those restrictions. However, it also requires positive action on the part of all the participants in the educational process. Two bases for positive action in the classroom will be discussed here.

Principle 1: Literacy is independent of dialect

The first principle underlying dialect-fair education is that instruction in basic literacy skills is not crucially dependent on any particular dialect. In particular, literacy is not dependent on facility with Standard English or on instruction in Standard English. The practical significance of the independence is that children can successfully acquire basic literacy skills no matter what dialect they speak when beginning the instruction, or when completing the instruction. Maintaining this independence is as important in reading instruction as it is composition instruction.

There are basically two different approaches to making materials for reading instruction appropriate for children who do not speak Standard English. One approach is to alter the language in the books to reflect the language that the children bring to the classroom. Another approach is to leave the textbooks unchanged, but to employ a set of phonics rules and teaching strategies appropriate for relating Standard English materials to the dialect spoken by the children. In the past decade there have been several attempts to introduce special reading materials for Black English speaking children. These have included reading texts which use Black English syntax, and in several cases special spellings to reflect Black English pronunciations. They have been praised by some educators and linguists, but vigorously resisted by most parents and many school people. This resistance is usually expressed in highly emotional terms. Schools have been forced to respond often by dropping the programmes. Using content and language that children feel comfortable with seems to have had great success in at least some instances, but there remain serious pedagogical problems with teaching materials that employ special spellings to accomodate the sound system of Black English. Special Black English spellings have been used very successfully by many black writers, but these spellings are appropriate for an audience that already knows the phonics of standard English, and is able to use that phonics system to assign Black English pronunciations to the text.

An alternative to altering spelling to make reading materials appropriate for speakers of Black English is to alter the set of phonics rules that relate the writing system to the pronunciation system of the dialect. Any writing system can be used with many different pronunciations systems. In English this is of course obvious when one observes that speakers of English around the world, with many variations in pronunciation, can all use one writing system. There are only very few differences in spelling conventions between American and British systems. The systems of rules that are used for stating the relationships between writing systems and pronunciation systems are generally termed 'phonics'. For any dialect of English it is possible to state the phonics rules that are necessary to relate conventional English spelling systems to the pronunciation system of that dialect. These phonics rules can be stated for Black English as easily as for any other dialect.

Over the past decades the idea has developed throughout formal schooling that English literacy means not just reading and writing, but reading Standard English and writing Standard English. This misconception has led to the assumption that phonics rules are absolute and universal: the only possible phonics rules are those which relate the English spelling system to Standard English pronunciations. Phonics rules can be specified for Black English; comparable rules could be provided for every contemporary dialect of English. The majority of the rules are shared across dialects; some are unique to each dialect.

Because the English writing system is dialect-neutral, any single written word may have many different pronunciations when read orally by different readers. The correctness of any reading must be judged by matching the reading pronunciation against the reader's normal spoken language or dialect. This might be characterized as a 'Read what you say' approach to reading instruction.

Such dialect-fair instruction contrasts with what many Black English speaking children actually confront. The instruction they receive is what teachers characterize as 'Read what you see'. Children subjected to this approach frequently find themselves caught in the following kind of interchange. Seeing the written word *mask*, the child uses the appropriate Black English phonics rules and says [mas]. The teacher hears this, interprets it as the homophone *mass*, and interrupts the child's reading, saying 'Read what you see.' The child looks, says the same thing again and gets the same response from the teacher. As this non-communication proceeds, the teacher's frustration at not getting the child to read what he sees is matched only by the child's frustration at not being able to persuade the teacher that he has done just that.

Exchanges such as this are viewed by most teachers as reading instruction. They are in fact an intrusion of dialect instruction into the reading class. Many educators assume that dialect intervention is a proper part of all language-arts instruction for Black English-speaking children. The dialect intervention is often not seen as such because of the overwhelming strength with which certain prejudices are held: if one is to read orally, one must use the phonics rules of Standard English; good compositions are mechanically correct and mechanically correct is defined as conforming to the rules of standard English. But literacy skills are of course quite independent of any particular dialect or language; they certainly have no necessary dependency on Standard English. Even when dialect intervention is seen to be such, it is still often thought to be properly included as an integral part of reading and composition instruction: the teaching of literacy skills provides natural practice for new language skills. However, for a number of reasons the 'Read what you see' approach results in both very weak reading instruction and ineffective dialect intervention.

Five reasons why 'Read what you see' is poor reading instruction

1. Standard English phonics can interfere with comprehension of words

Most contemporary theories of reading argue that learning to get from the visual representation of a word on paper to its meaning involves going through the sound of the word. For the early stages of reading this is a conscious process; for more experienced readers it is a much more automatic process and proficient adult readers often might not use this process at all. In any event, beginning readers use the sound of words to get at their meanings.

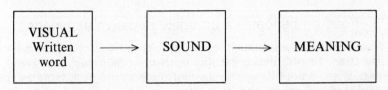

Standard English pronunciations, which are unfamiliar to the Black English speaker, do not assist in finding word meanings. This problem would not usually be great enough to actually prevent comprehension. More likely, it simply slows down the process while the child figures out what his natural pronunciation of the unfamiliar sound sequence is. In other words, comprehension has to wait while the child translates from Standard English back to Black English. For example, children know long before they begin to read that the teacher sits at something called a [des]. When they first learn to read the word *desk* the pronunciation [desk] is not associated with any meaning. Only when the child has realized that the pronunciation is comparable to Black English [des] can the experience be used to associate meaning with the written form.

2. Comprehension of grammar is reduced

When children read word by word, with pauses between words, they may well comprehend each word. For the earliest reading materials, that is often sufficient for comprehension in at least a general sense. As material becomes more complex, however, the grammatical relations among the words must be used in order to understand what is being read. If reading is too slow, it is not possible to use the grammar as a tool for understanding. It seems that reading must at least approach the speed of normal speech for comprehension to be maintained. The requirement of using an unfamiliar dialect often slows oral reading below this critical point. If the child is concerned about having to use unfamiliar pronunciations or has to make several attempts at producing a Standard English pronunciation, it is often not possible to maintain comprehension of the entire sentence. This bad habit in oral reading may also be carried over into silent reading as well. Well meaning teachers who force children to produce unfamiliar Standard English pronunciations have the same effect that some piano instructors have on their beginning students. The beginner is taught to hit all of the notes printed on the music, no matter how many attempts or how much time it takes. Ultimately the beginner may in fact get all the notes, but the melody is totally lost in the process. Similarly, the reader may get all the proper Standard English pronunciations, but the meaning of the sentence or paragraph is lost.

3. Reading becomes a uniquely negative experience

In many classrooms children receive more negative feedback for speaking Black English during reading instruction than during any other part of the school day. It seems that teachers are both more aware of dialect differences and less tolerant of them during reading. For example, at some point in the day a teacher may ask a child where her pencil is and the child responds. 'On my [des]' using the Black English pronunciation of *desk*. The response goes unchallenged because the teacher is more concerned about its content than its form. During reading instruction, however, teachers rarely hear anything new when children read. If the child uses exactly the same Black English pronunciation while reading aloud, the teacher is listening only to the pronunciation and often demands a standard English repetition. Teachers are not only more aware of Black English during reading instruction, but under the 'Read what you see' philosophy feel obligated to 'correct' the child. Many teachers are willing to continue this practice in the face of children's obvious frustration, sometimes reducing them to tears. Learning to read may well be the cornerstone of successful education. Many Black English speaking children find the experience too painful to care.

4. Reading becomes a culturally alien activity

If reading were something which could not be done in Black English it would be difficult for a black child to see how reading could have any relevance to himself or his culture. Reading becomes an activity which belongs to another world. Many black children come from homes where reading is not a highly valued or visible activity. In schools, they are exposed to reading materials that have little or no content with which they can identify. Insistence that oral reading must be done using an alien dialect serves only to make the activity even more remote from the rest of the child's experience.

5. Time alloted to actual reading instruction is decreased

Interrupting reading instruction for dialect intervention decreases the actual amount of reading instruction, as well as the quality of the instruction. The intrusion of discussions about Standard English pronunciation into reading instruction has an extremely disruptive effect. Often the amount of time spent on reading instruction is not increased to compensate for the time spent on dialect intervention. Paradoxically, the result of this is that the children who the teacher thinks are most in need of reading instruction actually get the least instruction.

Three reasons why 'Read what you see' does not work as dialect intervention

1. Reading programmes do not provide a systematic context for dialect intervention

A well-designed reading programme is designed to provide systematic instruction in reading. Most commercially available reading programmes have given no particular consideration to the special needs of Black English speaking children. As a result, these reading programmes do not support systematic instruction in standard English, at least not in most of the areas in which Black English speakers need instruction. When dialect intervention consists only of the instances of Black English that a teacher happens to notice during oral reading, no topic is ever pursued until children can demonstrate mastery of it.

2. Reading instruction does not provide the necessary sequencing of skills

Many reading teachers have found themselves confronting children in shouting matches that go something like the following:

Teacher: That word has a *t* at the end of it. P-A-S-T. Say *past*.
Student: That's what I just said. [pas]
Teacher: You said *pass*. The word is *past*.
Student: I know. That's what I said. How many times you want me to say it?

There is nothing absolute about the ability to discriminate speech sounds. People successfully discriminate the speech sounds that are a part of their dialect; other differences simply are not perceived. Any attempt to teach the articulation of sound sequences that do not exist in Black English must follow instruction leading to the ability to hear those sound sequences. Otherwise students will be totally mystified by the demands of the teacher. The bits and pieces of dialect intervention that get stuck into reading instruction almost never provide the student with this necessary sequencing of skills.

3. Phonics instruction is not articulation instruction

The phonics instruction used in reading classes is designed to teach children the alphabetic symbols that are associated with the sounds and sound sequences that they already use with ease. Teachers frequently attempt to use phonics instruction to teach Black English speakers new sounds or new sound sequences. For example, once children have learned the sound value of the letters *s* and *k* as single consonants or as parts of double consonants (as in *sick* and *kiss*), relatively little instruction is needed to teach them to read the word-final consonant blend *-sk*, e.g., ma*sk* and de*sk*. However, when children have always pronounced these words with a final [s] sound, this phonics instruction is woefully inadequate for teaching them that they must now pronounce a consonant sequence that is totally novel to them. A whole new sequence of articulatory movements needs to be learned. As any foreign language teacher knows, such instruction is often very difficult and requires a tremendous amount of practice on the part of the learner. Conventional phonics instruction in reading programmes gives neither sufficient time nor appropriate kinds of instruction to teach these articulatory skills. This is not the fault of reading programmes. It is the inevitable result of attempting to use reading instruction to accomplish something for which it was not designed.

Using Black English phonics

There are two different levels at which the Black English phonics rules may be used in reading instruction. The rules themselves may be taught to the students as a regular part of the instruction. Alternatively, the teacher may not overtly teach the rules, but simply use them for monitoring the appropriateness of oral reading. Several considerations are involved in choosing between these two approaches. First, if the reading programme being used does not teach any phonics at all, there seems to be little reason to single out the Black English phonics rules. Second, some teachers will find no difficulty in using the rules passively to determine appropriate reading but will find they have great difficulty in bringing themselves to teach their students overtly that, for example, final *d* may be silent. A third consideration is the heterogeneity of the students in the classroom. Some teachers will find it difficult to rationalize teaching one rule to some students and a different rule to others. Actually this should present no difficulty, either for teacher or students. This has the advantage of using the integrated classroom to raise the children's awareness of the diversity of dialects. In an atmosphere where all are accepted equally this functions to increase respect for all the dialects in the classroom.

The teacher needs to know Black English pronunciations for each new word in the reading programme in order to distinguish between differences in pronunciation due to dialect and those due to mistakes the child makes in decoding the word. There are several ways for the teacher who is not a Black English speaker to get this information.

1. Learn (memorize) the Black English pronunciations of each word in the reading lessons. This places an unacceptable burden on the working teacher. Teachers simply do not have the time required.

2. Learn the Black English phonics rules. There are less than thirty rules the teacher needs to account for virtually all the differences in consonant pronunciation between Black English and other dialects. The learning problem is greatly reduced. Teachers must decide whether they will actually teach Black English phonics rules or simply use the rules in evaluating children's reading.

3. There is a third way for a teacher to learn the Black English pronunciation of particular words during reading instruction. That is simply ask the children. One does not ask directly, 'What is the Black English pronunciation of this word?' Rather, the information is obtained indirectly by asking the child to use the word in other contexts. The pronunciation used for a word in these other contexts is the pronunciation to be expected when the child reads the word.

Some advantages of using Black English phonics

1. Black English phonics makes clear and explicit the systematic nature of Black English pronunciation. It is much easier for teachers to appreciate the systematic nature of the pronunciation their Black English speaking children use both in classroom conversation and in oral reading. Seen as part of a language system, teachers have an alternative to viewing these pronunciations as 'errors'.

2. The simplest form of the Black English phonics rules apply to conventional spellings of both simple and complex words. For example, rules stating the word-final *t* and *d* may be silent correctly predict that *t* is silent in *post* but not in *poster*.

3. The use of Black English phonics is not subject to the kind of community protest that the use of Black English readers with special spellings are. There is also no problem in transferring reading skills to use with any written English outside the classroom.

4. The same student reading-books can be used by all the children in the classroom. This reduces the need to segregate students by dialect for reading instruction. What is individualized from student to student is the teacher's expectations of the way the child will read. When explicit phonics instruction is given, it too may be individualized, or couched in relativistic terms: 'Sometimes some of us don't pronounce the final *t* or *d*.'

Introducing new words

Frequent practice in early reading instruction is to introduce new words using either flashcards or a blackboard. Typically the words are presented totally without context. Not until every child in the reading group is able to read the word is the word placed into contexts that make its meaning apparent. The very high proportion of homophones in Black English make this a hazardous procedure for use with Black English speaking children. Children assign meanings to words as soon as they see and pronounce or hear them. The possibility that wrong meaning associations will be made is very high. For example, the words *bin*, *Ben* and *bend* all have the same pronunciation in Black English. When any one of these is first introduced as a reading word the child must be provided with definitions or context to make sure that the appropriate meaning is associated with the written form of the word. Most teachers are highly sensitive to the special problems caused by standard English homophones (e.g., *two*, *too*, *to*); the same consideration is required for the much larger set of Black English homophones.

Reading grammatical markers

Many teachers who are willing to accept Black English pronunciations of single words (e.g., [kas] *cast*, [wif] *with*) are not willing to accept Black English use of grammatical markers. It seems that for these teachers it is acceptable for the final *t* to be silent if it is part of the root of a word (e.g., guest), but if the same sound is a past tense marker (e.g., *guessed*) it must be pronounced. They seem to feel that not pronouncing the [t] sound in this latter case indicates some failure to understand past tense. There is no linguistic support for this assumption.

There is a situation in French that is somewhat similar to Black English in this respect. A number of French words need a plural marker in their written form, but this plural marker is not pronounced. The written forms of the singular and plural are different, but the spoken forms are identical. Two examples which have also been borrowed into English are *beau/beaux* and *chateau/chateaux*. In French the plural forms are pronounced exactly like their singular counterparts.

The use of grammatical markers in Black English is not exactly parallel to these French examples. There are no well established conventions for writing Black English that require grammatical markers to be used in all possible cases: different authors use different conventions. Black English also differs from the French example in that the grammatical markers are sometimes used in speaking. The point is that there is no logical necessity in languages that written grammatical markers be pronounced in oral reading. When Black English speaking children read texts that conform to the grammatical rules of standard English, they must be allowed to use the Black English rules that govern pronunciation of grammatical markers. This applies to tense markers on verbs and plural and possessive markers on nouns. It also applies to the verbs *is* and *are*, which function in Black English very much like the other tense markers.

Clearly the differences between Black English and Standard English are far greater than can readily be accommodated through a distinctive set of Black English phonics rules. However, most of those other divergences do not become problems in reading instruction, as they do in composition. For most Black English speakers, the distinctive Black English forms alternate with comparable constructions that are identical in form, if not always in all aspects of meaning, with standard English forms. For example, Black English speaking children have no trouble either reading or understanding sentences such as, 'They haven't done it yet.' or 'I don't have it.' even though their preferred conversational expression of the same content may well take the forms, 'They ain't done it yet.' or 'I ain't got it.' Children who use such expressions as 'My mother working.' or 'My mother be working.' also use and understand the generally equivalent sentence that appears in reading texts: 'My mother is working.'

There are several exceptions to the general adequacy of using Black English phonics for dealing with texts written as Standard English reading texts. One of these problems relates to the use of multiple negatives within a sentence. Some Black English-speaking children do not use the word *any* in sentences like, 'They didn't bring any food.' In normal conversation these children use only the forms *no* and *none* in these contexts. Most Black English speakers do not use the word *there* to indicate existence as in, 'There was a big mountain.' In sentences such as this the *there* is understood to indicate location rather than existence because the comparable Black English form uses *it*, as in 'It was a big mountain.' Some other constructions may be treated as exceptions to general phonics rules, or may be treated as particular lexical differences. For example, for most Black English-speaking children the word *does*, *has* and *says*, are not used, and the words *do*, *have* and *say*, respectively, generalize to the Standard English uses of the former.

Principle 2: Dialect Intervention is Optional

For all the reasons listed here, and perhaps more besides, the integration of dialect intervention into basic literacy-skills instruction has not given many children who speak Black English effective mastery of literacy skills. It has also produced a history of chronic failure as a means of teaching the conventions of Standard English. Nonetheless, teachers pursue this approach with a vengeance, often with the blessing of principals, reading consultants and not a few black parents. Many parents and educators feel strongly that black children must develop some facility with standard English. They argue that it is the only way children will gain any economic or social mobility. However, any such mobility is even more dependent on the child's ability to read and write. Integrating dialect intervention with reading instruction only decreases the likelihood that children will become successful readers. The way out of this dilemma is simple and obvious. It is the second principle of dialect-fair education. Instruction in the use of Standard English must be available to children who want it. This instruction must be independent of basic literacy instruction. Equally important, it must be an optional part of the curriculum available to children when they and their families want it, but not forced on children whose families find it objectionable.

This second principle of dialect-fair education is important in its own right. However, it is also a necessary adjunct to the implementation of the first principle. Many teachers and parents feel strongly about the necessity of teaching Standard English. The only way they could ever be persuaded to allow dialect-fair reading instruction is to provide them with another context in which to channel dialect intervention.

Goals of dialect intervention

Before outlining strategies for successful dialect intervention within the context of dialect-fair education it is necessary to specify exactly what the goals of the intervention should be. In some schools the goal has been eradication of Black English. Conceivably a goal of eradication could be justified or at least rationalized if Black English were viewed as just a random collection of speech errors. Many advocates of eradication no doubt hold this view. When Black English is viewed in its proper perspective as an integral part of the culture of black America, however, the term eradication takes on social ramifications making it totally untenable. It is important to note in this context that any characterization of the use of Black English as an 'error' that needs 'correcting' is advocacy of the eradicationist point of view. People simply do not identify behaviour as *error* with the intent of reinforcing and maintaining it. The purpose of identifying errors is to eradicate them.

A far less objectionable goal is to make students *bidialectal*. In this case bidialectal implies that a student is able to operate in both Black English and the dialect taught in school, switching as the occasion demands. If the school can in fact help children achieve bidialectalism, the range of contexts in which they can operate successfully is potentially increased.

Some linguists have objected to talking about bidialectalism as a goal of education. They argue that the term just provides a cover for what in practice would be a policy of dialect eradication in the schools. The argument points out a very real danger. True bidialectalism is possible only if the school curriculum seeks actively to maintain the child's entry dialect, as well as teaching a new dialect. The dialect-fair approach to literacy skills instruction outlined here does in fact provide the necessary context for maintenance of entry dialect as well as a foundation for the dialect intervention that could produce truly bidialectal children.

While establishing the goals of dialect intervention it is necessary also to state exactly what dialect is being added to the children's repertoire. Must it necessarily be the Standard English of traditional education? Standard English has been identified throughout history with a culture highly alien to the cultural experience of most Black English speakers. An alternative goal would be to teach the dialect of those people in the black community who have best demonstrated academic, economic and political success in the larger context of mainstream society: the black middle class. This dialect has been described as 'Standard Black English'. Linguistically, it is virtually indistinguishable from the school's traditional Standard English. In a very real sense the distinction is chiefly in the label. But that label has important consequences in determining the acceptability and success of any dialect intervention. It also has subtle consequences for the way the intervention is approached in the curriculum.

Reasons a dialect intervention programme must be optional

The black community is as heterogeneous as any other segment of the American population, perhaps more so than many. As a result, the likelihood that any single programme will please all the people all the time is miniscule. Dialect intervention programmes have been no exception. Despite all the ineffectual approaches to dialect intervention that continue to be used in schools across the country, many black taxpayers still demand that schools teach Standard English to their Black English speaking children. Parents foot the bill for formal education and they have every right to make this demand of their schools. Some of these parents see discussions about preserving Black English as a luxury they cannot afford. They want to maximize social and economic mobility for their children. Education is seen as the key to this mobility and that education means learning to talk like people in the society to which they seek entrance.

Other segments of the black community take a radically different position. They see any attempt to change the way their children talk as a racist plot to destroy their cultural heritage. They also demand the right to influence the curriculum their children follow in school. The obligation and challenge to the schools is to meet both of these demands while still providing dialect-fair education in all other aspects of the curriculum.

The 'damned if you do, damned if you don't' dilemma has for too long afforded school systems a cover for not taking affirmative action to improve the language and language-arts instruction of black children. The only option not likely to arouse any segment of the community or the school staff is to avoid having any overt policy at all. As a result, black children do not receive dialect-fair education. Optional participation provides an alternative with minimal risk of community opposition. It is the only option that also allows dialect-fair education.

There is at least one other reason a dialect intervention programme should be an optional part of the school curriculum. If the intervention is not wanted by a child, and the child's family reinforces that negative attitude, the intervention cannot succeed in any event. It only wastes the child's time and the school's resources. Worse, the impact of this negative experience carries over into other aspects of the curriculum, increasing the possibility of alienating the child from the entire educational experience. Conversely, a programme that is available to children only when they and their familes express an active desire for it has the effect of increasing motivation to participate and succeed in the programme. The school's obligation to provide families with enough information to make intelligent choices requires that schools be sensitive to the families of their children and to their wishes. If carefully managed, continued contact with families could provide substantial reinforcement for learning.

Dialect intervention strategies

We have presented numerous arguments that instruction in basic literacy skills cannot be made contingent on a child first acquiring Standard English. It is possible to have successful reading instruction totally independent of the use of standard English. Quite the opposite argument can be made for dialect intervention measures. The most effective dialect intervention requires that Black English speaking children already know how to read. Prior knowledge of English writing and spelling conventions is an important resource for successful instruction in Standard English. In this sense the acquisition of a new dialect is like virtually all other school skills in being dependent on the acquisition of reading.

The advantage of knowing how to read before starting instruction in Standard English should be apparent from the following example. For the child who speaks Black English the following three words are all pronounced like the first: *mass, mast, mask*. If the child who does not read is taught that the standard English pronunciation for his word [mas] is [mask] in a context meaning 'covering for the face', the child has no way to know that the pronunciation [mask] does not extend to all other uses of his word [mas], including the contexts of boats and church services. On the other hand, the child who knows how to read can be taught that the reason *mask* is pronounced with a final [k] sound in standard English is that the *k* is pronounced in all final -*sk* blends. The example of *mask* then generalizes correcly to such words as *desk* and *task*.

The ability to read makes Standard English instruction much easier for the child. Before any instruction can begin in the pronunciation of Standard English sounds and sound sequences, however, the child needs to be able to hear the sounds in the speech of others. Training in auditory discrimination is a necessary first part of dialect intervention.

As the child begins to master the sound discriminations and then the pronunciation of the sounds and sound sequences of Standard English it is possible to introduce the grammatical markers of Standard English. There is little point in trying to teach the past and present tense markers on verbs until the child is able to hear and say the sounds involved. The Black English speaker does not need to learn a whole new system of grammatical markers. What needs to be learned is that the markers which are optional in Black English are obligatory in many contexts in Standard English.

Summary

Dialect-fair education is not and has not been available to many Black English speaking children. The reasons for this are numerous, but much of the problem centres around the substitution of dialect intervention for instruction in basic literacy skills. The basic literacy operations of reading and writing are totally independent of any particular dialect. With appropriate instructional materials and procedures, children who speak Black English can acquire literacy skills as readily as any other children can.

Schools should also present children with the option of learning the conventions of Standard English, if that is desired by students or their families. Only by allowing this instruction to be optional can the desires of all elements of the black community be accommodated. This instruction should be designed specifically as dialect instruction if it is to be effective. It cannot simply be an overlay on conventional reading and composition instruction.

Defining the principles that allow Black English-speaking children a dialect-fair education is one thing. Making it happen in the classroom is quite another. Change in education has always been slow and difficult to achieve. Changing attitudes as deeply rooted as feelings towards Standard and Black English will never be easy. It may in some sense seem easier to wait for a new generation of teachers, and to wait for some publisher to produce the ideal reading programme, than to persuade established teachers to change they way they use the materials already available. That, however, is a wait that has no end, and a wait that this generation of black children cannot afford.

References

BERDAN, R. 1980: 'Knowledge into practice: delivering research to teachers.' In M. F. Whiteman, (ed.), *q.v.*, pp. 77–92.

BRASCH, I. W. and BRASCH W. M. 1974: *A Comprehensive Annotated Bibliography of American Black English*. Baton Rouge, LA: Louisiana State University Press.

CULLINAN, B. E. (ed.) 1974: *Black Dialects and Reading*. Urbana, IL: ERIC Clearinghouse on Reading and Communication Skills, NCTE.

DESTEFANO, J. S. 1973: *Language, Society and Education: A Profile of Black English*. Worthington, OH: Chas. A. Jones.

DILLARD, J. L. 1972: *Black English. Its History and Usage in the United States*. New York: Random House.

HALL, W. S. and GUTHRIE, L. F. 1979: 'On the dialect question and reading.' Technical Report No. 121. Champaign, IL: Centre for the Study of Reading.

HEALEY, W. C. (ed.) 1972: 'Language and the black urban child.' Special Issue, *Language Speech and Hearing Services in Schools* **3** (4).

LABOV, W. 1972: *Language in the Inner City: Studies in the Black English Vernacular*. Philadelphia: University of Pennsylvania Press.

PIESTRUP, A. M. 1973: Black dialect interference and accomodation of reading instruction in first grade. Monograph **4**. Berkeley: Language-Behaviour Research Laboratory.

SMITHERMAN, G. 1972: *Talkin and Testifying. The Language of Black America*. Boston: Houghton Mifflin.

WHITEMAN, M. F. (ed.) 1980: *Reactions to Ann Arbor: Vernacular Black English and Education*. Washington, DC: Center for Applied Linguistics.

WOLFRAM, W., POTTER, L., YANOFSKY, N. and SHUY, R. 1979: *Reading and Dialect Differences*. Arlington, Va.: Center for Applied Linguistics.

Notes on Contributors

Robert Berdan has a PhD in Linguistics from the University of Texas at Austin. He has researched various dialects of English, both in the United States and in India. At SWRL Educational Research and Development he has been involved in a number of projects designed to accommodate Black English in instruction. He is presently co-ordinator of language acquisition research for the National Center for Bilingual Research.

Pam Czerniewska was, until recently, a lecturer at the Open University and Chairman of the in-service education course PE232 Language Development. She is the author of PE232 Block 1 'Understanding Speech' and co-author (with Sally Twite) of Block 2 'Patterns of Language'. Other publications are (with L. J. Chapman) *Reading: from Process to Practice* (1978) and (with Peter Gannon) *Using Linguistics* (1980). She is currently working in New York developing a literacy teaching and research programme for ex-offenders.

Derek Edwards has a BA and DPhil in Developmental Psychology from Sussex University. Since completing his doctoral research into the cognitive bases of language learning in young children, he has been lecturer in Social Psychology at Loughborough University. His major interests, both in teaching and research, are in the psychology of language, thought and communication in children and adults. He has recently been course consultant and contributor to the OU in-service teachers' course PE232 Language Development, from which has developed his current research interest in classroom education.

Mary Hoffman read English at Cambridge and Linguistics at University College London. Since 1975 she has ·been working for the Open University, writing distance-learning materials for teachers, on the teaching of reading and language development. She is a well known children's book critic, whose publications include *White Magic* (a novel for older children) (Rex Collings Ltd, 1975) and *Reading, Writing and Relevance* (Hodder & Stoughton, 1976).

Thomas Kochman is Professor of Communication at the University of Illinois in Chicago. He is the author of articles on the culture and communication patterns of black and white Americans, social and educational policy on language development in the schools and editor of the collection *Rappin' and Stylin' Out: Communication in Urban Black America.* He is presently completing a book on black and white cultural conflict. He received his PhD in Linguistics in 1966 from New York University. He has taught college since 1966 but also taught English in a Junior High School in New York City from 1961 to 1966.

Janet Maybin, BA(Durham), Dip.Ed.(Queen's, Belfast), graduated in Anthropology. She has experience in teaching at primary, secondary and higher education levels. In the Schools Curriculum Project in N. Ireland she was involved in action research in five schools, and contributed to reports and formative evaluation work. She is now a Field Officer at the Open University where her work has involved developmental testing of materials and preparation of television and radio programmes for in-service courses for teachers.

Liz Mercer has a degree in Psychology from Leicester University, and an MSc in Social Psychology from the London School of Economics. She now teaches Social Psychology at Loughborough University where she specializes in ethnic relations.

Neil Mercer is a lecturer in the Centre for Continuing Education at the Open University. He has a BSc in Psychology from Manchester University and a PhD in Psycholinguistics from Leicester University, where he taught Social Psychology until 1979. He has also taught in adult education, including teaching music in HM Prisons, and has published research in psycholinguistics and education. He was a member of the Open University PE232 Language Development course team, and the author of Block 4 of that course.

Katharine Perera teaches Linguistics in the Department of General Linguistics at Manchester University. She has a BA in English Language and Literature and an MA in Linguistics; she worked as a qualified teacher for seven years in Malaysia and on Merseyside before lecturing for three years in a College of Higher Education.

David Sutcliffe spent three years in advertising in Fleet Street before reading for an English degree, graduating in 1967. He taught in a multicultural school in Bedford for seven years and during this time became increasingly interested in West Indian children and their educational problems. He did research into West Indian children's language in Bedford for an MEd. at the University of Leicester. He resigned as Head of the Remedial Department of a Dunstable school to do full-time research into the black language background in the UK as an honorary associate at the London Institute of Education. The present focus of his research is on narrative styles.

Sally Twite graduated in English from Cambridge University. She spent a number of years teaching English as a foreign language and training teachers of English in Britain and in Israel. During her studies for an MA in applied linguistics she developed an interest in child language acquisition and has conducted research in British schools on the growth of metalinguistic capacities in young children. She joined the Open University in 1977 as a member of the PE232 Language Development course team. Her work there included co-authorship of units on grammar, meaning and the appraisal of language in the classroom. She has recently joined HM Inspectorate.

Silvaine Wiles read English for her first degree at Nottingham University. This was followed by a variety of teaching posts in London and Dakar. After completing her MA in Applied Linguistics at Essex University she joined the ILEA Centre for Urban Educational Studies. Following a further spell in Senegal teaching at Dakar University, she returned to CUES where she is currently Director of the Language Division. CUES, one of ILEA's specialist teachers' centres, is concerned with in-service training, research and curriculum development in the area of language, home/school links and multicultural education.

Index